# IoT and Big Data Analytics

## *(Volume 6)*

AF880217

# *Changing Competitive Business Dynamics Through Sustainable Big Data Analysis*

Edited by

**Sukanta Kumar Baral**

*Department of Commerce, Faculty of Commerce & Management,*

*Indira Gandhi National Tribal University (A Central University),*

*Amarkantak, Madhya Pradesh, India*

**Richa Goel**

*Symbiosis Centre of Management Studies, Noida,*

*Symbiosis International Deemed University, Pune, India*

**Tilottama Singh**
*Uttaranchal Institute of Management,*
*Uttaranchal University, Dehradun, India*

**Erdener Kaynak**
*School of Business Administration,*
*Penn State University, Harrisburg,*
*777 W. Harrisburg Pike*
*Middletown, USA*

&

**Vishal Jain**
*Department of Computer Science and Engineering,*
*School of Engineering and Technology,*
*Sharda University, Greater Noida, India*

**IoT and Big Data Analytics**

*(Volume 6)*

*Changing Competitive Business Dynamics Through Sustainable Big Data Analysis*

Editors: Sukanta Kumar Baral, Richa Goel, Tilottama Singh,

Erdener Kaynak, and Vishal Jain

ISSN (Online): 2972-4155

ISSN (Print): 2972-4147

ISBN (Online): 978-981-5256-65-9

ISBN (Print): 978-981-5256-66-9

ISBN (Paperback): 978-981-5256-67-3



First published in 2024.

need for a court order if at any point you breach any terms of this License Agreement. In no event will any delay or failure by Bentham Science Publishers in enforcing your compliance with this License Agreement constitute a waiver of any of its rights.

3. You acknowledge that you have read this License Agreement, and agree to be bound by its terms and conditions. To the extent that any other terms and conditions presented on any website of Bentham Science Publishers conflict with, or are inconsistent with, the terms and conditions set out in this License Agreement, you acknowledge that the terms and conditions set out in this License Agreement shall prevail.

**Bentham Science Publishers Pte. Ltd.**
80 Robinson Road #02-00
Singapore 068898
Singapore
Email: subscriptions@benthamscience.net

BENTHAM
SCIENCE

# CONTENTS

# FOREWORD

Industry 4.0 is built on a foundation of Big Data Analytics (BDA). It has become a practical tool for enhancing businesses' competitive advantages through better data-driven performance. While this is happening, firms are being forced to prioritize performance that is sustainable. The evidence also shows that BDA and innovation can boost business performance, giving it a competitive edge. This book makes the claim that big data analytics capabilities (BDAC) may increase innovation capabilities (IC) and, as a result, help create a sustainable competitive advantage (SCA) when combined with a high degree of data availability (DA). It serves as a comprehensive manual for exploring numerous dimensions with the aid of theories and models in order to gain a practical understanding from several varying points of view for its potential in society.The book employs a methodologically rigorous approach while ensuring that the content is understandable to all readers.

This book provides useful insight into the intellectual and practical effort and emphasizes the importance of re-thinking while analyzing the effects. It covers important topics like Big Data for Smart Cities, Sustainable Environmental Science and Technology, the Global Energy Crisis, Digital Manufacturing Support Processes, Digital Entrepreneurship, Workers' Healthcare using Big data Repository, the Internet of Things (IoT) in the Agriculture Sector toward Urban Greening, and Recent Advances and Perspectives in the Big Data Era.

This book, I believe, will be extremely valuable for a wide range of readers, corporate executives, entrepreneurs, and other professionals and masses in all sectors who want to expand their knowledge by learning about the underlying trends and activities in this book; it is not just for academics, postgraduate students, and research associates. Big data analytics is a novel topic with the ability to revolutionize entire industries; as a result, it will have an impact on everyone in the world in the next years.

It gives me great pleasure to write this foreword because the book's editors have worked tirelessly to find excellent answers and creativity. The chapters in this book were all chosen based on peer reviews by reviewers who were quite knowledgeable about the field.

**Prof. (Dr.) Mohammad Saeed**
Department of Business Administration
Minot State University, Minot, ND 58707, USA

# PREFACE

In the twenty-first century, digitization and the outcomes it produces hasten social change and the creation of sustainable societies. Our digital activities, judgments, and mere presence generate data, which opens up immense prospects for modifying present company procedures and practices. As a result, new theories, such as big data analytics, are desperately needed. The term "big data" refers to the process of creating increasing amounts of data in real time from several sources using modern industrial systems and advanced technology. To generate large volumes of data, modern enterprises increasingly rely on cutting-edge technology, which boosts a company's competitive advantage by extracting value from data and is based on rapidly developing digital technology research and the strengths that the information systems bring to the field. What it takes to achieve digital transformation is described in this book. An extraordinary rate of the adoption of big data analytics (BDA) is being observed in businesses in various nations looking for a competitive edge. This book's goal is to offer a conceptual framework based on resource-based theory (RBT) and dynamic capacity theory (DCT) that may be used to pinpoint the sources of competitive advantages, the interdependence of their constituent parts, and the methods for gaining competitive advantage.

The most recent results of the field's empirical study are presented in this book, along with important theoretical frameworks. In order to increase economic efficiency at the micro and macro levels, it reveals new and novel elements of big data analytics as well as how it might support industry competition. It is the perfect resource for academics, policymakers, businesspeople, organizations, and students. Big data has a variety of useful applications that are advancing both decision-making and industrial capabilities. However, for practitioners engaged in the study of stakeholders and their strategies, this book will be a valuable source of reference.

Further, this book has been organized in a reader-friendly way that makes it easy to understand the content. Important information that has been properly analyzed is underlined. The reader's access to materials in the book creates the possibility for more in-depth research. The case studies will offer a tried-and-true method for resolving typical issues in the subject area. The reader will be able to quickly grasp the chapters' major ideas and content.

**Chapter I talks about the Risk Analysis of Implementing Immersive Technology in the Healthcare System**

People can engage with a virtual environment in immersive situations. This technique has several medical applications. In medical applications, the use of immersive technology is still relatively new. Immersive technologies like virtual reality, augmented reality, and mixed reality have a variety of medical uses, including improving vision, treating behavioral disorders, rehabilitating patients, and developing personalized workout regimens. This chapter's goal is to evaluate the dangers of a technology-based healthcare system that is advantageous to both patients and professionals. Immersive training systems for the medical field are used to offer instruction and enhance patient care. We give a brief summary of the functional aspects of the system before doing risk analyses using Ishikawa, Fault Tree Analysis (FTA), and Causal Loop Diagram (CLD) to draw attention to three key system concerns. This chapter will also go over risk management and monitoring procedures.

**Chapter II talks about the Internet of Things (IoT) in the Agriculture sector toward Urban Greening**

By boosting production and efficiency, Internet of Things (IoT) technology utilization has the potential to significantly improve agriculture and farming operations. The most prevalent sub-verticals in IoT applications for agriculture and farming, according to this report, were crop management and water management. The study also found that sensor data for soil moisture was a common area of attention. The study also discovered that Wi-Fi, followed by mobile technology, was the most often employed technology in the creation of IoT applications. When compared to the farming industry, it was discovered that the agricultural sector received greater research focus. These results can serve as a reference for others in the farming sector who wish to enhance and broaden their usage of IoT in order to raise productivity. The paper also identifies key topics for further investigation, including scalability, heterogeneity, the architecture of IoT systems, data processing methodology, the size of the test site or agricultural area, and IoT security.

**Chapter III talks about Embodied Immersion: Exploring the Convergence of Haptic VR and Pervasive Visual Sensors**

In recent years, Virtual Reality (VR) technology has rapidly increased in importance and esteem. It offers users a virtual world in which they can form virtual habits or manage the objects in the scene with their limb movements. Users are looking for novel Human-Computer Interaction strategies as computers and information technology develop to offer a richer experience. In contrast, research on virtual scene modeling might make it easier for customers to access and have a more realistic experience. The intended article primarily focuses on the perspectives on AR and VR in the future on a global scale, taking VR strategies that depend on Scene Modelling, Statistical Analysis, and Sensor Networking and taking into consideration the research methods by examining the interactive VR technology from the perception of Visual Sensor Network (VSN), which tends to provide visual information to VR systems and also offers succinct and effective image data to aid in the creation of AR and VR. In addition, a wide range of uses tends to give the burgeoning VR business the assurance it needs to add greater value. A tried-and-true interaction mode is suggested that can significantly enhance user experiences, hence improving VR goods.

**Chapter IV talks about Post-Pandemic OTT Media Hegemony in India: A Socio-Economic Perspective**

As OTT media consumption spread to India after the COVID-19 pandemic, it revolutionized the entertainment market and changed how consumers watched entertainment. Customers were compelled to stay at home due to the lockdown. A paradigm shift in consumer behavior has been brought about by it. The ease of using OTT platforms for content consumption is fuelling this industry's expansion. As smartphone technology advances and internet usage rises, OTT services are benefiting the entertainment industry. The abundance of free time and thirst for entertainment during the pandemic have influenced the demand for OTT services. The study shows that during the pandemic, data usage, internet subscribers, and the proportion of internet subscribers all increased. Cheap data plans, a growing number of people using broadband, and rising smartphone sales are the major factors fueling OTT growth. It tries to evaluate the socioeconomic engagement of OTT media firms in their promotion and strategies.

### Chapter V talks about the Digital Disruption Model: Redefining the Healthcare Sector with Innovation

Healthcare executives are gaining the necessary benefits for patients thanks to innovations like the combination of artificial intelligence and machine learning, advancements in virtual reality, robotic process automation, and the use of bio-sensors in mobile devices, among others. With startups introducing new business models, key disruptive innovation is occurring, and the future appears promising, with investments totaling US$ 679 million in 2018. However, there is a dearth of literature on this phenomenon in the context of India. The current chapter aims to spark discussion within the Indian healthcare industry about disruptive and digital innovation to identify what types of disruption agents, such as technological enablers, business models, and value networks, appear to be emerging from various innovation clusters in relation to their digital transformational efforts and to assist policymakers in making informed decisions.

### Chapter VI talks about a Study on Digital Transformation Empowering Human Resource Management

Businesses and employees are under pressure to adapt as a result of quick globalization and expansion of digital technology. In the business world, the phrase "digitalization" today refers to the need for organizations to adopt it if they want to stay updated. Prior studies have focused on the impact of digitalization on marketing and organizational success, including consumer preferences, buying patterns, and customer relationship management. Academic research, particularly that on HRM, tends to give less weight to how it affects internal business. Consequently, the goal of this research is to learn more about human resource management in the digital age. The goal of this study is to show how digital HRM can improve organizational effectiveness.

### Chapter VII talks about an Investigation of Industry 4.0 with Client Value Added in the Business Industry

Industry 4.0, which was established in 2011, refers to a more advanced level of industrialization in which the entire process is managed by automatic or artificial intelligence-enabled machinery with very little room for human interaction. With the help of this technology, a networked channel for continuous data flow has been established between the production unit's machines and electronic retailers (E-retailers). Based on the data these retailers receive from the production unit's machines over the network, they offer services like cloud computing and other services. Data from customers, manufacturers, and workers, among others, is shared among machines *via* the internet; these machines send data *via* sensors from client machines/computer systems to service provider organizations, and these service providers analyze massive amounts of data using high-tech computer systems. The rationale behind this is to provide more customized services as well as add more value for clients; this will establish trustworthy relationships between clients and service providers, enhancing client loyalty towards the e-retailer and consumer loyalty towards the manufacturing unit at the same time.

### Chapter VIII talks about the Innovations in Environment and Science: A Study on Models of Sustainable Environment across the World to Achieve SDG-9

In today's society, digitalization is an instrument, but it is also a means of survival that opens up new options, such as knowledge without time constraints through continuous education. This current study delves in to the unique ideas, practical examples, and models that have been adopted globally as disruptive technologies of their outcomes and related problems, thus demonstrating the fundamentals of sustainability with its implementation in modern society. The study critically assesses the benefits and challenges of contemporary transformation as well as the effectiveness of these technical processes. The aspect of UN SDG-9 has also been discussed in the study that how current technologies are working towards achieving this digitalization in industries to satisfy this United Nations target.

**Chapter IX talks about the Understanding of General Population toward Global Energy Crisis: A Qualitative Study**

When it comes to global energy requirements, consumption, and energy sources, the last century and recent past were heavily reliant on various types of fossil fuels. These fossil fuel energy sources have long served humans, powering the Industrial Revolution in the 17th and 18th centuries. However, like other natural resources, fossil fuel supplies are rapidly declining and are anticipated to run out in the near future. The world is currently experiencing its worst energy crisis in history. In recent years, important events like the COVID-19 pandemic, the post-pandemic economic recovery, the recent Russia-Ukraine war, and harsh weather conditions caused by greenhouse gas emissions and global warming have resulted in a severe energy crunch in terms of fossil fuels. This has had a significant impact on the lives of the common populace. As a result, an attempt has been made to ascertain the general population's comprehension of numerous ideas linked to energy and its sources, problems and solutions in terms of the global energy crisis.

**Chapter X talks about Changing Competitive Business Dynamics of OTT Platforms' Viewership for Transformational Digital Engagement: Post-Pandemic Entrepreneurship**.

This chapter seeks to comprehend the potential factors that influenced the audience and acceptability of OTT platforms during the COVID-19 pandemic. The general public's consumption of entertainment, as well as their perception of it, has grown rapidly over the years. The demand for such services is growing all the time, resulting in high acceptance rates among the general public. The onset of the COVID-19 pandemic has favorably impacted the OTT landscape in terms of consumer viewership, content generation and distribution across OTT platforms, and customer involvement on the part of service providers. In comparison to the previous year, the subscription growth rate for OTT Service providers surged seven times around March 2020. It might be assumed that OTT platforms have inexorably become a part of the common person's life. Many factors have influenced the inclusion and expansion of this service, including Intention of Use, Accessibility, Content Quality, and Free Time, to name a few.

**Chapter XI talks about Women-Driven Innovation in Industry 5.0 Post Pandemic**

Women have disproportionately been affected by the COVID-19 outbreak, undoing decades of progress toward gender equality. Women-led firms have suffered badly economically, particularly in the pandemic-affected industries. The Sustainable Development Goals (SDGs) are a call to action in the United Nations 2030 Agenda to foster prosperity by addressing global challenges such as poverty and inequality (SDGs 5 and 9), with a special emphasis on catalyzing women's innovation-led entrepreneurship, resulting in economic empowerment for the world's future. Recent research has revealed the type of assistance that women-owned businesses require the most in order to recover and continue operation. These include government grants and stimulus funding, as well as private sector capital and financing, innovation assets for implementing cutting-edge technology and participating in technology-intensive activities, programs and trainings to advance digital and entrepreneurial skills. It is critical to actively support and promote public-private initiatives that assist women entrepreneurs in adapting to new technologies, innovating, developing digital skills, and improving access to financing and financial support. In light of Industry 5.0, the goal of this research is to identify the crucial characteristics that can support innovation driven by female entrepreneurs.

**Chapter XII talks about Managing Knowledge Processes and Conceptual Review for Higher Education Institutions**

Higher education is the backbone of any country, determining where we stand and where we wish to go. The goal of higher education is to offer students a platform to improve their knowledge, skills, and attitude in their chosen field of study. Each course has its own set of objectives and learning outcomes that should be expected upon completion. Despite these attempts, there is a significant gap in terms of the skill set required to make a student employable. This is one of the bottlenecks in the overall teaching-learning system. Through this research chapter, the author seeks to identify systemic gaps and proposes a redesigned approach to achieving higher education's goals.

**Chapter XIII talks about the Implementation of the Internet of Things (IoT) in Human Resource Management: An Overview**

One of the most important technological developments in recent years is the idea of the Internet of Things (IoT). The Internet of Things, to put it simply, is a system whereby all people, organizations, and objects are connected to one another across a network segment to continuously exchange data without the need for human involvement, fully stoking business. The ease of tracking efficiency has never been greater, thanks to technology. More than ever, communication tools, wearable computing devices, trackers, and other technologies are influencing business and daily life. This chapter tries to provide a history of IoT deployment in HRM. The emergence of mobile job seekers and the use of microchips to manage personnel are just two examples of how the expansion of the Internet of Things (IoT) is expected to change the way businesses and human resources departments function.

**Chapter XIV talks about Artificial Intelligence (AI): A Metamorphic Transformation in Healthcare Services**

All facets of human existence are significantly influenced by artificial intelligence, and technology is supposed to enhance human welfare. Healthcare is a significant area in this regard, and artificial intelligence is accelerating development. With the help of smart gadgets, AI can deliver improved healthcare services. Using the Internet of Things (IoT) and artificial intelligence, small, portable gadgets are now improving the quality of life for people. These tools are used to diagnose and treat a variety of brain illnesses in addition to assisting in the diagnosis of diseases like Alzheimer's disease. The survey is conducted to better understand how patients and healthcare professionals (doctors and nursing staff) feel about artificial intelligence. Super specialty private hospitals in Vizag, Andhra Pradesh, and the capital region of Odisha are included in the study's scope.

Thus, the goal of this book is to provide a high-quality publication with unique insights and techniques of application for current scholars and readers. This book provides an excellent summary of how Big Data analytics transforms organizations and organizes long-term competitive innovation.

**Sukanta Kumar Baral**
Department of Commerce, Faculty of Commerce & Management
Indira Gandhi National Tribal University (A Central University)
Amarkantak, Madhya Pradesh, India

**Richa Goel**
Symbiosis Centre of Management Studies, Noida
Symbiosis International Deemed University, Pune, India

**Tilottama Singh**
Uttaranchal Institute of Management
Uttaranchal University, Dehradun, India

**Erdener Kaynak**
School of Business Administration
Penn State University, Harrisburg
777 W. Harrisburg Pike
Middletown, USA

&

**Vishal Jain**
Department of Computer Science and Engineering
School of Engineering and Technology
Sharda University, Greater Noida, India

# ACKNOWLEDGEMENTS

First and foremost, we would like to express our gratitude to our Almighty God. We became more conscious of how genuine this writing ability is while putting this book together. You gave us the confidence to chase our dreams and pursue our passions. We would not have succeeded if you had not believed in us. We owe a debt of gratitude to our family members, who have been staunch supporters of our efforts to complete this book.

The editors would like to thank everyone who is associated with this book project, especially the writers and reviewers who participated in the assessment process. This book would not have been possible without their cooperation. The editors take the time to thank everyone who has contributed. We are grateful to the chapter writers who generously contributed their time and abilities to this publication. The editors are thankful to the reviewers for their considerable, unceasing contributions to the quality, coherence, and structuring of the information in the chapters.

We were inspired to provide explanations, investigate particular insight work components, and provide evidence for particular ideas by those who provided extensive and incisive criticism on a few chapters. We also want to express our gratitude to everyone who has helped us learn about and use the science and art of networking throughout the years.

# List of Contributors


| | |
|---|---|
| **Ashima Bhatnagar Bhatia** | Vivekananda Institute of Professional Studies – Technical Campus, New Delhi, India |
| **Arun Velu** | Equifax, Atlanta, USA |
| **Ashish Joshi** | Graphic Era Deemed To be University, Uttarakhand, India |
| **Ashutosh Priya** | Department of Applied and Regional Economics, Mahatma Jyotiba Phule Rohilkhand University, Bareilly, Uttar Pradesh, India |
| **Aurodeep Kamal** | KIIT School of Management, KIIT University, Bhubaneswar, Odisha, India |
| **Arpita Nayak** | KIIT School of Management, KIIT University, Bhubaneswar, Odisha, India |
| **Abhiraj Malia** | KIIT School of Management, KIIT University, Bhubaneswar, Odisha, India |
| **Biswajit Das** | KIIT School of Management, KIIT University, Bhubaneswar, Odisha, India |
| **Bhubaneswari Bisoyi** | Sri Sri University, Cuttack, Odisha, India |
| **B.C.M. Patnaik** | KIIT School of Management, KIIT University, Bhubaneswar, Odisha, India |
| **Chitra Krishnan** | Symbiosis Centre for Management Studies, Noida, Symbiosis International Deemed University, Pune, India |
| **Debendra Nath Das** | Mahatma Gandhi National Council of Rural Education, Hyderabad, India |
| **Flavio De Sao Pedro Filho** | Department of Management and Economics, Federal University, Rondonia, Brazil |
| **Hitaishi Singh** | Department of Home Science (Extension Education & Communication) ANDNNMM (CSJM University) Kanpur, India |
| **Ipseeta Satpathy** | KIIT School of Management, KIIT University, Bhubaneswar, Odisha, India |
| **Isha Pant** | Department of Computer Science and Engineering, THDC Institute of Hydropower Engineering and Technology, Uttarakhand, India |
| **Jaya Bharti** | Department of Psychology ANDNNMM (CSJM University) Kanpur, India |
| **Jasmine Mariappan** | UTAS, Ibra, Oman |
| **Kari J. Lippert** | The University of South Alabama, Mobile, USA |
| **Madhuri Yadav** | Department of Commerce, Indira Gandhi National Tribal University, Madhya Pradesh, India |
| **Mohammad Nasfikur R. Khan** | The University of South Alabama, Mobile, USA |
| **Navita Mahajan** | Amity University, Uttar Pradesh, India |
| **Neha Rastogi** | Doon Business School, India |

| | |
|---|---|
| **Neeru Sidana** | Amity School of Economics (ASE) Amity University, Noida, U.P., India |
| **Pragya Baluni** | THDC Institute of Hydropower Engineering and Technology, Uttarakhand, India |
| **Preetiraj Pattnaik** | Centurion University of Technology and Management Bhubaneswar, India |
| **Pawan Whig** | Vivekananda Institute of Professional Studies - Technical Campus, , New Delhi, India |
| **Prasanta Kumar Mohanty** | Centurion University of Technology and Management Bhubaneswar, India |
| **Robert J. Cloutier** | The University of South Alabama, Mobile, USA |
| **Rabinarayan Patnaik** | Faculty of Management Sciences, Siksha 'O' Anusandhan (SOA) Deemed University, Bhubaneswar, India |
| **Richa Goel** | Symbiosis Centre for Management Studies, Noida, Symbiosis International Deemed University, Pune, India |
| **Rajeev Ranjan** | Uttaranchal University |
| **Ravi Kumar Gupta** | Department of Humanities and Management Science, Madan Mohan Malaviya University of Technology, Gorakhpur, India |
| **Sukanta Kumar Baral** | Department of Commerce, Indira Gandhi National Tribal University, Madhya Pradesh, India |
| **S. K. Baral** | Department of Commerce, Indira Gandhi National Tribal University, Madhya Pradesh, India |
| **Supriya Lamba Sahdev** | ISBR Business School, Bangalore, India |
| **Shama Kouser** | Department of Computer Science Jazan University, Saudi Arabia |
| **Tilottama Singh** | Uttaranchal Institute of Management, Uttaranchal University, Dehradun, India |
| **Udit Maheshwari** | Department of Humanities and Management Science, Madan Mohan Malaviya University of Technology, Gorakhpur, India |
| **Yusuf Jibrin Alkali** | Federal Inland Revenue Service, Nigeria |

# CHAPTER 1

# Risk Analysis of Implementing Immersive Technology in the Healthcare System

**Mohammad Nasfikur R. Khan**[1,*], **Kari J. Lippert**[1] and **Robert J. Cloutier**[1]

[1] *The University of South Alabama, Mobile, USA*

**Abstract:** An immersive environment allows people to interact with a virtual environment. Despite its relatively short history, immersive technology still finds applications in medicine. There are numerous medical applications of immersive technologies like virtual reality, augmented reality, and mixed reality, including the improvement of vision, treatment of behavioral disorders, rehabilitating patients, and creating customized fitness routines. The objective of this chapter is to assess the risks associated with a technology-based healthcare system that benefits both patients and professionals. In addition to delivering training and improving patient care, immersive healthcare training systems help facilitate the delivery of training. Our first step is to describe how the system functions, followed by risk analysis, such as Ishikawa, Fault Tree Analysis (FTA), and Causal Loop Diagram (CLD), to highlight the three biggest risks associated with the system. Further, this chapter will discuss the monitoring and management of risks.

**Keywords:** AR, CLD, FTA, FMEA, Ishikawa, Immersive technology, Risk management, VR, Virtual environment.

## INTRODUCTION

Immersive technology allows for the rendering of a computer-created environment immersively. Medical sciences is among the fields in which immersive technology is most useful. Immersive technology is still in its early developmental stages in the medical field. It has already been reported that VR systems have been introduced to aid doctors and medical staff in their learning process. In addition to training and rehabilitation, immersive technologies like VR are also helpful for visually impaired people, people suffering from psychiatric disorders, and amblyopia sufferers. At the moment, there are no technology-based immersive experiences that are suitable for both patients and healthcare professionals. The focus of this chapter will be on an immersive and interactive

* **Corresponding author Mohammad Nasfikur R Khan:** The University of South Alabama, Mobile, USA; E-mail: mk2121@jagmail.southalabama.edu

**Sukanta Kumar Baral, Richa Goel, Tilottama Singh, Erdener Kaynak & Vishal Jain (Eds.)**

digital healthcare system. A variety of devices and sensors are incorporated into this system, as well as immersive gadgets. Consequently, users can use it anytime throughout the day. This chapter also discusses several important aspects of the immersive technology-based medical system.

- Describe immersive technologies.
- Discuss how immersive technologies are used in medical sciences.
- How can immersive technologies be used in medical education?

It is possible to use this technology with a variety of devices, including immersive glasses, wrist watches, and sensors. Users can access the system according to their needs. By using this system, educators can upload content according to their preferred time. On the other hand, learners can access this content according to their needs. Furthermore, clients can seek medical providers based on their specific requirements. Clients may also trade data with them, receive comments, contact specialists, obtain surgical aid, exchange psychological information, and ultimately, access an emergency system.

The first step in understanding this system is to examine its background. In the next section, we discuss how the system operates, revealing its working process. Next, we use different risk assessment procedures to reduce the chance of failure using risk assessment techniques. This section discusses and explains the processes for handling risk and maintaining it.

## BACKGROUND

### Immersive Technologies

To create new experiences, immersive technology combines the physical world with a virtual or simulated one. There are two main types of immersive technologies: augmented reality (AR) and virtual reality (VR).

#### *VR*

The concept of virtual reality is a computer-generated simulation of a three-dimensional environment. VR technology allows users to experience a virtual world using a computer-based operating system and other technologies. This alternate world is simulated using different devices, which enhances the sense of realism in people.The use of VR technology has transformed the way students are trained and how teachers learn. Instead of focusing on teaching, teachers can focus on learning.Multimedia Cone of Abstraction (MCoA), a model of active learning based on Dale's Cone of Experience (CoE), occurs as learners engage in activities within a virtual world. As a replacement for the CoE's foundation level, "Direct Purposeful Experiences" demonstrate how students can interact with and benefit from highly realistic representations. The student may be able to gain a better understanding of work or concepts if he or she receives timely feedback and can improve at their own pace. In addition, patients can directly contact medical professionals to receive fast and rapid responses.The server can also be used by medical professionals for data collection and feedback.

### *AR*

AR continues to be the most popular technology trend due to the availability of handheld devices that show AR. It is an interactive multi-media technology that combines virtual and real elements, enables real-time interaction, and creates three-dimensional maps. First, AR and VR are contrasted, then computer-generated models in live-action movies are discussed, and annotations and overlays on videos are shown.

To design and develop technologies that mediate human communication, it is useful to have a theory of human communication behavior. Due to the lack of appropriate technology, social acceptance, usability, money, and time, as well as a lack of knowledge of what can be achieved with AR in medical sciences, augmented reality technology has yet to gain traction even though it has been on the market since the 1980s. Additionally, traditional augmented reality applications must also combine virtual and real-world information, be interactive, and support 3D registration.

## Immersive Technologies in Medical Sciences

In healthcare education, simulation training has been shown to improve knowledge acquisition and competency. VR training can help healthcare professionals teach medical students to avoid situations that could lead to poor outcomes in a patient-practitioner relationship. For medical students, VR technology has the potential to be a valuable interactive, experiential tool that can help them develop the skills needed in a real-life scenario, as well as a cost-effective approach to repeatedly practicing simulated clinical scenarios in healthcare. By using VR, students can practice without fear of making real-life mistakes, prepare for diagnosing sickness indicators, and even perform complicated procedures.

By providing a suitable training method, VR simulations eliminate the need for cadavers or animals to gain professional knowledge and create crucial practical skills in medicine. While there is still room for improvement in the haptic (touch) sense, procedural, visual, and aural senses can be trained by using this method.

Trainee surgeons can experience a variety of surgeries and procedures through the virtual reality system, including endoscopic surgery, laparoscopic surgery, neurosurgery, and epidural injections. According to Vaughan *et al.*, orthopedic VR training simulators provide surgeons with an excellent platform to develop and improve their skills in a safe, risk-free, realistic operating room.

For doctors with less experience in surgery, VR simulations may be an effective tool to teach essential procedures for orthopedics and other types of surgery. Patients and their primary caregivers may respond better to traditional instructional approaches, such as giving a verbal presentation of information or providing written materials. Interacting with a patient should be tailored to their language ability, ethnicity, socio-economic background, level of education, and cognitive ability. There is evidence that these patient characteristics influence risk factors and patient outcomes.

For relevant and understandable patient knowledge, education must be designed to meet the specific needs of patients who experience acute or chronic conditions.To reduce recurrent strokes and maximize rehabilitation, Thompson-Butel *et al.* developed customized virtual reality rehabilitation sessions for stroke survivors and their primary caregivers. In their study, the researchers assessed whether VR sessions were effective in providing post-stroke education.This study found that using VR sessions resulted in "various significant improvements in technical expertise in areas such as neurodevelopment and physiology, cognitive impairment and healing, and stroke-specific instructions such as personalized stroke risk factors, as well as acute therapy advantages" for the victim and their caregivers.

Several studies have examined the current state of virtual reality simulations in dentistry training.Their research suggests that VR equipment can be used in dentistry education to provide opportunities for flexibility and self-learning. VR devices enable learners to participate in their education in a variety of ways: They can perform simulations whenever and wherever they want, and they can keep track of and re-visit their work after they have completed it. Moreover, incorporating virtual reality technology into the classroom reduces anxiety and boredom and enhances student engagement and retention. Additionally, students from all dental disciplines may benefit from more efficient and realistic pre-clinical practices with VR due to its rapid technological advancements.

Technological advancements enable the improvement of all aspects of human life, but health will suffer the greatest consequences. There is a need to re-think healthcare studies due to the healthcare crisis. Effective use of technology can improve the efficiency of healthcare organizations. Augmented reality has proven to be effective in providing enhanced healthcare to patients. This technology is expected to have a significant effect on the healthcare field.The reason for this is that augmented reality makes use of sensors, displays, and embedded electronics.

## CONCEPT OF OPERATIONS (CONOPS)

There are various CONOPS guidelines, models, and methodologies that can be used depending on the situation or environment. The risks associated with the system will be discussed in this section. According to the Whiting School of Engineering at Johns Hopkins University, this decision can be made based on a set of criteria derived from SE analysis:

- Risks associated with programs
- Designed to meet the needs of customers
- Constraints on funding
- Considering the market
- Aspects of technology
- System's environment

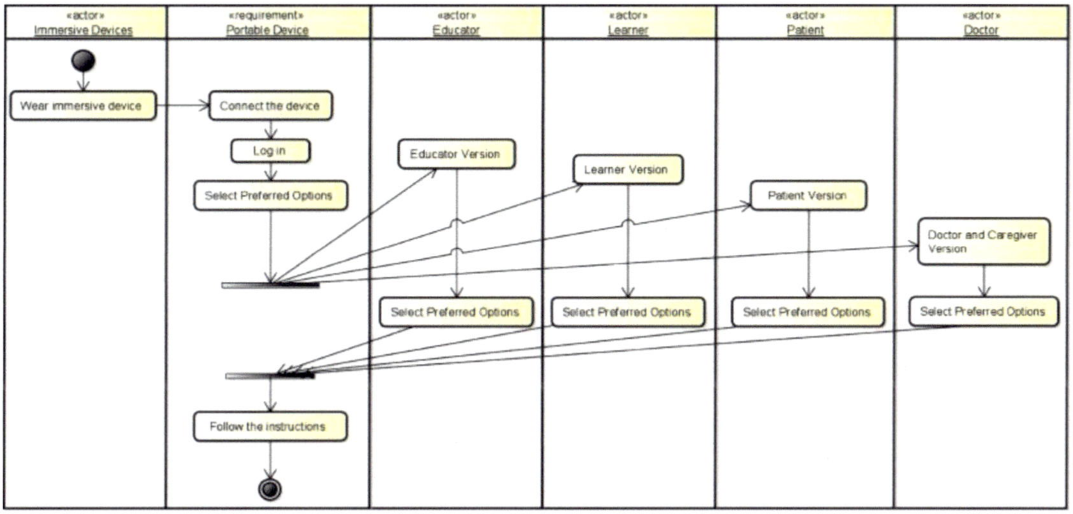


**Fig. (1).** An activity diagram of the proposed system.

Fig. (**1**) illustrates a simplified activity diagram of the proposed system, which illustrates how it will operate. Immersive devices used by educators, learners, patients, and medical professionals are linked to smartphones that must be registered before use. To access a particular area of medical sciences, users can log in as either an educator, learner, patient, or medical professional. After choosing certain options and following the instructions, using the system is straight forward. Through this system, patients can pick the specific specialists and services they need. Medical professionals such as doctors have access to the data of their patients 24/7 and can provide healthcare-related support. Meanwhile, educators and learners can easily communicate through a virtual environment created by the system. Students and educators can also easily assess each other using this system.

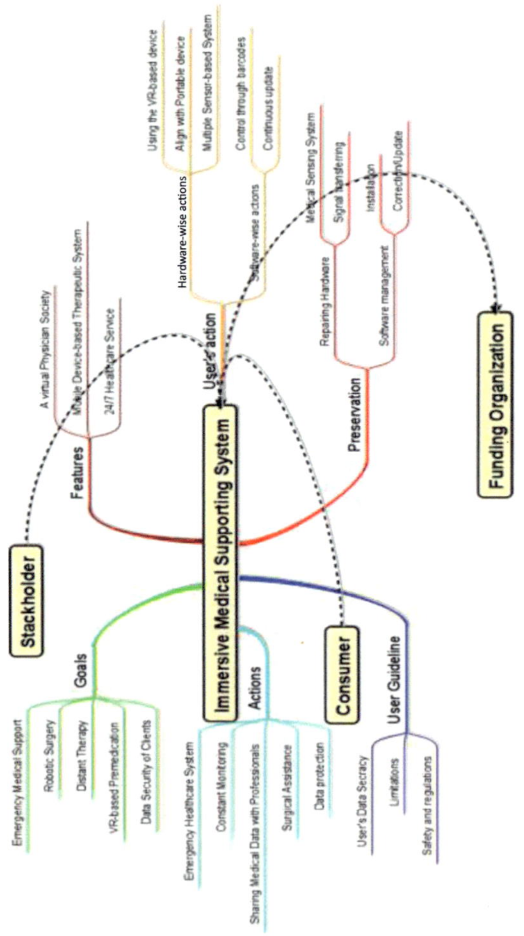


**Fig. (2).** A mind map of the proposed system.

Next, we mapped out our ideas regarding the recommended system in a mind map (Fig. **2**), which helped us visualize them. The mind map visually organizes information into a hierarchy, with representations of links between pieces of the whole. It is often made around a single concept, which is drawn as a center image on a blank page. The images, words, and parts of the words are added as representations of the concept. Major ideas are connected directly to the central concept, and other ideas branch out from those major ideas.Drawing mind maps by hand or using a computer is an effective way to follow lectures, participate in meetings, or prepare for planning sessions. Our system's mind map states that the funding organization will fund hardware and software development while developers will create it. Additionally, they will provide maintenance to ensure the system operates efficiently. To promote and deliver the system to specific consumers, it is necessary to engage a group of vendors.

## STAKEHOLDERS

The stakeholders of the system are listed in this section. The system of interests considers two types of stakeholders: active and passive. As soon as the system is operational and in use, users, companies, and other systems will engage in active interactions with it. Several factors can influence a system's success, such as individuals, organizations, policies, procedures, and guidelines, which can be considered passive stakeholders. A user group involves learners and educators, management (funding and management authority), experts, and technical support staff, as well as those involved in hardware and software maintenance. The state government plays a passive role in the development and research of immersive and portable devices, as do developers and researchers, and consumers and users.

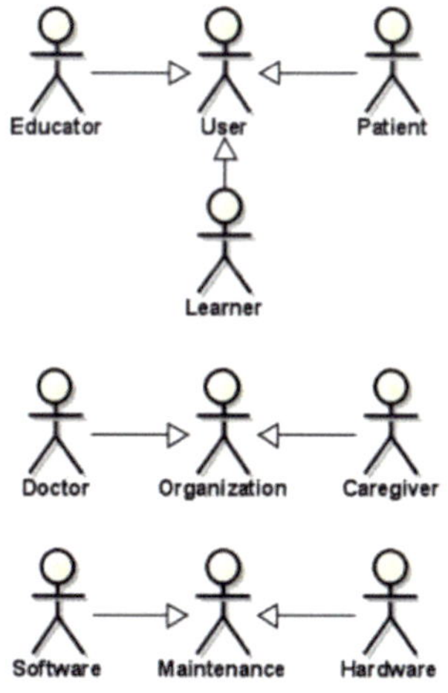


**Fig. (3).** Lists of active stakeholders.

A passive stakeholder is represented in Fig. **4**, while an active stakeholder is represented in Fig. (**3**). The three categories of active or involved stakeholders are organizations, users, and maintenance.

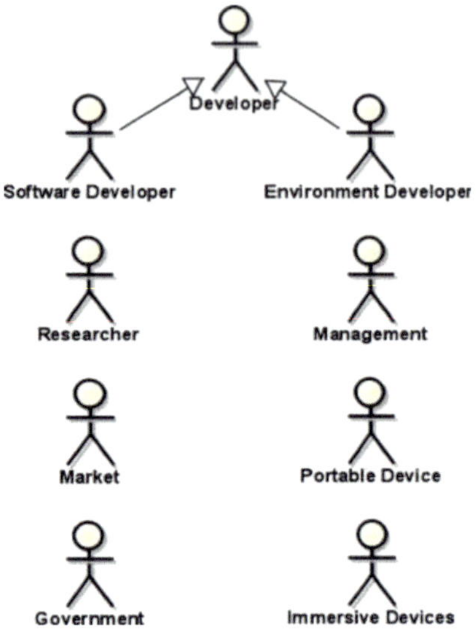


**Fig. (4).** Lists of passive stakeholders.

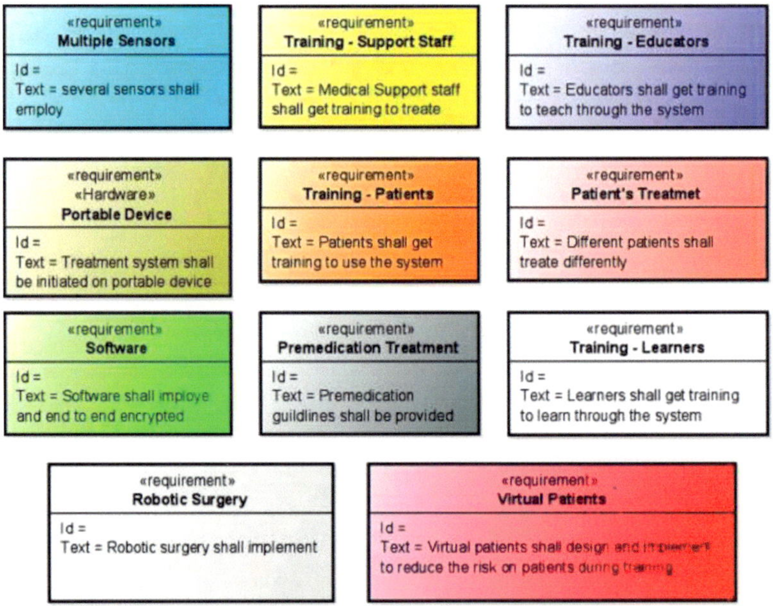


**Fig. (5).** The desirements diagram of the system.

### Desirements of the Stakeholders

Developing a new system begins with a stakeholder's desire or need that a current system cannot meet. These expectations are called stakeholder desirements when they are merely wanted rather than required. It has been shown through research that stakeholders looking for immersive medical systems seek specific features that pertain to their preconceived notions. This section assesses and represents stakeholder expectations, desires, and requirements as the basis for system validation - what stakeholders want the system to accomplish.

An example of the stakeholder's desires is shown in Fig. (**5**). The implementation of immersive technologies involves multiple sensors and devices to implement certain desires. The applications include therapeutic solutions, healthcare for children, surgical aid, pre-medication, robotic surgery, psychiatric counseling, and autism therapy. The concern for patient differences is expressed in the cultural requirement. In addition to the system requirements listed here, data security and privacy considerations also need to be considered.

## RISK IDENTIFICATION

Determining risks begins with outlining goals and objectives so that all project members are aware of what matters most for success. The identification and assessment of risks are enabled because of the creation of the necessary knowledge and scope. In this article, a series of techniques will be examined for identifying risk.

Systematic and effective risk management is essential for preventing and minimizing accidents. ISO 31000 defines risk management as the process of identifying, analyzing, managing and controlling risks. The process is as follows:

### Assessing the Context

To conduct a risk assessment, you must understand and evaluate the context. There are different perspectives on what the most important assets are from different roles and departments, so it is a good idea to get input from more than one source. The most important asset in a virtual environment is the server, while the most essential asset in this proposal is data sharing. Virtual environments would benefit most from immersive technology, whereas the proposed system would benefit most from sharing data.

Our next step will be to classify our contextual assets and key stakeholders within each department. It is necessary to consider their sensitivity and strategic significance. To get accurate and complete information, all major sub-systems must be aligned across all departments.

### Risk Identifying

Considering the risk of hackers to private data security, the risks associated with sharing data are usually at the top of the list, but threats come in many shapes and sizes. While breaches exploiting weaknesses in a business' firewalls or website security programs were very common in 2019, there were many other types of threats that led to data breaches in 2019. While compiling the list of all the unique threats your business faces, it is important to take into account many different types of threats.

Taking into account not only malicious but also accidental human actions, such as users accidentally deleting data or clicking on malicious links, is crucial. It may also be necessary to take into account the risk of system failure based on the quality of the hardware and information systems.

Natural catastrophes and power outages can also cause havoc in the same way humans can, so we should also take these kinds of threats into account. By the end of this step, we should have compiled a comprehensive list of assets that might be at risk.

### Analyzing the Risk

After identifying risks and estimating levels of uncertainty, we now have the basic framework for how to conduct a risk analysis. All our inputs are users' uncertainties, and we can build a complete model based on them. Next, we evaluate the outputs, which are the outcomes of the uncertainties and the probability of them occurring during the project. In this case, our outputs will be ranges rather than exact outcomes since users have provided estimated input values.

With the use of a computer program, we can investigate the outputs further. An algorithm can calculate the probability of each outcome by identifying each risk and its probability. Using the uncertain inputs as a starting point, each program calculates the model's outputs using the input value. The goal of the simulation is to produce an average value, but they may also be used to examine the range of possible outcomes, especially when there are different sources of uncertainty that might interact unexpectedly during the simulation.

## Evaluate the Risk Factors

Depending on the type of risk we are assessing, we can determine what interpretation is best based on the results. Make a chart or graph that summarizes the potential outcomes. Charts and graphs make complex statistical information easier to understand.

Analyzing the results of a risk analysis model using sensitivity analysis involves using mathematical software to assign different levels of uncertainty to the input assumptions of the model.

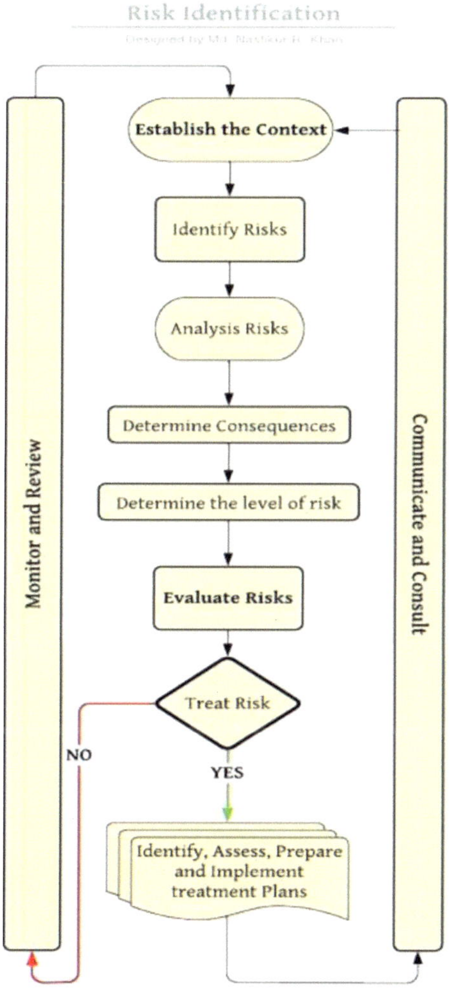


**Fig. (6).** Risk Identification and Management Process.

## Assessing the Risk

The solution with the least level of risk should be implemented. If that is the case, then the project might be limited by certain conditions or the project might not be initiated because the risks are greater than the rewards. During the process, there are likely to be other challenges that we did not manage to account for in our analysis. The project should be reviewed regularly so we can make sure we are staying on track with the proposed solution and make adjustments if any changes occur.

Fig. (**6**) shows a system's risk management process. This process makes use of brainstorming to identify potential risks. Furthermore, we employ several methods of risk assessment, including the FTA, the Ishikawa Diagram, and the CLD.

## RISK ANALYSIS

Risk analysis identifies and analyzes potential issues that could adversely affect key business initiatives or major projects. These analyses are performed to help organizations manage or mitigate those risks. The following methods are widely used to assess the risks in a project.

Risk assessments are done by engineering professionals in several different ways. Depending on the function, professionals may use only one or several of these types. Multiple risk assessment approaches can be implemented simultaneously. An analysis of this system's risks could be conducted using some risk analysis techniques. Some of these techniques include FMEA, CLD, and FTA.

### FMEA (Failure Mode and Effects Analysis)

The FMEA method is a risk assessment tool that can be applied to a variety of environments, such as medical devices, machinery, automotive, and so on, but it is most appropriate when utilized in component-based projects. There are different ways that products and processes can fail. A failure can have many effects, including waste, defects, or harmful outcomes for the customer. An FMEA identifies, prioritizes, and limits these failure modes. The FMEA is not a substitute for engineering quality.

By assessing a product or process' risk of failure, the knowledge and experience of a Cross-Functional Team (CFT) enhance good engineering. FMEA has two broad categories: Design FMEA (DFMEA) and Process FMEA (PFMEA).

Nevertheless, we did not apply this method to this situation since we lacked sufficient data to conduct an FMEA.

## CLD (Causal Loop Diagram)

A CLD illustrates cause-and-effect patterns from a system's perspective (also known as a system thinking diagram). The fishbone diagram may assist in revealing the categories of causes behind a problem. The causal loops indicate the interrelationship between causes and their effects. After completing the diagram, the positive and negative reinforcements that describe the system of behavior are identified. A good characteristic of causal loops is they depersonalize learning. It may be wise to point out the arrows that are reinforcing the problem instead of pointing at individuals.

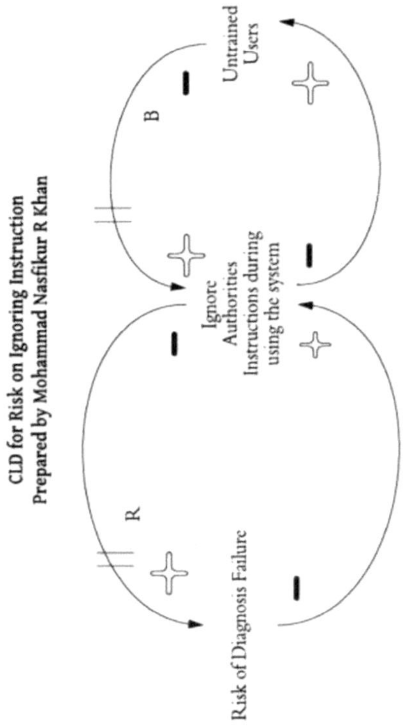


**Fig. (7).** CLD for Ignoring Instruction while using the system.

The model becomes a model of the system behaviors that produce the system's outcomes. A CLD provides a visual representation of how different variables in a system interrelate. There are nodes and edges in the diagram. There are nodes corresponding to variables, and edges corresponding to links connecting the two variables. The link with a positive marking indicates a positive relationship, while the link with a negative marking indicates a negative relationship. An example of a positive causal link is when both nodes of a graph move in the same direction, so if the node in which the link starts decreases, the other node decreases as well.

In the same way, if the node from which the link starts increases, the other node does too. Negative causal links refer to changes that occur in the opposite direction of the node in which the link originates, *i.e.*, if the node in which the link starts increases, the other node decreases, and *vice versa*.

As illustrated in Fig. (**7**), CLDs result from the possible consequences of ignoring instructions while using a system. This diagram illustrates how, if a user is not trained and ignores the instructions, there is a risk of a wrong diagnosis, which can cause severe health complications.

## FTA (Fault Tree Analysis)

System failures can be explored graphically by using FTA. It combines a series of lower-level events using boolean logic and is a top-down approach to identifying failures at component levels (basic events) that cause system-level failures (top events). There are two main components of fault tree analysis: "events" and "logic gates" related to the top undesired event. In comparison to FMEA, fault tree analysis takes into account all possible failures of a top event within the system. In contrast, FMEA analyzes all possible modes of failure, regardless of severity.

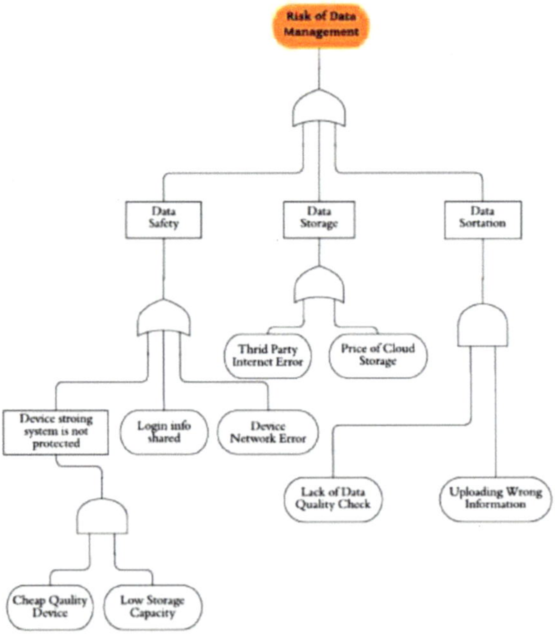


**Fig. (8).** FTA to assess the risk of the proposed system.

To identify the root cause of an undesired state that exists in a system using the FTA method (Fig. **8**), multiple events are combined at lower levels. As a result of this section, we will attempt to assess the risks associated with using data. Risks associated with data management are classified into three categories. These include data safety, data storage, and data sortation.

A secure data storage system requires sharing login information, preventing device errors, and securing device storage data. The device storage system is dependent on the device's quality and storage capacity. A cloud-based storage system is also prone to internet errors because of a third-party provider and since it is more expensive. Last but not least, the data sortation-based threats depend on a lack of quality-checking systems and uploaded data. There are times when users share wrong data based on their assumptions, which creates a risk for the system running smoothly.

The FTA method enabled us to investigate the root cause of the problem. Among them are a few that stand out: poor device quality, low storage capacity, shared login information, data quality checks, and incorrect data being uploaded.

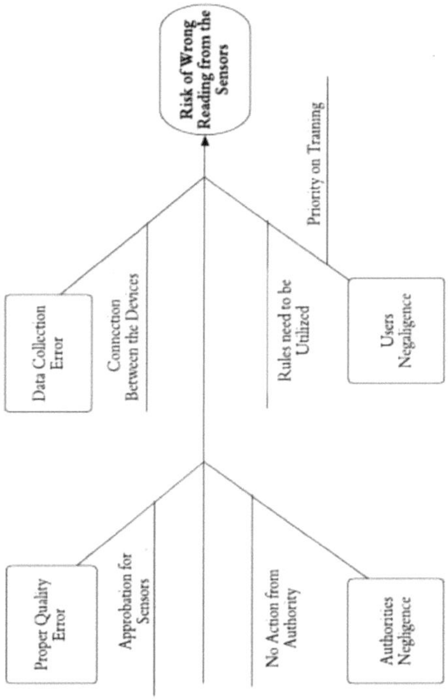


**Fig. (9).** Ishikawa Diagram for the Risk of Reading Wrong Information.

## Ishikawa Diagram

An Ishikawa diagram can be used to identify the causal link between a problem and a solution. It helps illustrate the causes of the phenomenon, the factors that affect these problems, and how the issue can be resolved using a picture. In Ishikawa, the causes and effects of a relationship are drawn like a fishbone. Determining the difference between solutions and problems is very difficult. Users can use Ishikawa diagrams to gain insight into the causes and effects of problems and to rank the causes and effects to accurately identify the causes.

The following diagram shows how we attempted to determine the risk of reading incorrect data from the sensors (Fig. **9**). As a result of the errors in the data collection process, the poor quality of the data, negligence on the part of the authority, and ultimately, negligence on the part of the user, this situation occurred. Training is necessary, rules must be followed, authorities should take action if any part of the system violates the rules, and sensors must be approved before use to manage this risk.

## RISK HANDLING AND MONITORING

To manage risk, five basic methods are employed. It is important to keep in mind that risk management applies to various aspects of our daily lives, like avoiding, retaining, sharing, transferring, and reducing loss, and will pay off in the long run.

### Avoiding

As a rule, avoiding something harmful is the same as not participating in it. A common example is smoking. We propose a system that will encourage users to stay away from unauthorized sensors and devices in order to reduce the risk of data loss or misinterpretation. It will be easier for the users and service providers to collaborate with a better awareness, which will lead to the best outcome for everyone.

### Retention

A retention strategy acknowledges the inevitable risks involved in certain fields, such as healthcare, which may mean selecting a less expensive internet plan that does not cover everything that matters most to the user. In order to accomplish that, we will provide guidelines and align with various internet service providers so that they cover the areas of our clients.

### Sharing

It should also be prohibited for users to share their login information since this can lead to security breaches. The user will be provided with a concrete security system to sign in so that the login information is not shared. It is necessary to provide the user's preferred email address and password in the first place. Afterward, the devices should be registered so that the data can be transferred.

They must also choose a few randomly chosen questions and answer those that only they know. Then, they will receive a one-time password for confirmation.

### Transferring

Any unauthorized transfer of data between devices can result in data loss when using the proposed system. As we discussed previously, it is important to register devices that the users will use to share and transfer data. The data sharing and transferring system will be more secure with the ability to use 3 devices simultaneously. To add a new device after the third one, the user will have to remove one of the previously registered devices. Thus, the system will ensure that necessary data is scrutinized and only authorized data is transferred.

### Prevention

As a final concern, if we prevent sharing data constantly to ensure minimal misuse, we might sometimes lose essential data during emergencies. For the implementation of complete AI, the system may need to accumulate data throughout the process. We recommend users utilize the device throughout the day so that they can take full advantage of it. We also encourage them to use no more than a minimal number of devices, which will help them feel comfortable and make them carry the devices easily without any hassle.

## CONCLUSION

Immersive environments provide people with the opportunity to interact with a virtual environment. This technology can be used in medical settings. The use of immersive technology in medical settings is still in its infancy. The medical applications of immersive technologies like virtual reality include improving vision, treating behavioral disorders, and developing custom fitness routines.

This chapter investigates the risks associated with a technology-driven healthcare system that is both beneficial and efficient. The first part of the chapter provides a brief overview of the system of interest. The second section discusses risk identification and risk management. A few risk assessment processes are then included in the report after the risk analysis. Moreover, the article explains how to manage the system as well as how to deal with these issues.

## BIBLIOGRAPHY

Alsuraihi, A.A. (2022). The effect of implementing mind maps for online learning and assessment on students during COVID-19 pandemic: a cross sectional study. *BMC Med. Educ., 22*(1), 169. [http://dx.doi.org/10.1186/s12909-022-03211-2] [PMID: 35279151]

Baukal, C.E., Ausburn, F.B., Ausburn, L.J. (2013). A Proposed Multimedia Cone of Abstraction: Updating a Classic Instructional Design Theory. *Journal of Educational Technology, 9*(4), 15-24.

Bloom, B.S. (1974). Time and learning. *Am. Psychol., 29*(9), 682-688.
[http://dx.doi.org/10.1037/h0037632]

Boaz, A., Hanney, S., Borst, R., O'Shea, A., Kok, M. (2018). How to engage stakeholders in research: design principles to support improvement. *Health Res. Policy Syst., 16*(1), 60.
[http://dx.doi.org/10.1186/s12961-018-0337-6] [PMID: 29996848]

Bracq, M.S., Michinov, E., Jannin, P. (2019). Virtual Reality Simulation in Nontechnical Skills Training for Healthcare Professionals. *Simul. Healthc., 14*(3), 188-194.
[http://dx.doi.org/10.1097/SIH.0000000000000347] [PMID: 30601464]

Brown, R.G., Easterfield, T.E. (1951). A Proposed Definition of Operations Research. *J. Oper. Res. Soc., 2*(2), 21-24.
[http://dx.doi.org/10.1057/jors.1951.8]

Eckert, M., Volmerg, J.S., Friedrich, C.M. (2019). Augmented Reality in Medicine: Systematic and Bibliographic Review. *JMIR Mhealth Uhealth, 7*(4), e10967.
[http://dx.doi.org/10.2196/10967] [PMID: 31025950]

Gadelha, R. (2018). Revolutionizing Education: The promise of virtual reality. *Child. Educ., 94*(1), 40-43.
[http://dx.doi.org/10.1080/00094056.2018.1420362]

Haller, G., Stoelwinder, J., Myles, P.S., McNeil, J. (2009). Quality and safety indicators in anesthesia: a systematic review. *Anesthesiology, 110*(5), 1158-1175.
[http://dx.doi.org/10.1097/ALN.0b013e3181a1093b] [PMID: 19352148]

Hoffmann, T., McKenna, K. (2006). Analysis of stroke patients' and carers' reading ability and the content and design of written materials: Recommendations for improving written stroke information. *Patient Educ. Couns., 60*(3), 286-293.
[http://dx.doi.org/10.1016/j.pec.2005.06.020] [PMID: 16098708]

Johnson, J.K., Barach, P. (2009). Patient care handovers: what will it take to ensure quality and safety during times of transition? *Med. J. Aust., 190*(S11), S110-S112.
[http://dx.doi.org/10.5694/j.1326-5377.2009.tb02614.x] [PMID: 19485869]

Khan, M.N.R., Lippert, K.J. (2022). A Framework for a Virtual Reality-Based Medical Support System. In: Anisha, P.R., Reddy, C.K.K., Nguyen, N.G., Bhushan, M., Kumar, A., Hanafiah, M.M., (Eds.), *Intelligent Systems and Machine Learning for Industry.* CRC Press.

Khan, M.N.R., Lippert, K.J. (2022). Immersive Technologies in Healthcare Education. In: Anisha, P.R., Reddy, C.K.K., Nguyen, N.G., Bhushan, M., Kumar, A., Hanafiah, M.M., (Eds.), *Intelligent Systems and Machine Learning for Industry.* CRC Press.

Khan, M.N.R., Shakir, A.K., Nadi, S.S., Abedin, M.Z. (2022). An Android Application for University-Based Academic Solution for Crisis Situation. In: Shakya, S., Balas, V. E., Kamolphiwong, S., Du, K., (Eds.), *Proceedings of ICSADL 2021, 1408*, 653-663.
[http://dx.doi.org/10.1007/978-981-16-5157-1_51]

King, C.L., Suamani, J., Sanuku, N., Cheng, Y.C., Satofan, S., Mancuso, B., Goss, C.W., Robinson, L.J., Siba, P.M., Weil, G.J., Kazura, J.W. (2018). A Trial of a Triple-Drug Treatment for Lymphatic Filariasis. *N. Engl. J. Med., 379*(19), 1801-1810.
[http://dx.doi.org/10.1056/NEJMoa1706854] [PMID: 30403937]

Lavanya, N., Malarvizhi, T. (2008). Risk Analysis and Management: A Vital Key to Effective Project Management.

Majid, B., Khan, R., Junaid, Z., Khurshid, O., Rehman, S.H., Jaffri, S.N., Zaidi, B., Zehra, J., Batool, S., Altaf, S., Jatoi, A., Safina, F. (2019). Assessment of Knowledge About the Risk Factors of Chronic Liver Disease in Patients Admitted in Civil Hospital Karachi. *Cureus, 11*(10), e5945.
[http://dx.doi.org/10.7759/cureus.5945] [PMID: 31799087]

Mascia, A., Cirafici, A.M., Bongiovanni, A., Colotti, G., Lacerra, G., Di Carlo, M., Digilio, F.A., Liguori,

G.L., Lanati, A., Kisslinger, A. (2020). A failure mode and effect analysis (FMEA)-based approach for risk assessment of scientific processes in non-regulated research laboratories. *Accredit. Qual. Assur., 25*(5-6), 311-321.
[http://dx.doi.org/10.1007/s00769-020-01441-9]

Norris, M.W., Spicer, K., Byrd, T. (2019). Virtual Reality: The New Pathway for Effective Safety Training. *Prof. Saf., 64*(06), 36-39.

Riva, G., Baños, R.M., Botella, C., Mantovani, F., Gaggioli, A. (2016). Transforming Experience: The Potential of Augmented Reality and Virtual Reality for Enhancing Personal and Clinical Change. *Front. Psychiatry, 7*, 164.
[http://dx.doi.org/10.3389/fpsyt.2016.00164] [PMID: 27746747]

Sacks, R., Perlman, A., Barak, R. (2013). Construction safety training using immersive virtual reality. *Construct. Manag. Econ., 31*(9), 1005-1017.
[http://dx.doi.org/10.1080/01446193.2013.828844]

Sánchez-Cabrero, R., León-Mejía, A.C., Arigita-García, A., Maganto-Mateo, C. (2019). Improvement of Body Satisfaction in Older People: An Experimental Study. *Front. Psychol., 10*, 2823.
[http://dx.doi.org/10.3389/fpsyg.2019.02823] [PMID: 31920858]

Shafiee, M., Enjema, E., Kolios, A. (2019). An Integrated FTA-FMEA Model for Risk Analysis of Engineering Systems: A Case Study of Subsea Blowout Preventers. *Appl. Sci. (Basel), 9*(6), 1192.
[http://dx.doi.org/10.3390/app9061192]

Simsekler, M.C.E., Ward, J.R., Clarkson, P.J. (2018). Design for patient safety: a systems-based risk identification framework. *Ergonomics, 61*(8), 1046-1064.
[http://dx.doi.org/10.1080/00140139.2018.1437224] [PMID: 29394872]

Thompson-Butel, A.G., Shiner, C.T., McGhee, J., Bailey, B.J., Bou-Haidar, P., McCorriston, M., Faux, S.G. (2019). The Role of Personalized Virtual Reality in Education for Patients Post Stroke—A Qualitative Case Series. *J. Stroke Cerebrovasc. Dis., 28*(2), 450-457.
[http://dx.doi.org/10.1016/j.jstrokecerebrovasdis.2018.10.018] [PMID: 30415917]

Ustun, A.B., Yilmaz, R., Yilmaz, F.G.K. (2020). Virtual Reality in Medical Education. *Mobile Devices and Smart Gadgets in Medical Sciences.* IGI Global.
[http://dx.doi.org/10.4018/978-1-7998-2521-0.ch004]

Vaughan, N., Dubey, V.N., Wainwright, T.W., Middleton, R.G. (2016). A review of virtual reality based training simulators for orthopaedic surgery. *Med. Eng. Phys., 38*(2), 59-71.
[http://dx.doi.org/10.1016/j.medengphy.2015.11.021] [PMID: 26751581]

Vertinsky, I. (2008). Operations Research. *The New Palgrave Dictionary of Economics.* (pp. 1-8). London: Palgrave Macmillan.
[http://dx.doi.org/10.1057/978-1-349-95121-5_1370-2]

Wiederhold, B.K., Riva, G. (2012). Positive technology supports shift to preventive, integrative health. *Cyberpsychol. Behav. Soc. Netw., 15*(2), 67-68.
[http://dx.doi.org/10.1089/cyber.2011.1533] [PMID: 22320253]

Wong, K.C. (2011). Using an Ishikawa diagram as a tool to assist memory and retrieval of relevant medical cases from the medical literature. *J. Med. Case Reports, 5*(1), 120.
[http://dx.doi.org/10.1186/1752-1947-5-120] [PMID: 21447163]

Yatsyshyn, S., Kabachenko, D., Korchynska, O., Seniv, L., Churikanova, O. (2023). Management Decision-Making as a Mechanism for Reducing the Level of Global Risk and Its Redistribution. *Khazar Journal of Humanities and Social Sciences, 26*(1), 107-118.
[http://dx.doi.org/10.5782/.kjhss.2023.107.118]

Yeung, A.W.K., Tosevska, A., Klager, E., Eibensteiner, F., Laxar, D., Stoyanov, J., Glisic, M., Zeiner, S., Kulnik, S.T., Crutzen, R., Kimberger, O., Kletecka-Pulker, M., Atanasov, A.G., Willschke, H. (2021). Virtual and Augmented Reality Applications in Medicine: Analysis of the Scientific Literature. *J. Med. Internet Res.,*

*23*(2), e25499.
[http://dx.doi.org/10.2196/25499] [PMID: 33565986]

Zhang, J., Peng, W., Wang, L. (2018). LeNup: learning nucleosome positioning from DNA sequences with improved convolutional neural networks. *Bioinformatics, 34*(10), 1705-1712.
[http://dx.doi.org/10.1093/bioinformatics/bty003] [PMID: 29329398]

CHAPTER 2

# Internet of Things (IoT) in the Agriculture Sector toward Urban Greening

**Pawan Whig**[1,*], **Shama Kouser**[2], **Ashima Bhatnagar Bhatia**[3], **Arun Velu**[4] and **Yusuf Jibrin Alkali**[5]

[1] *Vivekananda Institute of Professional Studies - Technical Campus, New Delhi, India*

[2] *Department of Computer Science Jazan University, Saudi Arabia*

[3] *Vivekananda Institute of Professional Studies – Technical Campus, New Delhi, India*

[4] *Equifax, Atlanta, USA*

[5] *Federal Inland Revenue Service, Nigeria*

**Abstract:** The use of Internet of Things (IoT) technology has the potential to greatly improve agricultural and farming operations by increasing productivity and efficiency. This study analyzed recent developments in IoT applications in agriculture and farming and found that the most common sub-verticals were water management and crop management. Additionally, the study identified sensor data for soil moisture as a prevalent area of focus. The research also found that the most commonly used technology in the development of IoT applications was Wi-Fi, followed by mobile technology. The agricultural sector was found to receive more attention in terms of research compared to the farming sector. These findings can be used as a guide for those in the farming industry who want to improve and expand their use of IoT to increase efficiency. The study also highlighted areas for future research, such as scalability, heterogeneity, IoT system design, data processing methodologies, the size of the experimental land or farming area, and IoT security.

**Keywords:** Agriculture, IoT, Security, Surveys, Technology.

## INTRODUCTION

The need to improve productivity in farming has become imperative due to various factors such as a rapidly increasing global population, which requires a 70% increase in food production by 2050, diminishing farming land and natural resources, and decreasing yields of key crops. The situation has been further compounded by the scarcity of resources such as fresh water and arable land and

* **Corresponding author Pawan Whig:** Vivekananda Institute of Professional Studies - Technical Campus, New Delhi, India; E-mail: pawanwhig@gmail.com

**Sukanta Kumar Baral, Richa Goel, Tilottama Singh, Erdener Kaynak & Vishal Jain (Eds.)**

the decreasing agricultural workforce. The reduction in the number of agricultural workers has led to the use of internet connectivity solutions in farming practices. IoT technologies are aimed at addressing this issue by helping farmers ensure successful harvests, financial stability, and environmental conservation. Precision agriculture is the use of IoT technology to achieve optimal resource allocation for high crop yields and reduced costs. Fig. (**1**) illustrates how precision agriculture employs IoT technology to ensure optimal resource allocation results in high agricultural output and lower operational costs.

**Fig. (1).** IoT technologies in agriculture.

According to a BI Official estimate, there would be 75 million IoT systems in use in the agricultural industry by 2020, with a 20% annual growth rate. The best farming sector is anticipated to double in size from a little over $5 billion in 2016 to $15.3 billion in 2025.

The usage of fertilizer, the number of visits made by personal vehicles, and the efficient use of resources like electricity and water are just a few examples of how IoT-based precision agriculture helps gardeners and farmers reduce waste and increase productivity. IoT smart farming solutions use sensors to monitor agricultural land while managing the watering system. Farm owners can monitor the condition of their farms from any location. They can select between manual and automatic methods for carrying out the necessary actions based on the data. If the moisture level lowers, the farmer can utilize sensors to initiate irrigation. Fig. (**2**) illustrates the effectiveness of smart cropping.

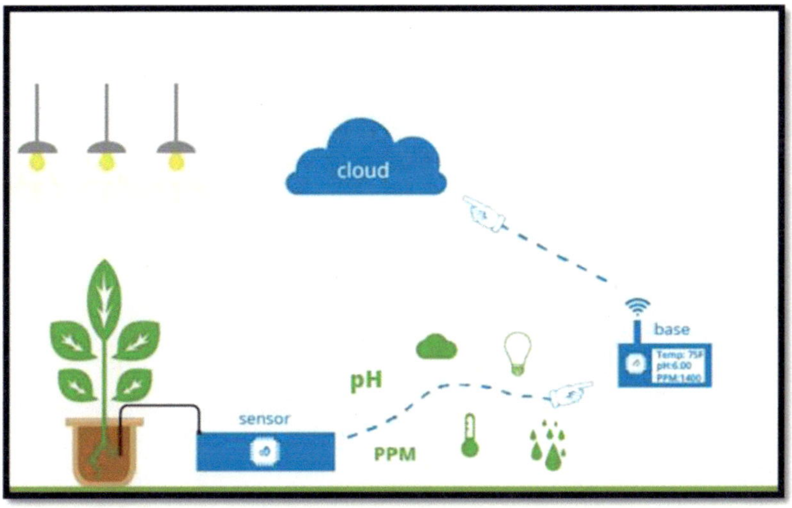


**Fig. (2).** Intelligent farming.

Agriculture is one of several industries that have been negatively impacted by the Industrial Internet of Things (IoT) to date. By the end of 2018, the connected agriculture market had a value of USD 1.8 billion and was continually expanding. It is projected to reach USD 4.3 billion by 2023 with a CAGR of 19.3%.

IoT technology is used to create automated machinery, networked gadgets, autonomous vehicles, and smart wearables. The IoT has, nevertheless, had the most impact on agriculture. 1.9 trillion people will live in the world by the year 2050, according latest statistics. And in order to feed this vast population, the agriculture industry is compelled to use the Internet of Things. Among the difficulties are those caused by climate change and extreme weather. The late 20th century saw the introduction of mechanical advancements like tractors and harvesters into agriculture operations all across the world. And because of the consistently rising demand for food, the agriculture industry largely depends on fresh ideas.

Agricultural productivity has increased at a lesser cost thanks to the Industrial IoT. IoT-powered smart solutions will become more prevalent in agriculture operations during the coming years. In fact, according to a few recent reports, the agriculture sector would have an IoT device installation growth rate of 20% CAGR. And by 2024, there will be 225 million connected agricultural devices, up from 13 million in 2014.

A vendor of IoT solutions and business owners in rural or underdeveloped areas had difficulty implementing their solutions since there was a lack of a consistent and dependable communication network infrastructure. However, by offering satellite connectivity and expanding cellular networks, numerous network providers are making it possible. An IoT comprehensive model is shown in Fig. (**3**).

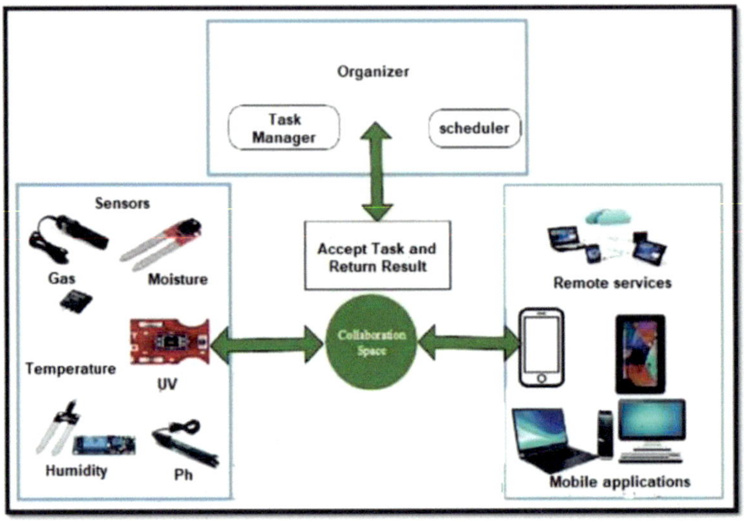


**Fig. (3).** IoT comprehensive model.

## IoT (Internet of Things)

In 1999, Kevin Ashton, who was then working for P&G, came up with the phrase "Internet of Things". Ashton, a supplier optimization specialist, made the decision to alert high management about a cutting-edge, intriguing RFID technology. He titled his presentation "IoT" since it seemed logical given that the internet was the largest new activity in 1999. Although Kevin captured the attention of certain P&G managers, the term "Internet of Things" did not become widely known for the decade that followed. Fig. (**4**) displays an illustration of an IoT system.

In 2010, when the term "Internet of Things" gained popularity, it was revealed that Twitter's OpenStreetMap software not only produced 360-degree films but also saved a tonne of Wi-Fi network data. People wondered if this was the start of a new Google strategy to index both the real world and the web. During the same year, the Chinese government proclaimed that the IoT would be a strategic focus in its five-year plan. The "IoT", a brand-new technical phenomenon, was added to their list in 2011 by Gartner, the market research company that created the well-known "excitement for new technologies". The next year, Monsieur, the biggest online event in Europe, focused on the Internet of Things. At the same time, well-known tech publications like Bloomberg, Quick Company, and Newsweek started to adopt the term "IoT" to describe the phenomenon.

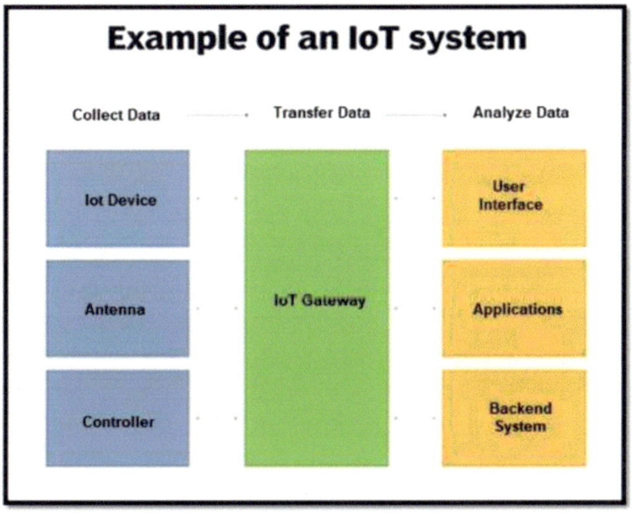


**Fig. (4).** Example of the IoT system.

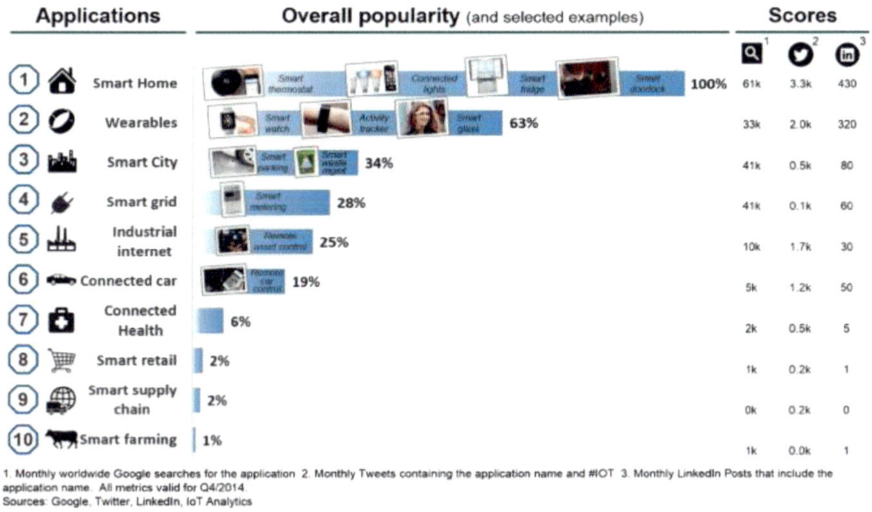


**Fig. (5).** Various applications of IoT.

In the current era of technological advancements, there is evident expansion in the realm of connected devices, highlighting a significant emphasis on device interoperability. The primary objective is to facilitate the integration of sensors, devices, and information systems across various industry verticals and organizational setups, fostering the emergence of new business models. To achieve this, IoT technology places a heightened focus on incorporating sophisticated networking mechanisms and middleware, allowing for the convergence of device networks and applications. The increasing complexity of

IoT demands more intricate solutions to enable seamless integration and functionality. Fig. (**5**) depicts the overall popularity of different groups within the IoT based on scores.

- IoT technology plays a pivotal role in crafting smart homes, encompassing a multitude of applications. These applications empower users to oversee and regulate various home appliances, such as smart LED bulbs, air conditioners, televisions, kitchen appliances, door locks, and more, as depicted in Fig. (**6**). For instance, with smart LED lights, users can effortlessly adjust light intensity and control the lights' ON/OFF functions without requiring manual intervention. In the context of a smart bathroom, users can dictate water temperature through simple audio commands. Furthermore, within a smart kitchen setup, devices are capable of sending notifications to users' phones, providing details regarding the expiration dates of products stored in the kitchen.

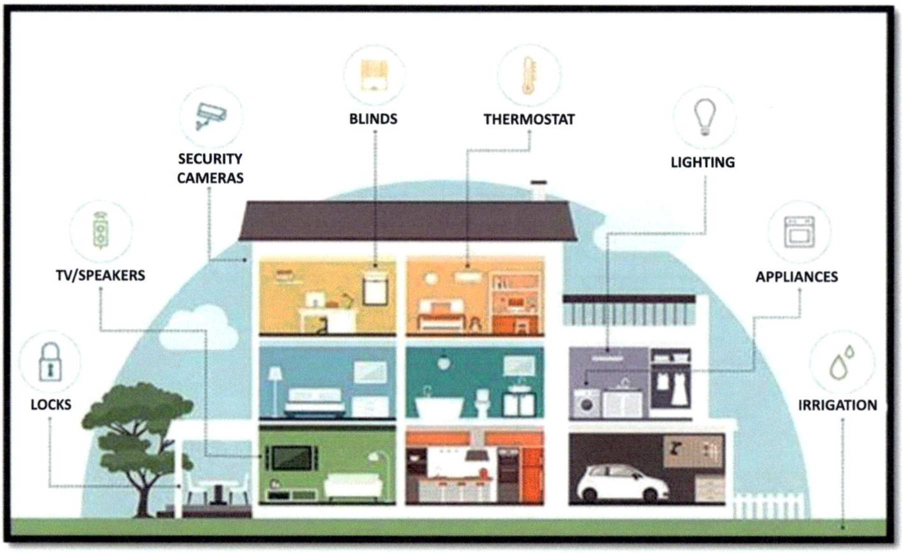


**Fig. (6).** Example of a smart home.

- Wearable devices refer to smart gadgets designed to be worn externally, integrated into clothing or the human body. These devices include a wide array of items such as smart belts, watches, clothing, fitness trackers, sunglasses, jewelry, accessories, tattoos, stickers, and more, each capable of being "smart". The initial surge of wearable technology in the market primarily featured health activity trackers following Bluetooth headphones, smartwatches, and web-enabled glasses. Subsequently, the gaming industry introduced more wearables, including virtual reality and augmented reality headsets. Notably, in wearable device technology, the most impactful applications significantly revolve around fitness management and medical usage. Fig. (7) illustrates various smart wearable devices available in the market.

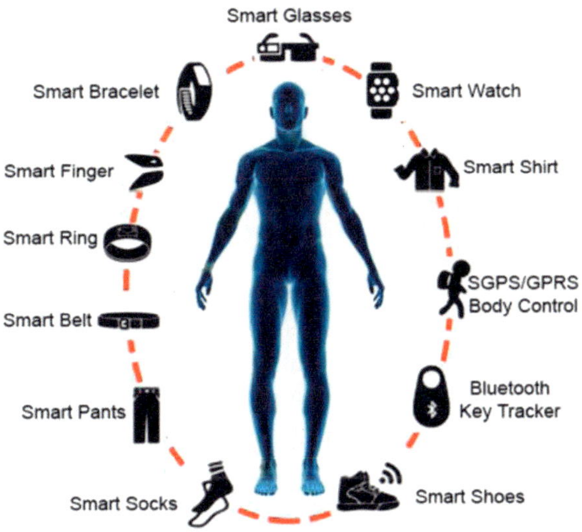


**Fig. (7).** Various smart wearable devices.

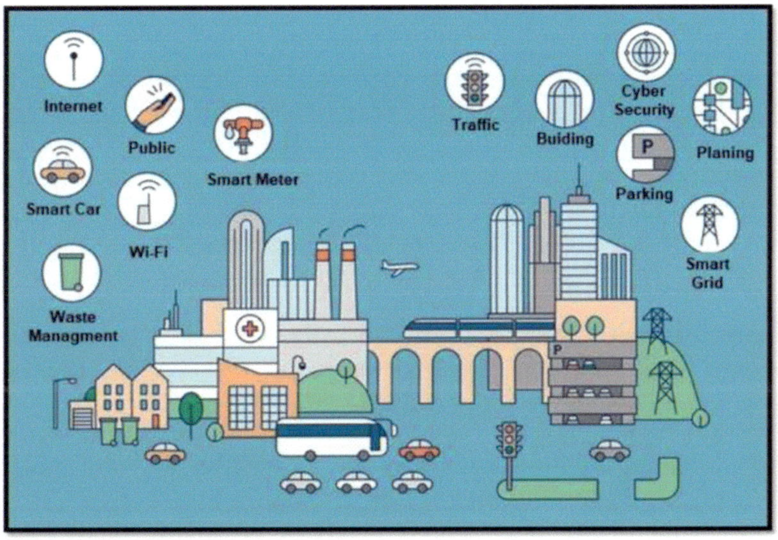


**Fig. (8).** Example of a smart city.

- Smart cities utilize IoT devices like wired cameras, lamps, and meters to collect and analyze data, which is then leveraged by communities to enhance infrastructure, public services, and utilities. Notably, cities employ this data to automate traffic control systems based on congestion density, implement smart waste bins capable of signaling when full, and regulate streetlights according to light intensity or traffic flow. Recently, London has announced plans to experiment a smart parking initiative, aiming to simplify parking spot location for drivers and alleviate urban traffic congestion by reducing wait times for available spaces. San Diego has implemented camera-equipped streetlights to monitor pedestrian movement, redirecting vehicles during peak hours to mitigate pedestrian accidents and alleviate traffic congestion. This proactive approach aims to track pedestrian activity and optimize traffic flow. An illustrative example of a smart city setup is depicted in Fig. (**8**).

- Integrated with smart energy infrastructure, the smart grid system automates various functions, including monitoring traffic, signage, parking spaces, and road warnings. It enables early detection of natural disasters and efficiently manages power demand in real-time using advanced smart meters. This capability aids in predicting and addressing sudden demand fluctuations, thereby reducing power outages.
- Any vehicle equipped with internet connectivity falls under the category of a connected car. IoT facilitates vehicle-to-vehicle communication, remote parking, geo-fencing for location tracking, and multimedia applications.
- Connected health technologies establish remote connections between physicians and patients. IoT-based healthcare applications contribute to cost reduction, enhanced quality, and personalized, accessible, and affordable healthcare for patients.
- IoT technologies such as RFID tags and GPS sensors provide comprehensive insights into product flow within retail environments, aiding in foot traffic management, facility maintenance, demand forecasting, and more.
- Efficient supply chain management optimizes market inventories, regulates material costs, and ensures high-quality service delivery, meeting consumer expectations while enhancing operational efficiency.
- Employing advanced technology, smart farming offers a sustainable approach to enhancing agricultural yield and quality. Technologies like GPS, water and temperature management, automatic irrigation, precision fertilization, and data management optimize farming practices. Devices like smart drones assist in watering, plant health monitoring, and livestock surveillance. Fig. (**9**) showcases the framework of smart farming practices.

## Methods and Techniques for Smart Agriculture

For ages, humans have attempted to enhance food production in order to fulfill food demands. To accomplish this goal, they are implementing many modern agricultural practices. Following the introduction of IoT, sophisticated farming methods such as vertical agricultural, hydroponics, and phenol-typing substantially improved their routine by incorporating IoT and its integral component. It is lucrative and can assist us in managing resources efficiently, including input resources, labor resources, and operational resources, while also providing a high output. Geospatial and chronological sample and charting, nursing and smart fertilization are all areas of technological applications. Sensors, UAVs, IoT-based machinery and communication, and other technologies and equipment are commonly employed. Some techniques used in agriculture using IoT are shown in Fig. (**10**).

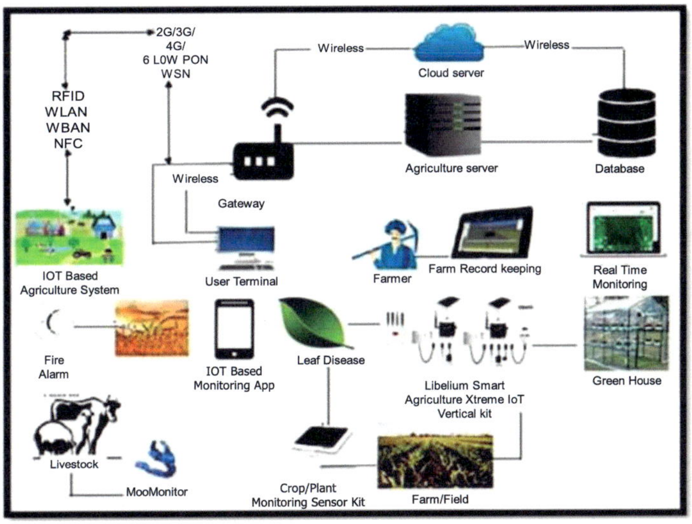


**Fig. (9).** Framework of smart farming.

## Precision Farming

Precision farming is not feasible for minor and average agriculturalists. The challenges in farming include climate change, a gap in food demand and supply, development, and deteriorating arable land, which are inevitable. In this context, the introduction of IoT allows a new measure in precision farming by combining skills, such as WSN and RFID. Precision agriculture is concerned with the effective use of natural resources while also conserving the environment.To implement precision agriculture, four steps must be completed: characterizing the degree and gauge of erraticism in soil and crop qualities, understanding the meaning and reasons of erraticism, handling erraticism on a three-dimensional and chronological foundation, and resolving the consequences of erraticism, which can only be accomplished efficiently with the IoT, and spatial and temporal models, as shown in Fig. (**11**).

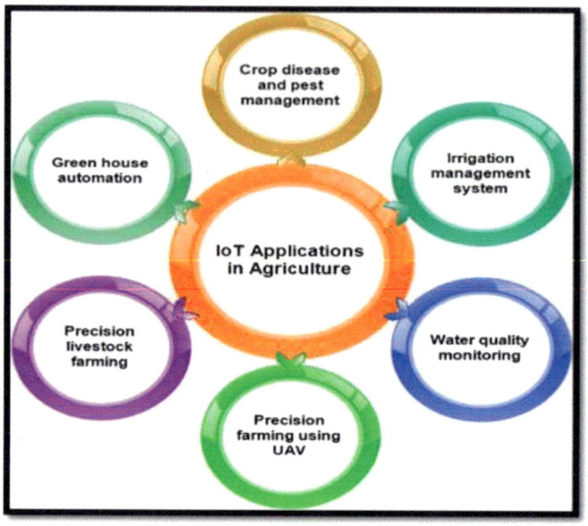


**Fig. (10).** Various techniques used in agriculture using IoT.

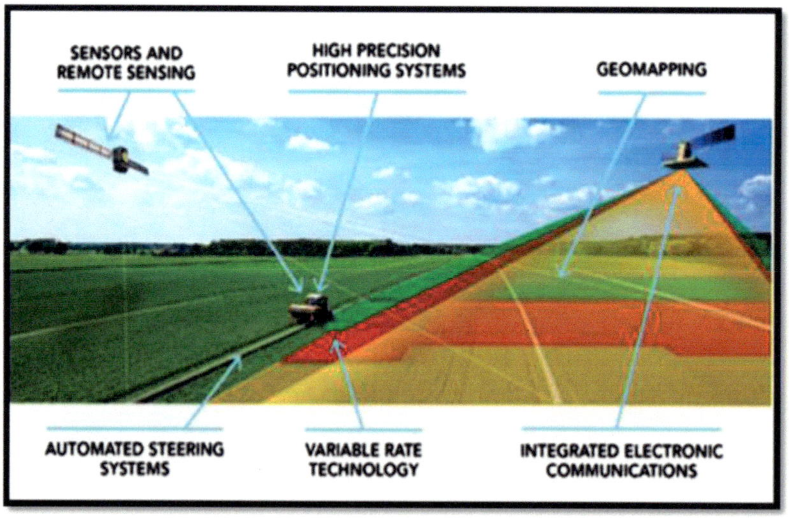


**Fig. (11).** Temporal models used in IoT.

## Farming in a Greenhouse

Greenhouse farming is comparable to precision farming, although there are some minor distinctions and goals. Without IoT and smart systems, accurate and continuous monitoring and control are impossible. Greenhouse agriculture takes up less space than fields yet produces more crops than traditional techniques.

## Farming in Cities

More people are moving to cities, and cities are large consumers of food products. Climate change and water shortages, on the other hand, have a severe impact on agriculture and pose substantial challenges to long-term food security. Another difficulty is the considerable distance between food producers and food consumers, which results in transport and chain source budgets that impair nourishment quality while also producing extra pollution from conveyance buses. Subsistence farming is a way in which individuals may produce food in their neighbor hood to have fresh and inexpensive food.

## Case Study

### *IoT: Fundamentally Redefining How Business Is Done in the Twenty-First Century*

Several significant industrial sectors have undergone a swift and profound transition as a result of the rise of breakthrough technology. Through a network of internet-connected gadgets that can interact with one another without requiring human intervention, the Internet of Things (IoT), a significant developing technology, links the real and virtual worlds. In this case study, various methods are discussed for smart agriculture.

## Agriculture IoT Applications

Precision agriculture is a basic and important application that may be utilized for crop field evaluation and mapping. The precision agriculture model is shown in Fig. (**12**). Weed control systems, water stress evaluations, and vegetation indices are examples of applications that rely on geographic and temporal sampling. It may also be used to measure geographical variability. It was initially pricey and not as efficient as it is today. UAVs are more lucrative and effective, and they might be used as the initial step in precision farming by agriculturalists in underdeveloped nations such as Pakistan.

## Intelligent Irrigation

As the globe faces the problem of water scarcity, the number of water-stressed countries is increasing. Weather-adaptive smart irrigation systems may be developed utilizing IoT and smart technologies, reducing the use of valuable aquatic reserves. Smart irrigation is crucial to conserving water as it only provides water when essential, based on crop and soil stress levels. UAV is an excellent instrument for dealing with the unpredictabile nature of water. The smart irrigation model is shown in Fig. (**13**).

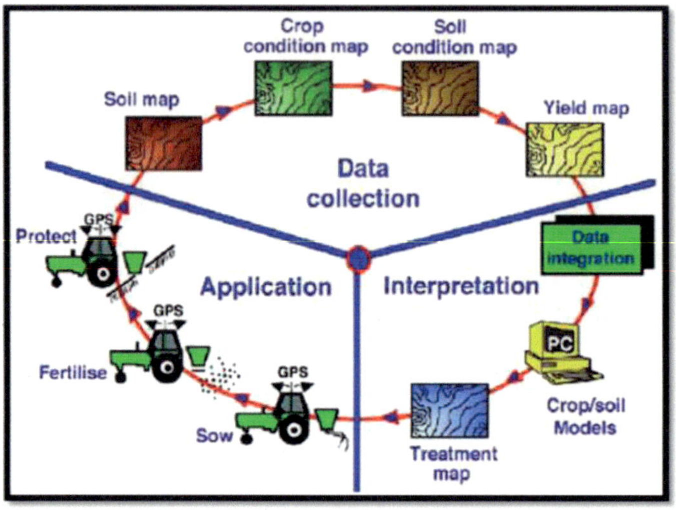


**Fig. (12).** Precision agriculture method.

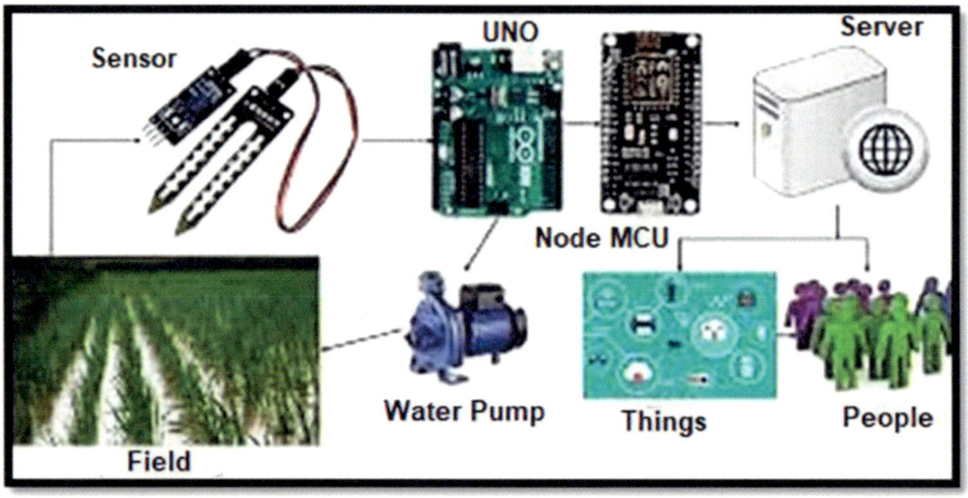


**Fig. (13).** Smart irrigation model.

## System for Pest and Weed Control

Pests, weeds, and diseases may all have a negative impact on agricultural output, with weeds alone reducing productivity by up to 30%. Pesticides and herbicides, on the other hand, diminish profit and deteriorate product quality, which is a major issue for consumers, as shown in Fig. (**14**). IoT and smart systems can detect diseases, pests, and weeds in crops early on and notify farmers. They are also capable of eliminating pests and diseases by precision agriculture.

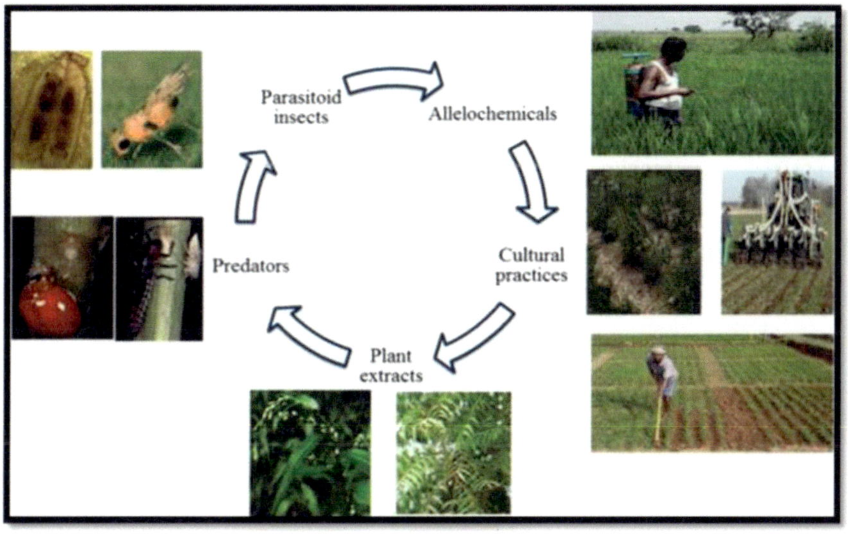


**Fig. (14).** Pest and weed control system.

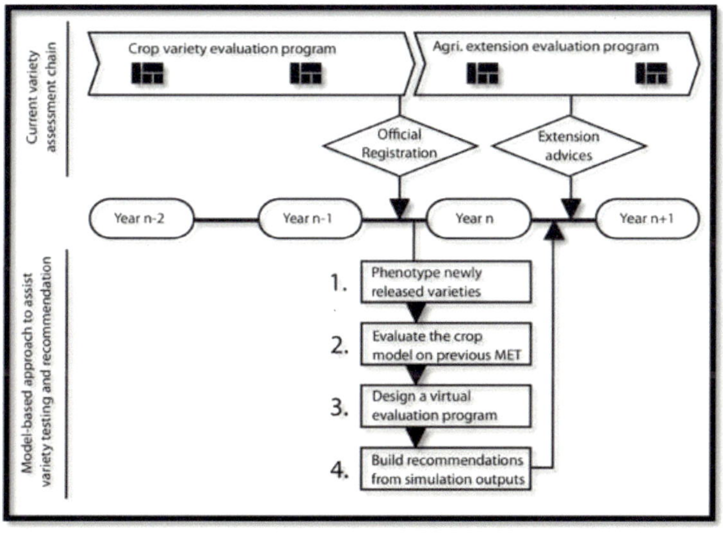


**Fig. (15).** Crop evaluation model.

## Crop Evaluation

The most important aspect of smart agriculture is yield evaluation. The initial stage in any form of assessment is data collection. Only IoT, WSNs, and UAV imaging provide precise and continuous monitoring of biotic and abiotic variables. All of these gadgets produce massive volumes of unstructured data. The collected data may be used for disease prediction, crop prediction, and harvest planning. Farmers may use these apps to minimize labor and operating costs, perform error-free disease and pest assessments and forecast. The crop evaluation model is shown in Fig. (**15**).

## Fertilization with Pinpoint Accuracy

Another significant contribution of IoT in farming is the ability to save both cash and the location. Imbalanced fertilization can produce multi-impact harm; for example, certain plants require fewer nutrients; hence, excessive use of fertilizers may generate salt in the earth, rotting the vegetable, decreasing output, costing more, and also causing weather alteration. Also, fertilizers containing various components such as N, K, and P, as well as water, are important, and their proportions vary depending on the plant's kind.Various steps involved in precision agriculture are shown in Fig. (**16**).

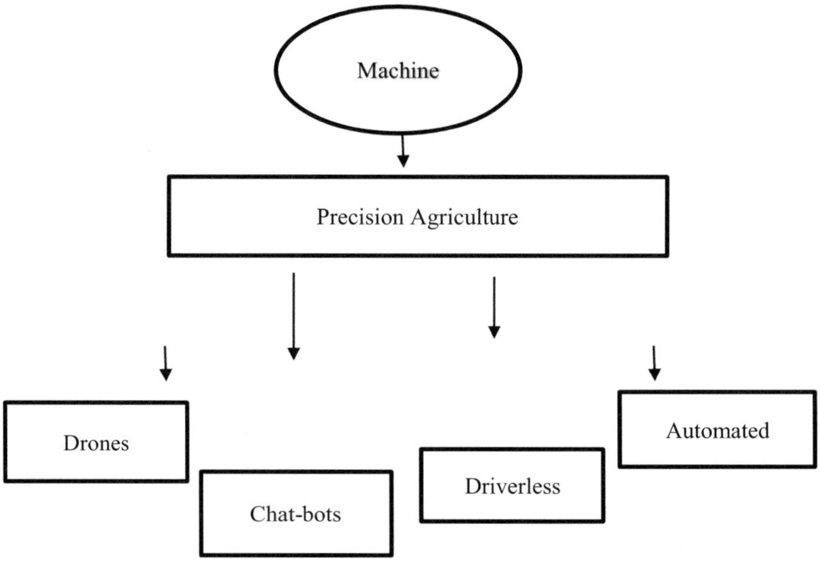


**Fig. (16).** Steps involved in precision agriculture.

## Challenges and Solutions

The major restriction of employing IoT strategies is battery life, and this is particularly true when using UAVs in husbandry. A comprehensive investigation has been conducted, and this one is open to different answers. Numerous investigators have sought to overcome these obstacles, proposing and testing their answers.

Ultralight-weight WPT systems were proposed to increase the flight duration of UAVs. The technology is adaptable enough to accommodate variations in air-gap geometry. The device can charge UAVs mid-air, increasing flight duration to roughly 7 minutes. With 10 W, their method can charge drones wirelessly. Another study used capacitive power transfer (CPT) technology to construct a wireless charging system for unmanned aerial vehicles. This system has a large charging space and can charge UASs.

Because of the efficiency and high-power transmission capabilities of the magnetic resonant coupling approach, a wireless charging system for UAVs utilized in agricultural areas has been suggested and developed. They obtained optimal transmission power and efficiency.

## CONCLUSION

This study discusses the relevance of IoT and its successful uses in agriculture, as well as obstacles and solutions. The ecology of IoT and the usage of UAVs, including their numerous forms and benefits, as well as changed proprieties and their merits and downsides for agriculture, are also discussed. IoT may be used in various smart agricultural approaches, such as precision agriculture, greenhouse farming, and urban farming, using case studies on food products. In addition, we highlighted several frequently utilized IoT applications in agriculture. Consider geographical and temporal mapping and crop sampling as the first step toward smart agriculture in any poor nation, such as Pakistan, where farmers face significant upfront costs. Following the overview, we concluded that Pakistan's agriculture is undertaking a number of measures to address climate change, water shortages, and food insecurity. The application of modern information technology, such as artificial intelligence, is often lacking in locally developed initiatives. Thus, Pakistan and other poor nations should shoulder the initial costs and R&D in the field of inter-agriculture and information technology; it would benefit them in the long run for sustained food security regardless of climate circumstances.

## BIBLIOGRAPHY

Alkali, Y., Routray, I., Whig, P. (2022). Strategy for Reliable, Efficient and Secure IoT Using Artificial Intelligence. *IUP Journal of Computer Sciences, 16*(2), 16.

Alkali, Y., Routray, I., Whig, P. (2022). Study of Various Methods for Reliable, Efficient and Secured IoT Using Artificial Intelligence. *SSRN.*
[http://dx.doi.org/10.2139/ssrn.4020364]

Anand, M., Velu, A., Whig, P. (2022). Prediction of Loan Behaviour with Machine Learning Models for Secure Banking. *J. Comput. Sci. Eng., 3*(1), 1-13.

Boukoberine, M.N., Zhou, Z., Benbouzid, M. (2019). A critical review on unmanned aerial vehicles power supply and energy management: Solutions, strategies, and prospects. *Appl. Energy, 255*, 113823.

[http://dx.doi.org/10.1016/j.apenergy.2019.113823]

Castaldi, F., Pelosi, F., Pascucci, S., Casa, R. (2017). Assessing the potential of images from unmanned aerial vehicles (UAV) to support herbicide patch spraying in maize. *Precis. Agric., 18*(1), 76-94. [http://dx.doi.org/10.1007/s11119-016-9468-3]

Chopra, G. (2022). A Clustering Approach Based on Support Vectors. *International Journal of Machine Learning for Sustainable Development, 4*(1), 21-30.

Dai, B., He, Y., Gu, F., Yang, L., Han, J., Xu, W. (2017). A Vision-Based Autonomous Aerial Spray System for Precision Agriculture. *ROBIO 2017-IEEE.,* 507-513. [http://dx.doi.org/10.1109/ROBIO.2017.8324467]

Diwate, S.K., Nitnaware, V.N., Argulwar, K. (2018). Design and Development of Application Specific Drone Machine for Seed Sowing. *IRJET., 5*(5), 4003-4007.

Faiçal, B.S., Freitas, H., Gomes, P.H., Mano, L.Y., Pessin, G., de Carvalho, A.C.P.L.F., Krishnamachari, B., Ueyama, J. (2017). An adaptive approach for UAV-based pesticide spraying in dynamic environments. *Comput. Electron. Agric., 138*, 210-223. [http://dx.doi.org/10.1016/j.compag.2017.04.011]

Feng, X., Yan, F., Liu, X. (2019). Study of Wireless Communication Technologies on Internet of Things for Precision Agriculture. *Wirel. Pers. Commun., 108*(3), 1785-1802. [http://dx.doi.org/10.1007/s11277-019-06496-7]

Hassan, M.A., Yang, M., Rasheed, A., Yang, G., Reynolds, M., Xia, X., Xiao, Y., He, Z. (2019). A rapid monitoring of NDVI across the wheat growth cycle for grain yield prediction using a multi-spectral UAV platform. *Plant Sci., 282*, 95-103. [http://dx.doi.org/10.1016/j.plantsci.2018.10.022] [PMID: 31003615]

Huang, H., Deng, J., Lan, Y., Yang, A., Deng, X., Zhang, L. (2018). A fully convolutional network for weed mapping of unmanned aerial vehicle (UAV) imagery. *PLoS One, 13*(4), e0196302. [http://dx.doi.org/10.1371/journal.pone.0196302] [PMID: 29698500]

Ivushkin, K., Bartholomeus, H., Bregt, A.K., Pulatov, A., Franceschini, M.H.D., Kramer, H., van Loo, E.N., Jaramillo Roman, V., Finkers, R. (2019). UAV based soil salinity assessment of cropland. *Geoderma, 338*, 502-512. [http://dx.doi.org/10.1016/j.geoderma.2018.09.046]

Jupalle, H., Kouser, S., Bhatia, A.B., Alam, N., Nadikattu, R.R., Whig, P. (2022). Automation of human behaviors and its prediction using machine learning. *Microsyst. Technol., 28*(8), 1879-1887. [http://dx.doi.org/10.1007/s00542-022-05326-4]

Kharim, M.N.A., Wayayok, A., Shariff, A.R.M., Abdullah, A.F., Husin, E.M. (2019). Droplet Deposition Density of Organic Liquid Fertilizer at Low Altitude UAV Aerial Spraying in Rice Cultivation. *Comput. Electron. Agric., 167*, 105045. [http://dx.doi.org/10.1016/j.compag.2019.105045]

Madhu, M. (2022). A Survey of Machine Learning and its Applications. *Int. J. Mach. Learn. Sustain. Dev., 4*(1), 11-20.

Mohsan, S.A.H., Othman, N.Q.H., Li, Y., Alsharif, M.H., Khan, M.A. (2023). Unmanned aerial vehicles (UAVs): practical aspects, applications, open challenges, security issues, and future trends. *Intell. Serv. Robot., 16*(1), 109-137. [http://dx.doi.org/10.1007/s11370-022-00452-4] [PMID: 36687780]

Maes, W.H., Steppe, K. (2019). Perspectives for Remote Sensing with Unmanned Aerial Vehicles in Precision Agriculture. *Trends Plant Sci., 24*(2), 152-164. [http://dx.doi.org/10.1016/j.tplants.2018.11.007] [PMID: 30558964]

Navia, J., Mondragon, I., Patino, D., Colorado, J. (2016). Multispectral Mapping in Agriculture: Terrain Mosaic Using an Autonomous Quadcopter UAV. *ICUAS'16.,* 1351-1358.

[http://dx.doi.org/10.1109/ICUAS.2016.7502606]

Park, S., Ryu, D., Fuentes, S., Chung, H., Hernández-Montes, E., O'Connell, M. (2017). Adaptive Estimation of Crop Water Stress in Nectarine and Peach Orchards Using High-Resolution Imagery from an Unmanned Aerial Vehicle (UAV). *Remote Sens. (Basel), 9*(8), 828. [http://dx.doi.org/10.3390/rs9080828]

Senthilnath, J., Kandukuri, M., Dokania, A., Ramesh, K.N. (2017). Application of UAV imaging platform for vegetation analysis based on spectral-spatial methods. *Comput. Electron. Agric., 140*, 8-24. [http://dx.doi.org/10.1016/j.compag.2017.05.027]

Sierra, G., Orchard, M., Goebel, K., Kulkarni, C. (2019). Battery health management for small-size rotary-wing electric unmanned aerial vehicles: An efficient approach for constrained computing platforms. *Reliab. Eng. Syst. Saf., 182*, 166-178. [http://dx.doi.org/10.1016/j.ress.2018.04.030]

Sona, G., Passoni, D., Pinto, L., Pagliari, D., Masseroni, D., Ortuani, B., Facchi, A. (2016). UAV Multispectral Survey to Map Soil and Crop for Precision Farming Applications. *Int. Arch. Photogramm. Remote Sens. Spat. Inf. Sci, XLI*(B1), 1023-1029. [http://dx.doi.org/10.5194/isprs-archives-XLI-B1-1023-2016]

Suprapto, B.Y., Heryanto, M.A., Suprijono, H., Muliadi, J., Kusumoputro, B. (2017). Design and Development of Heavy-Lift Hexacopter for Heavy Payload. [http://dx.doi.org/10.1109/ISEMANTIC.2017.8251877]

Tomar, U., Chakroborty, N., Sharma, H., Whig, P. (2021). AI Based Smart Agricuture System. *TLAI., 2*(2), 1.

Vanegas, F., Bratanov, D., Powell, K., Weiss, J., Gonzalez, F. (2018). A Novel Methodology for Improving Plant Pest Surveillance in Vineyards and Crops Using UAV-Based Hyperspectral and Spatial Data. *Sensors (Basel), 18*(1), 260. [http://dx.doi.org/10.3390/s18010260] [PMID: 29342101]

Verma, S., Bhatia, A., Chug, A., Singh, A.P. (2019). Recent Advancements in Multimedia Big Data Computing for IoT Applications in Precision Agriculture: Opportunities, Issues, and Challenges. *Multimedia Big Data Computing for IoT Applications: Concepts, Paradigms And Solutions.* Springer.

Whig, P., Sharma, R. (2023). Promoting Climate Change Mitigation, Advancing Collaboration, and Sustainable Development. *Int. J. Sustain. Dev. AI, ML and IoT., 2*(1), 1-18.

Whig, P., Kouser, S., Velu, A., Nadikattu, R.R. (2022). Fog-IoT-Assisted-Based Smart Agriculture Application. *Demystifying Federated Learning for Blockchain and Industrial Internet of Things.* IGI Global. [http://dx.doi.org/10.4018/978-1-6684-3733-9.ch005]

Whig, P., Nadikattu, R.R., Velu, A. (2022). COVID-19 pandemic analysis using application of AI. *Healthcare Monitoring and Data Analysis Using IoT: Technologies and Applications, 1*, 1-15. [http://dx.doi.org/10.1049/PBHE038E_ch1]

Whig, P., Velu, A.R.U.N., Sharma, P. (2022). Demystifying Federated Learning for Blockchain: A Case Study. *Demystifying Federated Learning for Blockchain and Industrial Internet of Things.* IGI Global. [http://dx.doi.org/10.4018/978-1-6684-3733-9.ch008]

Whig, P., Velu, A., Bhatia, A.B. (2022). Protect Nature and Reduce the Carbon Footprint with an Application of Blockchain for IIoT. *Demystifying Federated Learning for Blockchain and Industrial Internet of Things.* IGI Global. [http://dx.doi.org/10.4018/978-1-6684-3733-9.ch007]

Whig, P., Velu, A., Naddikatu, R.R. (2022). The Economic Impact of AI-Enabled Blockchain in 6G-Based Industry. *AI and Blockchain Technology in 6G Wireless Network.* Springer. [http://dx.doi.org/10.1007/978-981-19-2868-0_10]

Whig, P., Velu, A., Nadikattu, R.R. (2022). Blockchain Platform to Resolve Security Issues in IoT and Smart Networks. *AI-Enabled Agile Internet of Things for Sustainable Fintech Ecosystems.* IGI Global.

[http://dx.doi.org/10.4018/978-1-6684-4176-3.ch003]

Whig, P., Velu, A., Ready, R. (2022). Demystifying Federated Learning in Artificial Intelligence with Human-Computer Interaction. *Demystifying Federated Learning for Blockchain and Industrial Internet of Things.* IGI Global.
[http://dx.doi.org/10.4018/978-1-6684-3733-9.ch006]

CHAPTER 3

# Embodied Immersion: Exploring the Convergence of Haptic VR and Pervasive Visual Sensors

**Isha Pant**[1,*], **Ashish Joshi**[2] and **Pragya Baluni**[3]

[1] *Department of Computer Science and Engineering, THDC Institute of Hydropower Engineering and Technology, Uttarakhand, India*

[2] *Graphic Era Deemed To be University, Uttarakhand, India*

[3] *THDC Institute of Hydropower Engineering and Technology, Uttarakhand, India*

**Abstract:** Virtual Reality (VR) technology has exponentially gained significance in recent years, providing end users with a virtual world in which users can develop virtual habits or manipulate the items in the virtual scene using their limb movements. As computers and information technology advance, users are searching for innovative types of Human-Computer Interaction techniques to provide a richer experience. In contrast, virtual scene modeling research can help consumers have a more realistic experience and ease of access. This chapter will largely concentrate on the perspectives on Augmented Reality (AR) and VR in the future on a global scale, taking VR strategies that rely on Scene Modeling, Statistical Analysis and Sensor Networking and taking into consideration the research techniques by examining the interactive VR technology from the perception of Visual Sensor Network (VSN), which tends to offer visual information to VR systems, also leading to concise and effectual image data to aid in the creation of a digital model. Simultaneously, a diverse set of applications tends to give the booming VR industry the confidence to append more value.

**Keywords:** Human-computer interaction, Sensors, Scene modeling, Virtual reality, Visual visualization.

## BACKGROUND AND DRIVING FORCES

The origin of virtual and augmented reality technology can be traced back to 1838, when Charles Wheatstone invented the stereoscope, which superimposed an image over each of the user's eyes, culminating in a distant 3D image. Virtual Reality addresses the intricacies and pragmatism of realism and is demonstrated by virtual humans who glance, move, and act like real humans. It has the ability to be used in dynamic ways with far-reaching impacts across many research domains. Virtual reality technology is critical to the realization of telesensation. It

* **Corresponding author Isha Pant:** Department of Computer Science and Engineering, THDC Institute of Hydropower Engineering and Technology, Uttarakhand, India; E-mail: ishapant324@gmail.com

**Sukanta Kumar Baral, Richa Goel, Tilottama Singh, Erdener Kaynak & Vishal Jain (Eds.)**

features an intuitive simulated reality in which viewers can explore, walk around, and engage with virtual items (Chatzopou-los *et al.*, 2017). Virtual worlds, like the real world, show us a stereo vision image, relying on our vantage point.

We are constantly bombarded with screens. It is almost hard to get away from them. Virtual reality enables people to wear goggles or headgear in order to fully delve into the virtual world. While overlaying graphics on a tablet or smartphone is a more popular application of augmented reality than projecting visuals onto clear screens (Costa and Peixoto, 2021). Nobody had ever considered AR experiences or implementations on a smartphone before. This unforeseen utilization of mobile augmented reality validated the global consumer adoption of augmented reality. Within the last three decades, the Internet revolutions have had a profound impact on the growth and integration of new technologies, particularly e-collaboration. Human-Computer Interaction (HCI) analysis, like other fields of study, has become popular lately. In reality, interaction design is a multidisciplinary field that includes computers, pictures, cognitive sciences, psychology, and other fields. Wireless sensor networks (WSN) have received-great interest in the academic field in recent years. WSN is made up of numerous small devices known as nodes, which include sensing, refining, communication, and power distribution systems. Distributed networks help identify the physical setting and collect crucial data, which are then aggregated using wireless transmissions. Because of the growing demand for innovation, VSN combined with tiny cameras has rapidly become a major research area. The VSN may sample visual images in addition to the fundamental operations of the conventional WSN. This implies that VSN not only strengthens fundamental applications like conventional tracking and environmental monitoring, but it also expands into new domains. Furthermore, as a base, VSN has aided in the development and use of numerous technological innovations. In virtual reality, for example, programmers may use the VSN to get more precise parameters and visual information to construct a more sensible scene model or directly produce the impact of remote access scenarios with the aid of the remote VSN. Virtual scene creation indeed holds significant importance in the realm of VR goods. It serves as the foundation for immersive experiences in various applications, including gaming, entertainment, education, training, design, and more. This is why virtual scene creation is a major priority for VR goods. Leveraging a large-scale visual sensor system in the actual world is a big task that may be prohibitively expensive for the majority of academics intrigued by constructing and exploring sensor networks. Furthermore, most privacy laws prohibit the vigilance of individuals in public settings for research purposes. Aside from legal constraints and economic considerations, the use of realistic digital realities in network analysis includes significantly greater fluidity during the testing and evaluation cycle, thus speeding up the schematic design. For the purpose of visual sensor network algorithm validation, the virtual environment provides handy ground data. Because experiments in the virtual environment are fully reproducible, we can easily alter the methods and settings and quickly assess their effect. In the simulated environment, the harsh real-time restrictions of the actual world may be readily eased (Baker, 2017). These technological advances are still floundering in the commercial world due to the elevated production costs and the intricacies of AR/VR devices, but early advent has come. So, how near are we to mainstream adoption?

VR has been demonstrating several promising and impactful use cases across various industries, ranging from real estate to tourism. Even though augmented reality technology is somewhat less established than virtual reality due to constraints, lack of standardization, and increased costs, it is already being used in sectors such as manufacturing, logistics, and healthcare. Augmented reality perceptions are usually accomplished *via* headsets such as Vuzix, ODG, Meta, and HoloLens. Indeed, the indications suggest that VR technology is poised to reshape industrial and commercial marketplaces in significant ways. The coronavirus pandemic has boosted the adoption of hybrid reality perceptions, which combine in-person and digital aspects. Brands, marketers, and consumers are interested in XR technologies because they have ushered in the next era of human connection. Advancements like XR and motion capture have opened up a whole new world for visual story telling that links individuals to their surroundings and tend to make a labeled experience feel more rooted, genuine, beneficial, and interactive. Nevertheless, there is still much progress to be made before all these technologies can be widely embraced (Azuma, 2001).

## Perception and Reality

With the extended reality (XR) regime already in full swing, it is easy to foresee a future where the outline between the real and virtual worlds will become much more muddled than they are now. Everything that pertains to our view of things is the result of our senses. Subsequently, in essence, everyone's reality is distinct. Taking this a step further, it stands to reason that if you occupied your senses with additional computer-generated or simulated information, your experience of reality would alter, resulting in the emergence of a new, virtual one (Doerner *et al.*, 2022). Any interference with humans' natural sense of reality might be seen as "mediating" reality. Thus, different types of "mediating" realities existed long before the contemporary computer. To understand the notion and virtue of virtual reality, it is important to fully identify the notion of perception. Perception is the route through which man gathers and analyzes information about his surroundings. Perception involves both the senses and the brain. External senses and interior senses are the two kinds of senses. The exterior senses detect events occurring outside the body, whereas the internal senses detect phenomena occurring within the organism (hunger, exhaustion, pain, thirst). The exterior senses are classified as distant (heat, vision, hearing) and contact (smell, touch, taste). Only systems affecting the remote senses are highly refined in VR, while systems affecting the tactile senses are progressively evolving. The senses transmit sensory information while the brain analyzes what is received. In the digital era, we live multiple parallel lives (Makhataeva and Varol, 2020). While the real world remains the foundation of our individual world, a plethora of virtual worlds is rapidly occupying our imaginations. Not only can VR give vivid stereoscopic viewing of virtual worlds and sound effects, but it also allows players to interact with virtual items and the environment *via* feedback. No matter what sort of VR application is used, the impact and computer graphics are important to increase user engagement and, therefore, increase the efficacy of teaching and training. These worlds span from mainly 2D interfaces to multi-player 3D fantasy realms, ranging from websites to video games. Immersive graphics and audio-computer mediated worlds have the potential to intensify a wide range of emotions, including joy, tediousness, wrath, and rage because the player is forced to perform. Immersion, interaction, and imagination are key qualities of virtual reality. Immersion allows users to immerse themselves in physical space, while interaction allows users to manage virtual conduct. The cornerstone of the technology that delivers the three features listed here is the creation of a realistic virtual world with components such as interactions and noise. The volume of information acquired by visual means is the greatest, accounting for around 70% of the total (Lawson, 2015). Likewise, the visual feedback information is the most user-friendly and rational. As a result, visual modeling has emerged as one of the most crucial components of technology. Scene modeling and model optimization are the two main routes of the modeling process. Aside from the senses, experience, learning, emotion, and motivation all have an impact on perception. The primary notion behind cheating in the perception system is to substitute the genuine stimuli received by the senses with artificially produced ones. As a result, it appears that the perception model predicts the sensation of people's presence in an apparent, nonexistent world. Is the process by which information is retrieved from the material world? Obviously, it is vital for a VR setup. A sensor is a sort of transducer that transforms the energy it receives into an electrical signal. Depending on the circuit type, this might be a digital or analog signal. A sensor encloses a receptor that collects energy for conversion. Organisms work in an efficient manner. The sensor is referred to as a sense organ, with the eyes and ears being prominent examples. The sense organs transform energy into neural impulses because our circuits are made up of linked neurons. The spatial apparatus is the preferred method by which individuals obtain data from the environment, and sensory routes specify reality as we perceive it. According to

Sutherland *et al.* (2018), visual perception research dates back to the end of the nineteenth century, which inspired decades of reality mediators based on eyeglasses.

In the 1960s, Ivan Sutherland invented the idea of head-mounted displays or HMDs. These devices were known as the Ultimate Displays. Computer-Mediated Reality emphasizes the computer's role in producing or synthesizing these visuals. At the MIT Media Lab, Steve Mann suggested computer-mediated reality and was one of the first to think of wearable computing. Interacting with a digital environment is not a novel notion, as films such as Tron (1982) and Kids (2003) have brought hypothetical technology to life on the giant screen. Today, nevertheless, the same customers may now interact with their own social media sphere. Pursuit applications have always been one of the most significant uses of VR. The primary motive is that it has the potential to immediately generate significant money and profits for VR equipment and content providers, as well as the gaming business. People have wished for scenes in video games to be more realistic and lifelike since the invention of the medium. As a result, inexperienced video game developers do their preeminent in game interfaces. Conversely, the scale of optimization and the player's experience with the computer display are still restricted (Wild, 2016). However, technology bypasses the layer of interface barriers, allowing users to have a further realistic experience.

The list encompasses four crucial components:

## Targeted Tendencies

The entity having a familiarity which was intended by the designer. Watching a visual motion on a widescreen or wearing an HMD with a giant field of vision is an excellent approach to producing a self-motion feeling in VR.

## Artificial Sensory Stimulation

Using engineering, one or more of the organism's senses are co-opted, at least partially, and their normal inputs are replaced or augmented by artificial stimulation. Most organizational problems are underpinned by adequate posture and balance regulation, which is acquired *via* the timely development of cognitive sensory information. This integration, in hopes of preventing falls, necessitates the fast recalibration of visual data. This process is hampered by nervous system disorders and aging.

## *Perception*

During the experience, the organism appears to be unconscious of the disturbance, leading to the sensation of being present in the virtual environment. This state of unawareness leads to a sensation of being in another or alternate reality. It is seen as natural. In the future, we will most definitely encounter XR in ways we cannot yet imagine. But, for the time being, there is plenty of impending technical advancement to look forward to. VR technology will be faster, lighter, and more affordable. Wearable technology, its applications, and its prospective global impact are generating a lot of buzz. Pertaining to one optimistic prediction, the wearable computing industry will be a mega-dollar industry by 2030, including over 50 billion gadgets, over half of which will be devised by companies that do not yet exist. The use of alternative interfaces and the emergence of new virtual and augmented reality applications are features of wearable technology. Furthermore, advancements in smartphone technology (such as better processors and technological advancements) will enable us to relish smooth AR and VR experiences on our handsets (Wang *et al.*, 2017). Thanks to 5G wireless networks, we will be able to enjoy them almost anywhere on the planet. The purpose of AR/VR design is to provide a good user experience. The immersive, dynamic nature of AR/VR allows for the telling of tales that go beyond the flat world of 2D. The design process for AR and VR is a rigorous process since it provides a useful context for analyzing how to make portable sites and apps more accessible to people with disabilities, elderly groups, and those unfamiliar with advanced technologies (Blake, 2009). As technology evolves, it will become extremely relevant to deliver users with a diverse array of choices.

## Giant Leap with Visual Sensor Networks

Along with the new advances in CMOS tools and micro electro mechanical components, the classic Wireless Sensor Network (WSN) equipped with low-cost cameras has been adapted to sense and spread visual data and is now known as the Visual Sensor Network (VSN). Wireless sensor networks (WSNs) have piqued the interest of both academia and business for use in security, medical, military, environmental, industrial, and transportation applications (Thiago C, Costa and Portugal, 2020). A typical WSN design comprises dispersed sensors that gather, send, and receive data in order to serve users cooperatively *via* the base station, which typically serves as a gateway and helps coordinate the infrastructure. Wireless visual sensor networks (WVSNs), one of the most recent advancements in WSNs, significantly enhance the capacities of such networks with cameras installed on sensor nodes that allow the capture and processing of pictures and/or videos. This distinguishing feature differentiates WVSNs from regular WSNs in numerous respects, rendering the methods offered for traditional WSN deployment inapplicable to the WVSN deployment dilemma. Image acquisition equipment, storage units, memory, radios, and power supplies seem to be the hardware requirements of the visual sensors. A CCD webcam or perhaps a CMOS imaging device might be used to capture images (Gerschütz *et al.*, 2019). This same processing unit might be either non-programmable or programmed logic. The attached camera's sensory nodes are referred to as VS nodes, where each one is effective in capturing, manipulating, and transmitting image data to the sink node *via* intermediate forwarding of nodes in a multi-hop way. One of the classic techniques of creating geometric models is the use of visual sensor networks for automated assembly modeling. To begin, it employs ordinary vision sensors to acquire images from a pending model entity or model. The collected pictures are then processed and analyzed, and important 3D information and underlying structure are extracted from the model. Lastly, the geometric modeling technique is created automatically based on the inputs. In terms of capturing sensor data, camera sensors can gather more information than regular scalar sensors and can often do multi-angle imaging for the same object. The collection of visual pictures is mostly dependent on lenses, whereas the reception of image information necessitates the use of the following algorithms. Simultaneously, camera coverage has emerged as a research subject. Through computation, coverage optimization algorithms try to allot the functioning state of each node's visual sensor (Bolter, Engberg and MacIntyre, 2021). For example, if the viewing range of many vision sensors is the same, one or more of them can be turned off. On the other hand, energy demand may be decreased, while the quantity of information in the image information transfer stream can be reduced. VSNs are categorized into two sets: homogeneous visual sensor networks and heterogeneous visual sensor networks. The homogeneous VSNs are those where the camera sensors of every node in the network have similar capabilities; as a result, they can diminish a large VSN network's complexity. These sensors at every node differ in heterogeneous visual sensor networks, which also incorporate vibration sensors, temperature, or humidity. This VSN kind is more adaptable and may be used in a wider range of circumstances.

## DRIVING GROWTH OF AUGMENTED AND VIRTUAL REALITY

Conversational frameworks are altering how people communicate with the digital world. People's perceptions of the digital world are constantly changing due to extended reality. The anticipated immersive consumer experience is the result of a combination of changes in interaction models (Bassyouni and Elhajj, 2001). The pandemic has provided the impetus for the expansion of a virtual world in which we can participate in many of the same social events and interactions that are conducted in the physical realm.

## Escaping with VR Realm

Despite evaluating the tricky VR systems, the majority of configurations are divided into three major groups, and each category may be graded by some level of immersion it delivers. Immersion may be defined as how intensely the user focuses on the job at hand. Immersive computing is being used in a variety of disciplines, including disaster aid and restoration, thanks to its ability to immerse a viewer in a setting that elicits a direct situation than simply a photograph, providing viewers a greater emotional bond to an event they are watching (Jarmon and Traphagan, 2009). Immersion influence is typically thought to be the result of several constraints, including the intensity of interactivity, image sophistication, stereoscopic interpretations, area of regard, and display initial value. For example, offering a stereoscopic rather than a monoscopic perspective of the virtual environment will improve the user's sense of immersion. The most regarded technique might be to directly induce the feelings that comprised VR in the neurological system. The nervous system regulates how we engage with daily situations in functionalism/conventional science. As a result, we absorb all sensory information as neural impulses. It must be emphasized that no criterion is successful in isolation, and the state of immersion obtained is the result of the intricate interplay of the numerous elements involved. When investigating the genesis of sickness symptoms and the types of symptoms that may emerge, the type of VR system utilized is an essential issue. Non-immersive, semi-immersive and fully-immersive VR systems are used. Non-immersive devices, as the title implies, are the fewest immersive VR implementations. The virtual environment can be depicted as a high-definition display while using the desktop system. Interaction with the virtual world can be accomplished *via* traditional methods such as keyboards, mouse, and trackballs, or it can be amplified by the use of 3D interaction gear. Non-immersive systems still have the benefit of not requiring the greatest degree of graphical fidelity or special hardware and may be implemented on high-spec PC emulators.

This implies that these systems are the most affordable VR solutions that may be utilized for a broad array of applications. Semi-immersive solutions are an unexplored application of VR technology that draws heavily on innovations created in the realm of flight simulation (Yap and Yen, 2016). The semi-immersive framework comprises a moderately high-performance graphics processing system linked to a widescreen panel, a giant screen projector system, or a multiple television projection system. Such projection technologies are comparable to IMAX theatre in certain respects. These systems employ a broad peripheral vision to improve the user's sense of immersion or presence. The clarity of the reflected picture, on the other hand, is an essential factor. To avoid distortions, the geometries of the projected picture should be calibrated to the form of the panel, and the settlement can affect the quality of texture, colors, the capacity to specify shapes, and the user's ability to interpret the text on the screen (Wang and Ong, 2016). A fully immersive VR framework gives a far more firsthand experience with virtual surroundings. These are the most well-known VR implementations, in which the user presumably wears a head-mounted display (HMD) or utilizes a kind of head-coupled display, such as a Binocular Omni Orientation Panel. A head-mounted display (HMD) employs tiny monitors positioned in front of each eye to give stereo, binocular, as well as monocular pictures. Stereo pictures are delivered in a comparable pattern as shutter frames, with each eye seeing a slightly distinct image. VR headsets comprise sensors, one or perhaps extra image sensors, connectivity, very high displays at high frame rates and a wide field-of-view to send a realistic image and immersive experiences. The main distinction is that the two displays are situated close to the eye (50-70mm), even though the picture around which the user focuses will be considerably distant due to the HMD optical system. In the digital age, virtual reality modeling (VRM) is a crucial component of research. In addition, virtual reality models may be generated immediately on-site using digitally-mediated instruments (laser scanners, remote sensing technologies, drones, digital photogrammetry, and so on) or in digital labs employing 3D modeling software and presented through immersive systems. This entails the use of field-collected VRM datasets as well as the usage of VRM for restorations and electronic information.

### *VR Scene Modeling*

The conventional scene modeling approach is still mostly reliant on 3D geometric modeling of computer graphics. OpenGL is a modeling tool for creating virtual scenes. It can accomplish easy 3D model construction and real-time interaction with the associated graphic features. OpenGL offers a robust API for developers to use, and graphical transformation capabilities that can enable developers to quickly construct 3D visuals. Furthermore, development tools specializing in virtual reality modeling or visualization, such as AutoCAD, 3D Max, and so on, are alternatives. In comparison to older coding languages like OpenGL, VRML offers higher amalgamation and even more sophisticated modeling capabilities, and, at present, it is called the chief technique of scene modeling.

### *VR Model Optimization*

When compared to scene modeling, model optimization can result in an enhanced user experience. However, there exists a typical issue in which the image is not as genuine and smooth. The picture's unreality is mostly restricted by the modeling material and the specific manner of construction. The choppy image is not only due to the manner of constructing the model, but it also has to do with the pace of computer operations. In response to the user's activity, the visual display must alter the real-world scene. The preceding is the contemporary common model optimization direction.

**Objects duplicated**: It is not needed to reconstruct the recurring objects numerous times. To govern node and position modifications, numerical transformations can be employed.

**Texture projections**: Texture projection refers to altering the extent and direction of the geometry by combining advanced texture maps to improve the visual special effects. Furthermore, the texture project can strengthen object realism and refine modification despite increasing the number of modeling procedures.

**Blanking**: The user's visual field is circumscribed, whether in a real or virtual setting (Bolter *et al.*, 2021). When certain sceneries are obscured by others, the scene's complexity must be minimized by restricting the observer's range of vision and standpoint, thus decreasing the number of scene modeling processes.

## VIRTUALIZATION OF SENSOR NETWORKS

Virtual sensor networks (VSN) divide the standard wireless sensor network (WSN) services provider's functionality into two segments: Sensor infrastructure providers maintain physical sensory infrastructures, whereas sensor virtualization network operators create VSNs by pooling resources from various networks and providing a service to application-level consumers. The WSN virtualization revolution has indeed been fueled mostly by the realization that the majority of sensor devices in a WSN are inert most of the time. Wireless sensor virtualization is amongst the most effective methods of utilizing the actual sensor node. Numerous surveillance, tracking, and general-purpose monitoring activities benefit from wireless vision-sensing devices. Camera-enabled sensors collect visual data that may be used for public safety, surveillance systems, building control, environmental sensing, humanitarian relief, and traffic control, among other things. Furthermore, for some of these activities, surveillance might be crucial, necessitating robust availability all across the network's lifespan. Sensor virtualization provides a basis for the development, experimentation, and evaluation of new sensor network designs. Furthermore, by facilitating the shifting of sensor system resources amongst various service providers and server-side users, virtualization in WSNs is intended to enable a distinct demarcation of infrastructure and services and encourage new ways of doing things. Smart cameras, self-contained visual systems with more advanced imaging devices, onboard storage and transportation capabilities, power, and (wireless) networking technology will be the foundation of forthcoming visual sensor networks. This creates new potential for the development of sensor nodes suitable for-visually monitoring large public places, disaster areas, battlefields, and sometimes even ecosystems (Peters and Simó, 2021). Such multi-camera setups are at the crossroads of computer vision and sensor networks, posing difficult technological challenges to researchers in both domains. In fact, when the scale of a cam sensor network expands, it becomes impractical for human drivers to watch numerous video feeds and detect all occurrences of potential interest, and even to control individual units directly in order to sustain continuous monitoring. In a nutshell, sophisticated camera sensor networks executing sophisticated visual surveillance activities spontaneously or with minimum human involvement are required. Aside from legal constraints and economic factors, the utilization of genuine virtual realities in sensor network analysis includes substantially better adaptability even during the design and assessment cycle, thus speeding up the project development. For the objectives of visual wireless sensor algorithmic validation, the virtual environment affords easily available ground truth. Even though experimentation in the virtual environment is fully reproducible, we might easily alter methods and settings and quickly assess their effectiveness. In the simulated world, the harsh real-time restrictions of the actual world may be readily eased. Lastly, notwithstanding its complexity, our simulator works on holistic approach PCs, eliminating the need to deal with embedded systems.

## Testing the Boundaries with Visual Sensor Networking in VR Modeling

Researchers and practitioners have tackled the design objectives for designing effective virtualization in sensor networks. Visual sensors have been commonly used to create simulated view pictures. When the count of visual sensors rises, the quantity and variety of material also increase. WVSN leverages multi-cameras like visual sensors to deliver multi-view offerings, environmental management, multi-resolutions, and espionage. Visual sensor nodes in the WVSN service transfer recorded visual content to sink for subsequent operations appropriate to application purposes, which are created to suit constrained assets, including energy supplies and computing power. Nevertheless, users can still obtain accurate information (Jung, 2015). The more the sensors used to rebuild landscapes, the finer the outcomes. Yet, limitations in energy, processing power, and transmission bandwidth on WVSNs create barriers to receiving information from the multi-camera channel. Furthermore, owing to energy constraints, processing overhead, and bandwidth constraints, generating view pictures in a Wireless Visual Sensor Network context is indeed a difficult operation. Each one of the design requirements, such as network heterogeneity, flexibility, segregation, adaptability, legacy support, experimentation, and deployment facility, must be met in order to accomplish the difficulties underlying wireless sensor virtualization. Heterogeneity is an essential consideration while developing

VSNs. Because it supplies multiple types of sensors, heterogeneity is required when creating a federalized sensor network. This heterogeneity can be seen in the installation of sensor nodes or perhaps in the sensor network established by heterogeneous sensors. Versatility refers to the ability of a design to adjust to dynamic environments (Gorecky *et al.*, 2014). One must consider versatility when developing VSNs. The virtualization of sensor networks provide complete flexibility in all aspects of sensory networking. Every other sensor virtualization connection service provider should be allowed to use any virtual sensor network topology they choose (Javornik *et al.*, 2017). To increase failure, security, and privacy, sensor network virtualization requires guarantee isolation across existing VSN. The misconfigurations and execution problems are common in sensor operating systems. Sensor virtualization needs to guarantee that interruptions with one VSN stay inside that VSN and, therefore, do not influence adjacent VSNs that coexist with it. The isolation enables the rational separation of VSNs even when they dwell along the same physical substrate network system. Countless cases of unaltered sensing apps employ their virtual sensor as if it were a single dedicated sensor, thanks to device abstraction. Substantial isolation also increases efficiency since each recipient's effectiveness is determined by how much of the console's resources they share. Sharing ensures that a significant proportion of a sensor's assets are used. A key aspect of sensory network virtualization is the coexistence of numerous sensor networks. Scaling is an essential component of this strategy. To make a massive-scale federated sensor network, the VSN must be scalable, allowing for easy alteration or incorporation of additional physical sensor networks. When adopting any modern technology, legacy compliance, as well as backward compatibility, was and still is a major problem. In theory, sensor network virtualization may embrace historical support by treating the current WSN sector as yet another VSN in its assortment of sensor networks; however, how this can be implemented successfully remains an unresolved question. The researchers shall strictly adhere to this design aim. Longevity is critical for current wireless visual sensing devices, although it has received little attention. Because visual sensors gather sensory input in a directed sensing paradigm and sensor nodes have various relevancies, wireless sensor reliability principles are inapplicable to WVSNs. The premise of resiliency is distinct, necessitating a greater perspective of defective node replacement. Last but not least, any globally dispersed federated sensor network system is primarily built and validated in test laboratories in a controlled setting prior to implementation. Because simulating a genuine sensor network is prohibitively costly, testing is-confined to basic topologies and traffic patterns that do not necessarily match the physical environment (Xie *et al.*, 2008).

## Visual Data Accumulation Challenges

Visual data is substantially larger and more sophisticated, unlike scalar data in WSNs. Therefore, a more appropriate selection is necessary to capture/transmit/process visual data given the limited resources (hardware capabilities, bandwidth, and battery life) in WVSNs. Owing to the lack of field of view of visual sensors, it is sometimes important to formulate many visual sensors in random orientation to adequately absorb an item with WSNs. It is much more difficult to determine a minimal set of relevant sensors to adequately protect the item if visual sensors are randomly distributed in the target field. Whenever an event happens in a conventional WSN, all nodes inside that detection range of such event perceive the event and thus become data source stations, transmitting the sensor information back to the source (Edler *et al.*, 2018). In WVSN, the camera on that node may be unable to take the required photo due to its relative angle or obstructions between the item and the sensor node, even though the objects are inside the sensor node's field of view. A sensor node must record, analyze, and transmit sensory information rather than quantitative data; memory and processing demands for a WVSN are significantly greater than that for a WSN. Because of the severe memory and disk requirements, the majority of extant WSN platforms are inapplicable for WVSNs. As a consequence, owing to the limited viewpoint of the camera or the barrier obscuring the view, certain essential situations (for example, the identity of the invader or the license plate of the automobile for security video surveillance) may be missed. Such type of challenges necessitate the deployment of more edge devices. Nonetheless, with WVSNs, an additional essential requirement, Field-of-View (FoV), must be addressed in addition to the detection range (Grabowski and Jankowski, 2014). Each FoV is based on the fact that such a lens records visual information of an incident from a specific direction. In other words, in addition to perceiving range coverage, the receptors' FoV must embrace the act in order to gather visual input from the occurrence. Unless an event happens, adjacent sensors that capture the trigger will simultaneously communicate visual information to the base station. As these nearby sensing nodes are frequently closed geographically, clashes will occur while transmitting data in real time (Druga, 2018). The balance between visual data quality and process resource usage is determined by the platform's needs. A CCD webcam is now a superior alternative for situations that need improved picture quality (*i.e.*, face recognition during security monitoring). Designed applications need the capture of a large number of pictures but do not necessitate high definition. A CMOS is superior image equipment for some applications (for example, object recognition throughout wildlife monitoring). One option is to allow all visual sensor clusters whose field of view includes the item to send visual information to the base station. This strategy, though, would result in a large amount of erroneous visual data being broadcast back to the sink, which might result in substantial additional energy usage and communication bandwidth. Two kinds of WVSN platforms based on computing capabilities and system resource usage are present. One is a low-cost WVSN system created particularly for energy consumption. Another is the high-end WVSN framework, targeted for complex visual large datasets with greater system resources and power consumption requirements. This opens up new research avenues and prospects for developing new WVSN platforms capable of performing complex visual data processing in an energy-efficient manner. Further refined methods might include determining the smallest number of devices that can encompass the object from diverse perspectives constructively or eliminating duplicate visual information among visual sensors prior to relaying the sensor data back towards the base station.

## EMERGING AR AND VR TRENDS

Rapid innovations in high-speed information exchange and small portable computing systems have heightened prerequisites for profound human-digital interactions beyond conventional display technologies. The first surge in AR/VR took place in the 1990s, but it gradually faded due to the absence of adequate equipment and interactive materials. Over the last millennium, the notion of immersive displays has indeed been revived and re-energized (Mao, 2020). VR encapsulates a completely immersive environment, whereas AR stimulates interaction among the users, interactive resources, and the actual reality, showcasing virtual images while maintaining watching abilities. Through sensors in 'day-in- day-out- and not-so-everyday-devices', the Internet of Things (IoT) generates a colossal volume of information. The prominence of AR and VR can be imagined as follows:

**AI implementation in the AR/VR space**: Augmented, virtual, and mixed reality have all entered the corporate world and proved their worth (Rauschnabel, 2016). Nonetheless, leaders of VR/AR development companies and VR/AR programmers will look forward to sharing the prospects of their collaborative efforts in the decades ahead. Individuals will examine how rigorous machine ML algorithms or other AI strategies can help multiple computers visualize and absorb information effectively.

**Rising AR Avatars:** The prominence of virtual celebrities such as Brud's Lil Miquela and Activ8's Kizuna AI has gone up significantly. All such fictional characters have piqued the interest of customers and become virtual influencers. As an outcome, their overall market is anticipated to widen in the years ahead. Businesses and marketers must adopt these avatars into their workflows not only to lure customers but also to assist them in navigating both in and out of physical stores, adding a touch of elegance to their initial ordeal.

**Prepping for AR:** People are eager to utilize self-driving vehicles. However, what amazes automakers is that the assimilation of AR technology into these vehicles is expected. Numerous automobile sector executives will endorse the idea of using such two leading tech patterns to redefine how individuals migrate and commute in the form of voice assistants, in-car AR, and so on in the coming years.

**AR Buying Experiences:** In the retail industry, AR technology has diverse applications. Store mapping is one of many possibilities that is presently being realized. With AR, on-screen guidelines can assist a customer in navigating the store layout to access the information they require. All the consumer will just need to grab their phone to follow the augmented reality guidance through all the aisles to one's desired destination, the item.

**The Meta World:** Facebook's rebranding to Meta may have gone viral by storm. However the notion of the Metaverse and the tumult of digital information with extended reality space has been for a while. It is vital to be aware of the industry's shift toward the era of digital and virtual reality spaces. Still, the advantages of this model can be therapeutic efficacy and providing enterprises with a comparative edge in many industrial sectors. Even though the metaverse is concerned primarily with VR spaces, the notion is capable of transforming AR's use in corporate and personal situations as well.

**XR for the Future:** AR, MR, and VR are realigning the health sector by serving distinct functions. With the combination of various technologies, healthcare and medical personnel will be able to swipe among them within that application. With the world market for Extended Reality (XR) and its uses anticipated to be more than double by 2024, there are hardly a few sectors that do not benefit from this powerful training tool. Future AR/VR gadgets will offer customized, handy, and well-designed outlooks. A platform shift is undeniable as these aspects take hold. With this steady pace, we will see novel AR glasses with LTE abilities that will be a viable alternative to handsets in three years. The configuration of our total count of consumer electronics will then be altered with improved immersive innovation and AR capabilities. Augmented and virtual realities are expected to have a strong impact on global trade. In this case, being cognizant of AR/VR trends and the perspectives of top VR companies is insufficient. Augmented and virtual realities make data visible, contextual, and serviceable instantaneously. This creates a strong connection between IoT, AR, and VR. It also yields virtually limitless enterprise applications, such as order picking, augmented reality-enhanced surgical procedures, and digital twins, allowing for a next-generation framework for modeling and monitoring plant operations, supply chains, and other sophisticated methods. Technology is unavoidable. It creates an avenue for reliability, but it cannot function without people. Their instinct, spontaneity, and learning ability are critical. The destiny of supply chains will be all about collaboration in 2023 and beyond. The future may be defined as hyper-reality, which integrates AI, AR, VR, and MR. A need for large-sized headsets and the ability to connect to a stationary PC will no longer be a primary concern. The transition from the simulated environment to real life will be hyper-immersive.

## CONCLUSION

Virtual reality technology has been a popular concern in recent years. VR has received considerable attention owing to the fact that it permits people to actually escape. Some investigations have emerged in an unending flow, spanning from its theories and models to software or hardware and industrial applications. In the provision of specifications, the main difficulty right now is VR modeling. Individuals are always worried about how to create a realistic, low-volume visual world. The targeted chapter concentrated primarily on standpoints of AR and VR in the long term on a large scale, taking into account VR schemes that fall back on Scene Modeling, Statistical Analysis, Sensor Networking, and factoring research methods by examining the realities from the perspective of visual sensor networks, which generally tend to avail visual information to VR systems, resulting in providing succinct and effective image data to facilitate in the formation of the digital realm. Simultaneously, a diverse set of hypotheses gives the AR/VR sector the confidence to add value. While associated VR software applications are quickly evolving, we must also pay special attention to VR hardware progress. If you climb something elevated and look down, you are inclined to witness vertigo (Mekni and Lemieux, 2018). If you ever see an entity moving quickly toward your head, you will feel compelled to duck. To deepen the feeling of immersion, AR/VR inventors will soon broaden this sensory interception to other faculties, such as touch and smell. Simultaneously, the gadgets we use to access these imaginary environments will become less expensive and slimmer, expelling the friction that is presently a constraint. A familiar and pleasant interaction style may significantly affect consumer behavior, making VR goods even stronger.

## BIBLOGRAPHY

Azuma, R., Baillot, Y., Behringer, R., Feiner, S., Julier, S., MacIntyre, B. (2001). Recent advances in augmented reality. *IEEE Comput. Graph. Appl., 21*(6), 34-47. [http://dx.doi.org/10.1109/38.963459]

Baker, C. Artificial and Mixed Reality: New Frontiers in Performance. 2017 23rd International Conference on Virtual System & Multimedia, (pp. 1-10). IEEE.

Bassyouni, Z., Elhajj, I.H. (2021). Augmented reality meets artificial intelligence in robotics: A systematic review. *Front. Robot. AI, 8*, 724798.
[http://dx.doi.org/10.3389/frobt.2021.724798] [PMID: 34631805]

Blake, J., Gurocak, H.B. (2009). Haptic Glove With MR Brakes for Virtual Reality. *IEEE/ASME Trans. Mechatron., 14*(5), 606-615.
[http://dx.doi.org/10.1109/TMECH.2008.2010934]

Bolter, J.D., Engberg, M., MacIntyre, B. (2021). *The Genres of AR and VR. Reality Media: Augmented and virtual reality.* MIT Press.
[http://dx.doi.org/10.7551/mitpress/11708.003.0010]

Cruz-Neira, C., Sandin, D.J., DeFanti, T.A., Kenyon, R.V., Hart, J.C. (1992). The CAVE: Audio visual experience automatic virtual environment. *Commun. ACM., 35*(6), 64-72.
[http://dx.doi.org/10.1145/129888.129892]

Costa, D.G., Peixoto, J.P.J. (2021). On the mathematical modelling of visual sensors when computing coverage metrics in camera-based sensing applictions. *2021 IEEE ICA.,* XXIV Congress of the Chilean Association of Automatic Control.1-6.

Doerner, R., Broll, W., Jung, B., Grimm, P., Göbel, M., Kruse, R. Introduction to Virtual and Augmented Reality. In: Doerner, R., Broll, W., Grimm, P., & Jung, B. (Eds.), *Virtual and Augmented Reality (VR/AR)* (pp. 1-37). Springer.
[http://dx.doi.org/10.1007/978-3-030-79062-2_1]

Druga, M. (2018). Pokemon GO: Where VR and AR Have Gone Since Its Inception. *IEEE Potentials., 37*(1), 23-26.
[http://dx.doi.org/10.1109/MPOT.2017.2675498]

Edler, D., Husar, A., Keil, J., Vetter, M., Dickmann, F. Virtual Reality (VR) and open source software: A workflow for constructing an interactive cartographic vr environment to explore urban landscapes. *KN. J. Cartog. Geograp. Inform., 68*, 5-13.

Gerschütz, B., Fechter, M., Schleich, B., Wartzack, S. (2019). A review of requirements and approaches for realistic visual perception in virtual reality. *Proceedings of the Design Society: ICED., 1*(1), 1893-1902.

Grabowski, A., Jankowski, J. (2015). Virtual Reality-based pilot training for underground coal miners. *Saf. Sci., 72*, 310-314.
[http://dx.doi.org/10.1016/j.ssci.2014.09.017]

Jung, T., Chung, N., Leue, M.C. (2015). The determinants of recommendations to use augmented reality technologies: The case of a Korean theme park. *Tour. Manage., 49*, 75-86.
[http://dx.doi.org/10.1016/j.tourman.2015.02.013]

Wang, S., Parsons, M., Stone-McLean, J., Rogers, P., Boyd, S., Hoover, K., Meruvia-Pastor, O., Gong, M., Smith, A. (2017). Augmented reality as a telemedicine platform for remote procedural training. *Sensors, 17*(10), 2294.
[http://dx.doi.org/10.3390/s17102294] [PMID: 28994720]

Wild, F. (2016). The future of learning at the workplace is augmented reality. *Computer, 49*(10), 96-98.
[http://dx.doi.org/10.1109/MC.2016.301]

Xie, W., Cao, W., Meng, S. (2008). Coverage analysis for sensor networks based on Clifford algebra. *Science in China Series F: Information Sciences, 51*(5), 460-475.
[http://dx.doi.org/10.1007/s11432-008-0048-7]

Yap, F.G.H., Yen, H.H. (2017). Novel visual sensor deployment algorithm in occluded wireless visual sensor networks. *IEEE Syst. J., 11*(4), 2512-2523.
[http://dx.doi.org/10.1109/JSYST.2015.2446952]

# CHAPTER 4

# Post-Pandemic OTT Media Hegemony in India: A Socio-Economic Perspective

**Madhuri Yadav**[1,*] and **Sukanta Kumar Baral**[1]

[1] *Department of Commerce, Indira Gandhi National Tribal University, Madhya Pradesh, India*

**Abstract:** Following the COVID-19 pandemic, OTT media consumption made its way to India, revolutionizing the entertainment industry and altering how consumers consumed entertainment. The lockdown has forced consumers to stay home. It has brought about a paradigm shift in consumer behavior. The convenience of consuming content on OTT platforms is driving the growth of this sector. The entertainment sector is doing well with OTT services thanks to the rise in smartphone technical changes and rising internet usage. Due to the abundance of spare time and appetite for entertainment during the pandemic, OTT demand has been greatly influenced. India is a booming market, surpassing Australia, Germany, and South Korea and will become the sixth-largest market in 2024 with a CAGR of 28.6%, as per the PricewaterhouseCoopers report (PwC) published in August 2022. The OTT market continues to increase with growing demand in India. The data were collected from secondary sources. The research reveals that throughout the pandemic, both data usage and subscribers to the internet increased. The main drivers of OTT growth are cheap data plans, broadband penetration, and increasing smartphone sales. It aims to assess how OTT media companies are engaged in their promotion and strategy plans from a socio-economic perspective. The study shows that Hotstar has the highest market share, with 41%, followed by Eros Now at 24%. The findings show that the lockdown has brought socio-economic changes in the consumption patterns of consumers.

**Keywords:** COVID-19, Entertainment, Internet users, OTT media, Post-pandemic, Revenue market, Socio-economic.

## INTRODUCTION

Media has played a crucial role in shaping lives, views, and opinions. With the introduction of technology, the media and its forms have evolved. One such media platform is OTT. OTT stands for over-the-top; the name is given since OTT devices go over the cable box, unlike TVs, in an attempt to provide access to

* **Corresponding author Madhuri Yadav:** Department of Commerce, Indira Gandhi National Tribal University, Madhya Pradesh, India; E-mail: yadavmadhuri444@gmail.com

**Sukanta Kumar Baral, Richa Goel, Tilottama Singh, Erdener Kaynak & Vishal Jain (Eds.)**

video content to its end users. The customers can avail the streaming content directly over the web. The term is generally used to describe platforms for VOD programming; it refers to streaming audio, texting, and internet-based phone calling options. There are certain exceptions, but "OTT services" are generally monetized through paid subscriptions (Gomathi and Christy, 2021). Simply put, OTT is a medium by which TV and film content is provided on the internet, *i.e.*, individual experience based on and offered directly to viewers in a more personalized manner. In 2008, it was seen that Reliance Entertainment launched BigFlix as its first OTT platform to capture the viewers in the market. However, OTT started flourishing in India in 2013 after the launch of Zee TV and Sony Liv. Since Disney Hotstar was launched in 2015, it has become the most popular OTT platform. Similarly, Netflix came into the Indian market in 2016. With the emergence of OTT, the entire process of media churning (particularly entertainment) has changed as now the users are not required to wait to watch a show like a traditional TV system. They can subscribe to any OTT platform, select the genre they like, and watch their chosen content. Simply put, entertainment is enjoying oneself, usually with close friends and family. In the modern world, one of the most important sectors is entertainment., including the sub-fields of theatre, dance, film, literary publishing, music, fine arts, opera, dance, television, and radio. "Over-the-Top (OTT) entertainment, as this technology came to be known, is burgeoning into a multi-billion-dollar industry in India, cannibalizing smoothly into the established bastion of traditional television, cinema theatres, radio, and other traditional forms of entertainment" (MICA, 2021). The consumer has shifted from traditional TV to OTT platforms due to three factors: technological flexibility, customer-centric, and user behavior (Patnaik *et al.*, 2022). The study focuses on the emergence of customer behavior in the pandemic era in a specific industry, namely OTT or over-the-top services. It is a part of the entertainment sector, which is very big. Notably, the pandemic-induced lockdown fuelled the demand for OTT.

## OTT in India and COVID-19 Pandemic

The COVID-19 pandemic outbreak confined people to their respective homes. Everything was impacted, from schools and colleges to theatres and offices. The world subsequently shifted to the internet. People solely relied on these OTT platforms for entertainment. The pandemic has changed how audiences consume media because OTT platforms offer convenience, productivity, and low cost. The OTT market continues to increase with growing demand in India (MICA, 2021). According to IBEF, the pandemic-induced lockdown fuelled the growth of these platforms even more, and people consumed entertainment themselves staying at their respective homes. Further, the subscription video on demand will significantly generate revenue, rising at a CAGR of 30.7% (Jain, 2021). The pandemic impacted consumer behavior globally, and digital media assumed greater significance in keeping the public informed and entertained within the four walls of their homes. It can be observed that from the start, OTT platforms have flourished and grown in popularity; during the pandemic, it gained more popularity because of sudden changes in the consumption pattern of consumers (Patnaik *et al.*, 2022).

As per the PWC report, India is one of the 10 largest markets of OTT platforms in terms of revenue, where mobile internet users would double from 406 million to 805 million in 2022. Furthermore, demand for consumer-generated content, declining internet costs, and portability demand drive the OTT video business. The secret to the Indian OTT market is a greater emphasis on locally produced content. Additionally, India has shown all the possibilities to surpass South Korea, Germany, and Australia in total video revenue and would be the 6th-largest market in 2024. The PWC report revealed that OTT, a video platform, has been growing in and beyond the four walls due to the penetration of smartphones and smart TVs. The main source of revenue will be subscription VOD, which would grow at a CAGR of 30.7 percent, from US $ 708 million in 2019 to US $ 27 million in 2024. In 2020, after the COVID-19 outbreak, the total OTT revenue more than doubled when public entertainment was absent, and people were forced to spend additional time at home. Despite a slowdown in growth rates, the market will still develop at a remarkable CAGR of 14.1% to reach INR 21,032 crore in 2026. Subscription services, which accounted for 90.5% of revenue in 2021 and are projected to account for 95% of revenue in 2026, are responsible for fueling this rapid growth.

## Literature Review

Sundaravel, E. and Elangovan, N. (2020) explored the emergence, benefits, and way forward for VOD streaming in India. They also introduced "OTT" varied services, growth drivers, technical knowledge, target audience features, content censorship, and anticipated future developments within the industry. The emergence of "OTT" has adversely affected the penetration of cable TV in India. Additionally, smartphones are the most widely used devices for watching OTT video content in India.

Fitzgerald, S. (2019) stated that Amazon and Netflix are engaged in a war in India, which will eventually cause the growth of the OTT market. Most of the users have been using YouTube as a free media library for video programming. The three forms of OTT apps in the Indian marketplace include communique services, software ecosystems, and video and audio content material. Various regional content creation channels have accelerated the OTT sector and media financial system within the country, including global leaders and broadcast community-backed platforms, OZeeTV and VOOT.

Saha, S. (2021) concluded that YouTube is the most frequently used application, with Netflix and Amazon Prime in second and third place, respectively, followed by MX player, Sony LIV, and other OTT platforms. Internet penetration, the increasing provision of content quality, the availability of foreign and regional languages, and break-free shows contribute to the OTT rise in the country. The future is much more trustworthy than virtual platforms, where customer touchpoints have changed drastically.

Rahul, M. and Dinesh Babu, S. (2021) mainly focused on how the censorship of OTT platforms in India works. With the growth of OTT platforms, censorship emerged, affecting the Indian OTT sector as well. In 2021, the central government established three levels of regulation for the "OTT platforms". The authors also compared the censorship and control policies of OTT platforms in India with those of the world. A comparison of OTT platforms worldwide is not intended to explain how good the censorship of OTT platforms in India is but rather to compare how censorship in India differs from the rest of the world. It is intended that India's censorship system is unique in that it has implemented methods for viewers and OTT companies.

Jain, M. K.'s (2021) study showed how customers demanded entertainment during the lockdown and how their plentiful free time due to the pandemic increased their subscriptions to popular OTT series. Due to the lockdown, the filming of TV shows and movies was halted, which caused a shift in consumer behavior toward OTT services and a rapid increase in their demand. Due to the simplicity and diversity offered without commercials, people are now more at ease using OTT services. According to trends, the OTT market will also expand rapidly in the next few years. Businesses now have to deal with consumers' shifting choices for OTT platforms over traditional offline entertainment.

Song, M.'s (2021) paper analyzed and compared Netflix and Amazon on the basis of five success factors of innovation. Amazon is cheap and has lots of content to see, but the user experience is not pleasurable. At the same time, users have a pleasant experience with Netflix, and it has loyal customers with various trials and errors. Moreover, Amazon has bigger libraries than Netflix, with Netflix offering fewer movies but a high caliber. APV subscription provides multiple additional benefits such as free access to Amazon Prime Music, free shipping of the Kindle library, and other benefits. None of these, however, are associated with OTT movies or TV series.

Mondal, S. (2022) showed that data usage during COVID-19 increased the number of internet subscribers. Netflix memberships and revenue increased significantly over the same period. There is a very positive impact on data usage when it comes to Netflix viewership growth. In India, Netflix's revenue has also increased significantly due to the rising percentage of broadband users. This study clearly states that the use of over-the-top services has a significant impact on internet usage and data consumption, and the increase in the number of internet users significantly increases the revenue of OTT service providers. The study also shows that the pandemic and lockdown period are key factors in such outcomes.

Gomathi, S., and Vijaitha Christy, N. (2021) stated that OTT has a very bright future and added that video consumption, Internet, and mobile penetration are increasing daily. Due to the availability of on-demand video and foreign content, millennials are attracted to OTT platforms. Many OTT platforms have experienced significant growth due to Jio's entry and its free 4G service offer. However, it cannot be predicted whether OTT platforms will surpass traditional TV in India. The charges of OTT services are a little high for Indian users.

Patnaik *et al.*'s (2021) study explored the growth of OTT during COVID-19. It analyzed people's opinions of OTT platforms and consumption patterns and compared them with movies to see if "OTT platforms" are capturing traditional media. It turns out that people are using OTT platforms for entertainment. Most of them experienced increased time spent and were looking forward to OTT movies being released in cinemas simultaneously. Also, people had no problem watching movies on OTT rather than in cinemas. The study reveals OTT platforms have a lot of future potential, and the pandemic has a huge part to play in it.

Gupta, P. (2021) stated that people have shifted toward online series due to their higher quality and constant accessibility. Most viewers also appreciate that OTT is accessible from everywhere and that they can download it. People feel that these elements are missing in TV shows due to television programs' predetermined pacing and lengthy commercial interruptions. Most people believe online content or series is much better than TV shows. These are the main reasons web series have become more popular in India. The two main ways web series are promoted are through word-of-mouth and online marketing.

Kumar *et al.* (2020) defined the future of Netflix in terms of revenue as remarkably bright in India. Netflix emerged in India in 2017. In addition, it has gradually established a more substantial presence and taken on local competitors like Disney+Hotstar. It has made its largest investment in India to produce original stuff. Netflix offers three different subscription plans, basic, standard, and premium, each with advantages. It has approximately 100 million subscribers worldwide. Amazon Prime Video offers various services to their Prime subscribers, such as Kindle First, free shipping within two days, Music Prime, and Prime Photos.

According to Gowda, S. and Mandge, O. (2021), "Over-the-top (OTT)" is becoming one of the most prominent industries for providing entertainment and is regarded as a need. The number of OTT users has been increasing continuously. Moreover, Amazon Prime Video and Netflix are global OTT players with a larger customer base than Indian OTT platforms such as VOOT, Hotstar+Disney, and ZEE5. In India, Prime has begun to increase its market share. This study aims to comprehend the workflow for various OTT services. Technological foundation, audience distribution, content, and censorship affect growth.

Moochhala, Q. (2018), in his paper, aims to explore the future of various streaming entertainment media platforms in the Indian market. To delve deeper into the subject, the study used primary and secondary data to evaluate every platform on specific parameters. Notably, this reveals that internet users are slowly shifting from traditional media (TV and Cinema) to OTT (Over-The-Top) digital apps for entertainment. The study also aims to determine the impact of India's rebranding itself as Digital India and whether the country will be successful in this endeavor. It further attempts to find out the most emerging brand in the market and what are the significant reasons behind it.

### Objectives of the Study

- To understand the OTT platforms and their business in India.
- To discover the growing demand for OTT content after the COVID-19 pandemic.

## RESULTS AND DISCUSSION

### Results

As per the IAMAI report, India has 692 million active internet users; out of them, 341 are from urban areas, and 351 are from rural areas. Reports estimate that there will be 900 million internet users in India by 2025. Notably, digital transactions have increased by 50% because of the global pandemic. Fig. (**1**) depicts the number of internet users in India in millions (2015-2025).

From 2015 to 2020, the number of internet user increased drastically in India. A CAGR of almost 20% was registered to be 302 million in FY 15 and 743 million in FY 20. It is also projected to reach 975 million in FY 2025.

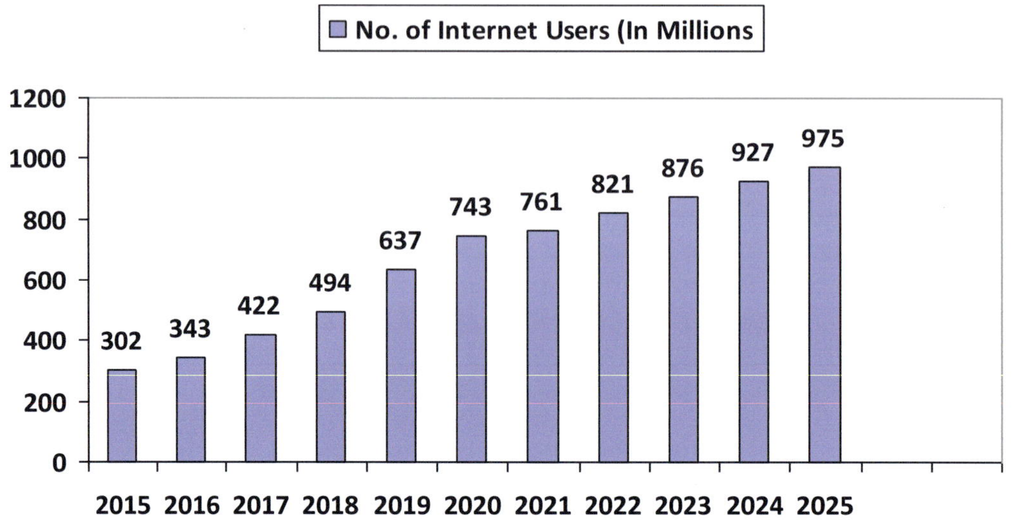


**Fig. (1).** Number of internet users in India in millions (2015-2025).
Source: Compiled by the researchers.

It has been seen that, in 2026, the users of the smartphone will be one billion. In 2021, smartphone users were 1.2 bn. It will likely overtake the second largest smartphone producer in the following five years. Fig. (**2**) shows the number of smartphone users in India in millions (2013-2025).

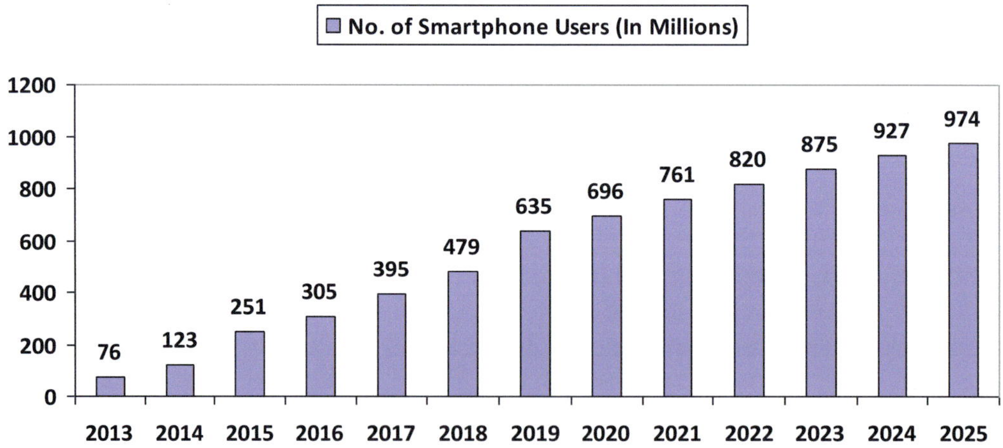


**Fig. (2).** Number of smartphone users in India in millions (2013-2025).
Source: Compiled by the researchers

In India, it has been seen that smartphone users increased to 696 million in FY 20 from 76 million in 2013, with a CAGR growth of ~37% during this period. The number is projected to reach 974 million in FY 25. Table **1** shows various internet subscribers in India.

**Table 1. Internet Subscribers in India (Million*).**

| | |
|---|---|
| Internet subscribers (Total) | 825.30* |
| % change quarterly | 3.79% |
| Subscribers (Narrowband) | 47.21% |
| Subscribers (Broadband) | 778.09* |
| Subscribers (Wired internet) | 25.99* |
| Subscribers (Wireless internet) | 799.30* |
| Internet subscribers (Urban) | 502.53* |
| Internet subscribers (Rural) | 322.77* |
| Urban subscribers (per 100 population) | 107.3 |
| Rural subscribers (per 100 population) | 36.24 |
| Internet subscribers (per 100 population) | 60.73 |

Source: Compiled by the researchers.

As per the MICA Report 2015, Internet subscribers were over 251.59 million, reaching 825.30 million in 2021. While 98% of urban India had access to the internet, close to 33% of rural India could consume content on the internet in 2020. Over 55% of urban Indians have a subscription to a movie or television show. The next most popular service is digital/satellite TV, with a 41% market share, which ranks second worldwide. The 450 million entertainment customers in India use smartphones for 4.6 hours daily (EY FICCI, 2021). According to the IAMAI or Internet and Mobile Association of India, India is the most promising OTT market. With 560 million internet users, India is the second largest internet market in the world, only behind China. Table **2** below explains the growing revenue of OTT in India.

**Table 2. Ever-growing revenue of OTT in india.**

| S. No. | OTT Platform | Market Share (Percentage) |
|---|---|---|
| 1 | Disney+Hotstar | 41 |
| 2 | Eros Now | 24 |
| 3 | Amazon prime video | 9 |
| 4 | Netflix | 7 |

*(Table 2) cont.....*

| S. No. | OTT Platform | Market Share (Percentage) |
|---|---|---|
| 5 | ZEE5 | 5 |
| 6 | ALT Balaji | 5 |
| 7 | SonyLIV | 3 |

Source: Omida consumer research. [https://www.theglobalstatistics.com/ott-platforms-market-share-india/].

As the table depicts, Disney + Hotstar has the highest market share with 41%, closely followed by Eros Now with 24%, Amazon Prime Video with 9%, Netflix with 7%, ZEE5 ALTBalaji with 4%, and Sonyliv with 3% of the market share.

Many OTT platforms exist in India, such as Disney+Hotstar, Netflix, Amazon Prime Video, ALT Balaji, Eros Now, SonyLIV, ZEE5, Jio Cinema, etc. According to Frost and Sullivan (2017–2022), the OTT market is anticipated to increase by 33.8% CAGR from INR 22.62 billion in 2020 to 93.67 billion in 2025 in India. The revenue from "OTT platforms" increased to around 19 billion Indian rupees in 2020. It was expected to touch 46 billion rupees in 2022. Further, in 2020, OTT revenue in India reached more than 2 billion USD and is anticipated to touch seven billion by 2026. According to Statista (2020), with 20%, both Netflix and Prime Video make up the highest OTT video revenue market share, followed by Hotstar, Zee5, etc. With a hike of 49 percent across the entertainment industry, the Highest Annual Growth for Indian Entertainment Digital Market was recorded in 2019-2020. India will show record growth in the coming decade, expanding by more than 20%. According to the report, 90% of subscribers of Eros Now were grouped. The company emphasized strategic alliances with domestic telecom companies such as BSNL, Idea Cellular, and Reliance JIO and paying TV agents, namely, Tata Sky Binge, Airtel, and Xstream (IBEF, 2021). In terms of revenue in 2022, India would become the 10th largest market for OTT, with a rise in mobile internet subscribers from 406 million in 2017 to 805 million in 2022. The number was expected to be doubled in 2022. Table **3** provides the number of OTT subscribers in India.

**Table 3. OTT subscribers in india.**

| S. No. | OTT Platform | Number of Subscribers (CRORES) |
|---|---|---|
| 1 | Disney+Hotstar | 14 |
| 2 | Amazon prime video | 6 |
| 3 | Netflix | 4 |
| 4 | ZEE5 | 3.7 |
| 5 | SonyLIV | 2.5 |

Source: Omida Consumer Research: https://www.theglobalstatistics.com/ott-platforms-market-share-india/

As per the Omida consumer research reports, the total number of OTT subscribers in India was 45 crore in 2022. Disney+ Hotstar has the highest number of subscribers with 14 crores, followed by Amazon Prime Video and Netflix with six crores and four crores, respectively. As per the Media Partners Asia (MPA) report, in 2022, OTT's worth would be $5 billion. Additionally, Netflix's revenue would be 67% from online VOD. Table **4** explains the different major OTT players in India.

**Table 4. Major OTT players in india.**

| Platform | Parent Company | Launch Date | Business Model | Subscription Price (Rs.) |
|---|---|---|---|---|
| Hotstar +Disney | Star India | 2015 | freemium | 99* |
| Amazon | Amazon | 2016 | SVOD | 179 |
| Netflix | Netflix US | 2016 | SVOD | (149, 199, 499, 649) |
| Voot | Network 18/Viacom | 2016 | SVOD | 299** |
| ALT Balaji | Balaji Telefilms | 2017 | AVOD | 100* |
| Sony LIV | Sony Pictures network | 2013 | AVOD | 299 |
| ZEE5 | Zee Entertainment/Essel group | 2018 | freemium | 699** |
| Eros now | Eros International | 2015 | AVOD | 49 |
| MX player | Times Internet | 2018 | freemium | free |

Note: OTT = over the top; SVOD = Subscription Video on demand, AVOD = Advertising Video on demand; *2 months, **Annually.

Some popular OTT platforms include Hotstar+Disney, Netflix, Amazon Prime Video, VOOT, etc. Moreover, OTT, or the Over-the-top market, is dominated by Hotstar in India in terms of market share; its business model is freemium, and the subscription price is just 99 rupees for two months. It is one of the popular platforms owned by Star India. It provides services such as movies, shows, news and sports, web series, and short movies (Jain, 2021). The viewers can make an account and view the free content with advertisements. However, it offers free content to international TV shows and movies for premium subscribers (RBSA, 2021). The subscribers of Disney+ Hotstar are approximately 43 million, which make it a comprehensive OTT platform in India. Notably, Hotstar dominates the OTT platform with 29% of total users. Netflix focuses on three major plans: basic, standard, and premium (Kumar *et al.*, 2020). Recently, Netflix has added a mobile-based subscription plan costing just Rs. 149. Amazon and Netflix are tough competitors; both want to capture the Indian market, and their business model is the same as SVOD, but their approach differs. Netflix is a little expensive, while Amazon Prime offers various services at affordable prices at 179 per month. Amazon Prime Video entered the Indian market in July 2016. It has approximately 100 million subscribers worldwide. It offers services such as the e-commerce platform Prime membership, free and fast delivery, discounts, and access to ebooks (Jain, 2021). Alt Balaji subscription price is very affordable, at 100 rupees for two months, and it also offers original web series and movies, which carved a niche in the Indian market. Table **5** explains the revenue model of OTT platforms in India.

**Table 5. Revenue model of OTT platforms in india.**

| Revenue Model | Particular | Platform |
|---|---|---|
| Advertising video on demand (AVOD) | Users can access stuff for free, and the Platform makes money from advertisements. | MX player, YouTube, VOOT, TVF |
| Subscription video on demand (SVOD) | Viewers have to pay some subscription charges and get access to the content. | Netflix, Amazon Prime Video |
| Freemium | It is the combination of both models, AVOD and SVOD models. | ALT Balaji, Hotstar, ZEE5, SonyLiv |
| Transactional video on demand (TVOD) | Viewers only pay for live events, movies, and series; no need to buy a subscription. | Veqta |

Source: Compiled by the researcher.

The OTT platform invests in creating and purchasing content, then sells content to make money from the users or audience who pay to watch. The revenue models differ from media and offer packaged services to their telco-backed OTT platforms like Jio Cinema, and Airtel TV. In India, OTT platforms adopted four monetized models to generate profits. Viewers are forced to watch advertisements that cannot be skipped while watching content, interrupting the viewing experience of watching their favorite stuff on the OTT platform. AVOD stands for "Advertising Video on Demand". Under this model, viewers can watch stuff free of cost. Platforms generate profit through advertisement, charging brands and companies to post advertisements on their platform. In addition, SVOD stands for Subscription Video on Demand. OTT platforms earn money by charging users a subscription fee to watch the content. The subscription cost may vary by platform. However, in the hybrid model, the OTT platform provides paid and free subscriptions for the users and earns profit by using both models, namely AVOD and SVOD. Moreover, TVOD is an abbreviation for Transaction Video on Demand. This model includes two steaming options for subscribers to select based on their choice.

## Socio-Economic Perspectives

While considering the socio-economic challenges, it is more important to understand the consumption pattern and adoption of the OTT platform in urban and rural areas. In tier 2 cities, OTT is struggling due to the limitation of smartphones, and internet penetration poses challenges in the OTT market growth (Sujata *et al*., 2015). Furthermore, 46% of OTT video platform users were from the top five metro cities, while another 35% belonged to tier I cities in July 2020. India has witnessed massive growth compared to the world market at a 28.6% CAGR across the forecast period (RBSA, 2021). Apart from that, studies showed that the majority of Indians prefer regional language-based content, particularly Hindi language. Notably, Hindi-based content accounts for more than 50% of total streaming. If OTT wants to reach every part of India, it should not depend on only one or two languages. Therefore, they must focus on the various regional languages. A considerable amount is invested in these OTT platforms to create original content in various languages according to consumer preferences (Patnaik *et al*., 2022). The consumer buys the package according to their need and capacity (Srna *et al*., 2020).

## DISCUSSION

The study's first objective was to understand the OTT platforms and their business in India. As Table **2** depicts, the OTT platforms in India, such as Disney + Hotstar, have the highest market share with 41%, closely followed by EROS NOW with 24%, Amazon Prime Video with 9%, and Netflix with 7%. Zee5 and ALT Balaji have 4%, and SonyLIV has a 3% market share. However, Hotstar has captured the OTT market. The number of paid subscribers is expected to jump from the current 102 million to a whopping 224 million by 2024. Fig. (**3**) shows subscribers of OTT in India. The main drivers of subscribers are smartphones with cheap data plans and broadband penetration. Additionally, the main reason for OTT growth is the growing digital population in India. Furthermore, the number of internet users in 2015 was 302 million, which is likely to increase to 975 million in 2025.

The study's second objective was to discuss the growing demand for OTT content after the COVID-19 pandemic. fig. (**1**) depicts India's OTT revenue from 2017 to 2022. The total revenue of the Indian OTT market was 277 million in 2017; it increased to 823 million in 2022. However, we see that Indian OTT revenue has been growing continuously. It will be a good indicator for all the OTT platforms in India. OTT platforms saw a significant increase in content consumption and subscriber count during the coronavirus (COVID-19) pandemic. As a result, they work to satisfy viewers' growing appetites for entertainment. According to estimates, original series has been watched by users on OTT platforms for at least 32% longer between March 20th and April 3rd, 2020, than between January 13th and February 2nd, 2020.

## CONCLUSION

The present studies reveal that OTT platforms have been continuously growing in India after the pandemic. However, the study also reveals several factors for the growth of OTT platforms, such as increased access to high-speed Internet, affordable data plan rates, penetration of smartphones, and the increasing use of online streaming services for content. By 2022, there were expected to be 829 million smartphone users in India, the second-largest smartphone market in the world. India surpasses the USA's mobile subscribers with over 400 million (Jagmohan, 2019). This study helps to assess researchers and service providers in shaping their promotion and strategy plans. However, OTT platforms must enhance their content according to the viewer's point of view and should reduce violence, nudity, and other content (Rahul & Dinesh, 2021). In India, most people prefer watching the OTT platform's free content (Gupta, 2019). Affordable internet access has fueled the expansion of OTT services across India. However, still, users are not switching to OTT platforms because they lack technological literacy and access to diverse content (Kumari, 2020). Therefore, the future of OTT platforms is quite promising, and video consumption will rise along with the growth of the Internet and mobile devices.

## BIBLIOGRAPHY

Dasgupta, D., Grover, D. Understanding adoption factors of over-the-top video services among millennial consumers. *Int. J. Comp. Eng. Technol., 10*(1), 61-71.

Fitzgerald, S. (2019). Over-the-top video services in India: Media imperialism after globalization. Media Industries Journal, 6(2).

Gomathi, S., Vijaitha Christy, N. (2021). Viewers' perception towards OTT Platform during pandemic (with special reference to Coimbatore city). *Int. J. Creat. Res. Thoug., 9*(8), 593-693.

Gowda, S., Mandge, O. (2021). OTT and growth of India's OTT platform. *Int. J. Adv. Res. Ide. Innov. Technol., 7*(3), 1246-1250.

Gupta, P. (2021). The factors affecting shift of Indian customers from TV series to web series-the future of OTT services in India. EPRA International Journal of Multidisciplinary Research (IJMR).

IAMAI, (2022). Internet in India 2021 https://www.business-standard.com/article/current-affairs/intern-t-usage-grows-faster-in-rural-india-knowhow-still-a-deterrent-122072801008_1.html.

IBEF, (2021). India To Have 900 million internet users by 2025. https://www.ibef.org/news/india-to-ha-e-900-million-internet-users-by-2025-report.

Jaganmohan, M. (2020). Smartphone users in India 2015-2022. https://www.statista.com/statistics/467163/forecast-of-smartphone-users-in-india/.

Jain, M.K. (2021). The Rise of OTT Platform: Changing consumer preferences. *EPRA Int. J. Multidiscip. Res., 7*(6), 257-261.

Khanna, V. (2017). A study on factors affecting subscription rates of Netflix in India: An empirical approach. *Delhi Business Review, 18*(1), 83-100.
[http://dx.doi.org/10.51768/dbr.v18i1.181201717]

Kumar, J., Gupta, A., Dixit, S. (2020). Netflix: SVoD entertainment of next gen. *Emerald Emerging Markets Case Studies, 10*(3), 1-36.

[http://dx.doi.org/10.1108/EEMCS-04-2020-0108]

Kumari, T. (2020). A study on the growth of over the top (OTT) video services in India. *Int. J. Latest Res. Human. Soc. Sci., 3*(9), 68-73.

MICA. (2021). *Indian OTT platforms.* https://www.mica.ac.in/indian-ott-platforms/indian-ott-platforms

Moochhala, Q. (2018). *The future of online OTT entertainment services in India..* Pune, India: Actionesque Consulting.https://actionesque.com/research-papers_pdf/QM-OTT-future-2018.pdf

Mondal, S. (2022). A Comparative Study between Over-the-Top (OTT) Media Service and Use of Internet in COVID-19 Pandemic.
[http://dx.doi.org/10.2139/ssrn.4004498]

Nijhawan, G.S., Dahiya, S. (2020). Role of COVID as a Catalyst in increasing adoption of OTTs in India: A Study of evolving consumer consumption patterns and future business scope. *J. Cont. Commun. Communic., 12*(12), 298-311.
[http://dx.doi.org/10.31620/JCCC.12.20/28]

Patnaik, R., Shah, R., More, U. Rise of OTT Platforms: Effect of the C-19 Pandemic. *PalArch's J. Archaeol. Egypt/Egyptol., 18*(7), 2277-2287.

Patnaik, R., Patra, S.K., Mahapatra, D.M., Baral, S.K. (2022). Adoption and challenges underlying OTT Platform in India during Pandemic: A Critical Study of Socio-Economic and Technological Issues. *FIIB Business Review, 23197145221101676*
[http://dx.doi.org/10.1177/23197145221101676]

PWC, (2018). PwC Global Entertainment & Media Outlook: 2018-2022. https://www.pwc.in/industries/entertainment-and-media/global-entertainment.

PWC, (2020). PwC Global Entertainment & Media Outlook: 2020-2024. https://www.pwc.com/gx/en/industries/tmt.html.

Rahul, M., Dinesh Babu, S. (2021). A Comparative Study on Ott Platform Censorship and Policies in India. *Ann. Rom. Soc. Cell Biol., 25*(6), 11160-11167.

RBSA. (2021). *OTT-A Paradigm Shift in Media & Entertainment.* https://rbsa.in/ott-a-paradigm-shif--in-media-entertainment/

Saha, S. (2021). Consumption pattern of OTT platforms in India. *Int. J. Mod. Agricul., 10*(2), 641-655.

Sujata, J., Sohag, S., Tanu, D., Chintan, D., Shubham, P., Sumit, G. (2015). Impact of over the top (OTT) services on telecom service providers. *Indian J. Sci. Technol., 8*(S4), 145-160.
[http://dx.doi.org/10.17485/ijst/2015/v8iS4/62238]

Sundaravel, E., Elangovan, N. (2020). Emergence and future of Over-the-top (OTT) video services in India: analytical research. *Int. J. Busin. Manag. Soc. Res., 8*(2), 489-499.

Sunitha, S., Sudha, S. (2020). Covid-19 conclusion: A media and entertainment sector perspective in India. *Vichar Manthan, 8*(24), 135-137.

Song, M. A Comparative study on over-the-tops, netflix & amazon prime video: Based on the success factors of innovation. *Int. j. adv. smart converg., 10*(1), 60-74.

Silverman, S., Etkin, J. (2020). When limits backfire: The ironic effect of setting limits on entertainment consumption. *ACR North American Advances.*

# CHAPTER 5

# The Digital Disruption Model: Redefining the Healthcare Sector with Innovation

**Preetiraj Pattnaik**[1], **Rabinarayan Patnaik**[2,*] and **Prasanta Kumar Mohanty**[1]

[1] *Centurion University of Technology and Management Bhubaneswar, India*

[2] *Faculty of Management Sciences, Siksha 'O' Anusandhan (SOA) Deemed University, Bhubaneswar, India*

**Abstract:** With innovations and developments in virtual reality as well as artificial intelligence, machine learning, robotic process automation, the use of biosensors in mobile technologies *etc.*, healthcare executives are seizing the required benefits for patients. The introduction of new business models by start-ups is causing considerable disruptive innovation, and with investments totaling US$ 679 million in 2018, the future appears bright. However, there is very little literature available on this phenomenon. This study focuses on instigating the discussion in the healthcare sector of India on the field of digital and disruptive innovation to spot what sort of agents of disruption can help policymakers make informed decisions. The scope of the study includes understanding the usage of this disruption, typically by the startups operating in the field of healthcare and so on. Further investigation found ventures from these companies in a digital context can be examined using the criteria of value for cost towards health services, the presence of a robust and sustainable business model, and a platform for customer-centric solutions. The approach was to see patterns that could show incumbents in the industry relying more on sustainable innovation and creating enough space to allow spectacular usage in the future with due changes in their traditional setups.

**Keywords:** AGG, Apps, DFR, DHR, Digital india, Digital transformation, Disruptive innovation, FODCAP, Healthcare sector, Health-tech start-ups, JTBD, Low-end sisruptions, MM, New-market disruption, Organizational culture, Profit formula, Resources, RPR framework, SAR, Sustainable innovation.

* **Corresponding author Rabinarayan Patnaik:** Faculty of Management Sciences, Siksha 'O' Anusandhan (SOA) Deemed University, Bhubaneswar, India; E-mail: patnaik.rabinarayan@gmail.com

**Sukanta Kumar Baral, Richa Goel, Tilottama Singh, Erdener Kaynak & Vishal Jain (Eds.)**

## INTRODUCTION

Disruptive innovation combined with digital transformation talk about the complete restructuring of an industry, including its business models, due to the advent of digital technologies and the transformation of products, services, and processes. It is hoped that the healthcare sector will be as disruptive as other industries through the adoption of digital transformation. Even though new technology is constantly introduced, this change has yet to materialize. The reason this happens is because established businesses focus on developing better products and services through sustainable innovation for those customers who are the most demanding and profitable ones. As a result, the needs of some segments are either exceeded or unmet. When a smaller new entrant is able to cater to the needs of the segments that were overlooked by the incumbents earlier and is able to gain a strong market share over the course of time by providing good enough functionality, preferably at a lower price, then it proves to be disruptive. Given the low-profit margin provided by these ignored segments, the incumbents (who prefer going after more profitable and demanding segments) tend to ignore the entrant and do not fight it aggressively. The entrant then slowly moves up the segments, providing the performance that the customers in the profitable segments require while maintaining the competitive advantage that drove their earlier success. The major challenges faced by these Indian healthcare operators can be the next game changer for them, typically because of ever-increasing demands for specialized treatments. However, the infrastructure necessities in this process have been a great challenge and will remain one of the most potential limitations if not addressed sufficiently as well as timely. The optimism in bringing down these limitations to a greater extent can be because of the application of digital tools and interfaces in creating an efficient system accessible to patients from all types of segments and spectrums.

## UNDERSTANDING DISRUPTION

Now, coming to answer one key strategic question, which is how the healthcare sector in India can respond to the digital changes to ensure sustainability? In order to answer this question, we need to know in detail about the theories of disruption and how they align themselves in the healthcare sector. Looking through the lens of understanding disruption, let us examine the healthcare sector of India. Before we begin, we need to understand that hospitals are not so easy to disrupt. The economic model of hospitals is unlike any other industry in the world due to its intricacy; it is not feasible in any other sector and, theoretically, should not even exist. Hospitals have historically marketed themselves as a one-stop shop with all the answers to anyone's health issues. In any other business, it will be difficult to do the same because of the complexity of the resources, which are very costly and capital-intensive. Even though, now, there are specialty clinics and hospitals that provide care, it still remains quite complex. It was predicted that, with 1.3 bn population, healthcare in India was expected to be a $372 billion industry by 2022, which would open a large, untapped market for new healthtech startups. Further, adding fuel to the fire are the low allopathic doctors-to-patient ratio (1:1596) and access to smartphones and the internet. From doctor consultation to lab diagnosis, healthcare services and tech-equipped medical devices, these startups have touched a variety of segments like diabetes, heart attack and even cancer. From standard X-rays to MRI scans, innovation has helped doctors see a better picture of the human anatomy and hence helped in giving a better diagnosis to the patient. Another such innovation is the Vacutainer for blood sample collection instead of a normal syringe. In both cases, the characteristics of sustainable innovation are fulfilled. Even though many technologies have been introduced in healthcare, there has not been any significant low-end disruption in the hospitals primarily because they have been utilized sustainably to help doctors and hospitals. These innovations cover little to reduce healthcare costs. For example, DocsApp, an approved tech-enabled multilanguage consultation service, was founded in 2015 by renowned doctors across India with expertise in more than 18 areas, such as general medicine, pediatrics, dermatology, gynecology, neurology, psychology, psychiatry, cardiology, oncology, sexology, and weight management and many more. The company says that around 65% of its user base is from rural India who were previously dominated by traditional channels. Currently, they are offering more than 100k consultations every month. Going ahead, it is looking to launch its interface in other regional languages and plans to make provisions that will enable the user to take unlimited specialist consultations for their family as well as introduce video doctor consultations. Even though it remains to be seen whether this company will be able to disrupt hospital business models because of the complexity of services at the higher end, for example, surgeries, it still is something to look forward to.

Earlier, the people of rural India were not able to consult good specialist doctors and get proper medical attention because of their geographical disadvantage and were mostly faced with scenarios where their loved ones suffered due to medical negligence, but now, due to the growth in technology, primary education, and cheaper data, people in rural India are able to afford smartphones. There are apps like Lybrate and Portea, which have changed the format; instead of the patient going to the doctors, now the doctors are coming to the patients through their smartphones and providing consultations through video and audio calls. This has created a fairly new market of patients who were previously unable to consult proper doctors at all. Posing a threat to incumbents by "flying under the radar" in the industry are consultation apps in the healthcare sector. Even though the application remains somewhat similar, they are catering to a new base of customers who previously were not able to go to the hospitals or clinics for consultations. Also, the distribution channel is different as they are present in a digital platform as opposed to brick-and-mortar hospitals and clinics. The healthcare sector as a whole has seen disruption from many angles. Be it health apps, prescription apps, consultation apps, or appointment apps that cause disruption through digital mediums or technical innovations in medical equipment, business processes in pharma *etc.* It can also be seen that the incumbents do not generally ignore these changes rather, they try to incorporate these changes in their business models, try to create a new company under their umbrella corporations, or even acquire the startups that came in with these new models. Even though in the earlier days, the incumbents ignored these new players, they soon accepted the change and adapted accordingly. Disruption theory suggests that incumbents will ignore start-ups whose services are considered inferior. It will be interesting to watch disruption play out over the next few decades as small entrants, like DocsApp, Liberate, Portea, and CircleUp, keep improving and moving up-market.

## ALIGNING INNOVATION AND DISRUPTION

In the healthcare sector, a huge opportunity lies in AI, blockchain and data analytics. If utilized properly by the incumbents in healthcare, then it has the potential of becoming a sustainable innovation, but if ignored, then these innovations have the power to be disruptive. If these innovations cause a disruption in the market, it will undoubtedly be a new one rather than a low-end one, as evidenced by the fact that millennials and residents of tier-2 and tier-3 cities—who are typically at the lower end of the spectrum—are adopting these technologies due to the dearth of more reasonably priced options and the convenience of being able to do things while on the go that wearables and AI apps provide.

Right now, these technologies are still an opportunity because the incumbents can use these technologies in their core business or its subsidiaries. And some are doing so too. But it will not be long before they become a threat. The players in the healthcare sector have two options to cope with the changes: either adapt early and live or ignore and die later. In order to adapt, the players cannot just go around and disrupt themselves by changing their core but rather invest in the startup, create a new unconnected subsidiary to merge with the new startups or else create one of their own (in short, acquire the disruptive technology, but silently) and let the business grow on its own in the market, and when the time comes when their core business becomes saturated, then shift to the new change that they have acquired and added value to over the years. But then the question arises: which technologies to acquire? They cannot just create subsidiaries for every new technology that comes. For this, they need to listen to the customers at the lower end and understand their changing needs because they are the ones who will help the disruptors to disrupt the market and then make the informed decision to look for disruptive technology.

## JOBS-TO-BE-DONE (JTBD) FRAMEWORK

One of the services hospitals offer is to provide patients with the required diagnosis, treatment and care as per the patients' requirements. To categorize customers on the basis of the service that they require in the healthcare sector, the following categorization has been made.

- Emergency- patients who come in critical conditions and require immediate attention.
- Check-ins- patients who come for regular consultations and check-ups.
- Undergoing treatment- patients who are currently admitted to the hospital and are undergoing treatment.
- Surgery- patients who have come in for surgery.

Traditional market segmentation is done by product category and other indicators like geography, as well as socio-economic status. Although these categories and indicatorsare often correlated with a customer's interest in a particular product, they do not cause the customer to buy the product. Rather, "jobs" arise in people's lives that they need to get done (or problems arise that they need to solve).

To understand this, let us briefly look at the automobile industry. For the high-end option, we can select a Rolls Royce, and for the low-end option, we can select Maruti Swift. Both the cars serve the same functional benefit, which is to move from point A to point B. In the case of a Rolls Royce, it also serves a social and emotional benefit of making a status statement and allowing the user to feel like a member of an elite club. But what it lacks is that it cannot be taken on every kind of road, the mileage is low, and it is extremely high maintenance. But in the case of Maruti Swift, even though it does not serve the emotional and social benefit as a Rolls Royce, it aces in providing the functional benefit of moving from point A to point B; it can be taken on the majority of the roads, it gives good mileage and is low maintenance. This also demonstrates the fact that different types of jobs play different roles in high-end and low-end products.

In the healthcare sector, historically speaking, in the early days, doctors used to do house calls to attend to patients, but it became inconvenient after some time due to the lack of necessary care being provided at home. Hence came infirmaries that had voluntary nurses who had acquired skills to look after ill patients, and doctors could do regular visits. From this, modern-day hospitals were born that marketed themselves as solution centers for all diseases. But when this became cumbersome, specialty hospitals emerged in the scene. Presently, in search of convenience, people are looking for ways to get personalized attention from doctors without having to leave their houses, and due to the advent of technology, the same is made possible through video-calling apps for doctors. Still, to get physically diagnosed, one still needs to go to the doctors, either at clinics or hospitals. So, in a way, the field is looking at a 360-degree change, but the job still remains the same.

## JOBS-TO-BE-DONE (JTBD) PYRAMID

The JTBD pyramid helps the company align itself according to the jobs that the customer wants to get done. Now, let us take a case study to understand the JTBD pyramid better.

A great illustration of jobs to be done is found in CVS Pharmacy's Minute Clinic. Minute Clinic originated with a simple job to be done and has grown into a successful business. They do this work because, in the US, it is very difficult to get medicines without the prescription of a doctor or a medical practitioner. The majority of the clinics take up most of the time of the day for minor conditions. But in the Minute Clinic, they have appointed certified nurses who can tend to such minor conditions due to their experience in the field, wherein they can provide the same treatment as the doctor for such minor conditions and can also prescribe medication in the least amount of time.

With a jobs-to-be-done perspective, a company can easily shift from a product-based company to a job-based company and can go beyond its core to satisfy the customers' need to get the job done. This leads them to the frontiers, where they find competitors whom they traditionally would not have considered had they remained in the core business. Considering Apollo hospitals in India, they have aligned themselves somewhat in the jobs-to-be-done format and have gone beyond their core to create many other companies like Apollo Cosmetics Clinic, Apollo Diagnostics, Apollo Fertility, Apollo Munich (health insurance provider), Apollo Pharmacy, Apollo Life (wellness FMCG products), Apollo Telemedicine Networking Foundation, and many more. They also have an app called "Ask Apollo" that integrates all the services from their group of companies and provides it in a single platform along with individual apps for each company. They have gone beyond their core, which is hospitals, and have integrated themselves in to the health spectrum well. From this case, some takeaways are:

- You need to reinvent yourself time and again so that you stay relevant and sustained in the times to come.

- In order to stay relevant, you must always look for the jobs to be done and find ways to get the job done from your available resources.
- To learn what the jobs are to be done, you should not just rely on data but observe the livelihood and behaviors of the consumer in reality to get the actual picture.

In the case of hospitals, the job to be done is based on "Help me to stay healthy." Understanding the job to be done, some ideas on how one might improve the way they develop or market the product include:

- The first thing that needs to be done is to find out the barriers in the purchase and usage process that frustrate the consumer and look for ways to remove those barriers.
- You need to talk to customers in order to get the reality of things and know the barriers.

One of the jobs that remains to be done in the healthcare sector revolves around rural India. The job to be done for them can loosely be considered as "help me get healthy in a way that I do not spend much". The affordability of healthcare is a major problem in rural India. Because of this, they do not want regular check-ups or preventive steps. Rather, they need quick solutions to their problems from a trusted and good doctor. So, if hospitals can develop simple healthcare clinics that are designed to serve the people in rural India with just the processes and personnel that they require in an affordable manner, then it can lead to new market disruption. A similar job can also be fulfilled *via* a digital medium, which can connect the patient with the nearest, well-reputed doctor virtually who can then carry forward the treatments as he sees fit. Digital mediums mostly help in reducing costs and making the service affordable for the customer. In the traditional route, the patient would have to travel a certain distance to reach the cities where such hospitals were mostly situated, bearing the cost of transportation, food, lodging and consultation fees. But if a digital medium were to be initiated, then the total cost for the patient could be reduced, hence making the service open for new markets.

## ORGANIZING ONESELF FOR THE INNOVATION

Every organization has a particular way or a particular culture in which it functions. The decision making driven mostly by cultural factors determines the interactions and the importance of these factors in the organizational context. For example, resources that are mostly flexible and transferable (Technology, people, products, facilities, equipment, brands, cash, *etc.*) or, let's say, Profit Formula, which is the criteria used in an organization to prioritize one option over another and to guide decisions such as which proposal to fund, which customer to call on, or which product feature to be developed first; for example, gross margin targets, ROI/ROA thresholds, utilization goals, types of orders or customers, *etc.*

### Key Resources in Healthcare

Hospitals can have as many of the latest technologies, build apps, have great customer relations, have a great location, the latest information, and so on. But everything will seem useless if they are not accompanied by qualitative medical practitioners like doctors, nurses, medical laboratory professionals, surgeons, *etc.*, along with the management team that runs the hospital. Now, one may say that technology can replace the human element, but it is only possible to a certain extent. For example, you cannot replace a surgeon with technology; there are some robots that can perform surgeries, but the assistance of a surgeon is still needed.

### Key Processes in Healthcare

In healthcare delivery, the production or execution process is a key process because, in hospitals, it is extremely important how healthcare is delivered. If the service is not executed properly, the customer becomes dissatisfied and will not hire the organization in the future for their job or somebody can even incur some serious health problems if the medical practitioners ignore some critical processes.

### Key Profit Formula in Healthcare

Now, this is something that is very difficult to decide. If you have two potential customers but have the capacity to serve only one, what are the criteria you will typically use in your organization to determine which customer to serve? With the key resources, processes, and profit formula in mind, if we look at the Apollo Hospital chain, their capabilities are to:

- Deliver industry-leading healthcare services
- Solve challenging and complex medical cases
- Provide an array of services like pharmaceuticals, diagnostic clinics, global consultancy capability, health insurance, *etc.*

All this has led them to become a multi-specialty hospital chain across India. With such high-end resources providing high-end services, something that they cannot do is:

- Drive the cost of their services down;
- Provide their complete array of services in rural areas.

Even though they are trying to provide some of their services in rural and semi-urban areas through Apollo Reach, it still has not been successful for them because of the high cost of resources, both people and technology. Some key takeaways from the case are:

- It is important to see the feasibility of the business and other factors with due consideration of profit formula and so on.
- A business cannot disrupt itself because disruption needs a different business model and culture for it to grow successfully.
- You need different sets of capabilities to cater to the different types of customers.

A core business can make it difficult for new innovations and ideas to be "nimble" because of their existing culture. If the culture of the core business is not able to accept the new innovation and ideas, then they will try to change it and might make it more complex, making it difficult for the new innovation to be nimble.

Apollo Hospitals have been somewhat successful in implementing new innovations because the processes are not driven by net profitability but are driven by the type of patient. But with nascent innovations like Telemedicine, they are still struggling because they change the entire process of healthcare delivery. Even though they have created a new unit called Apollo Reach for such innovations, they are still not able to implement it properly primarily because the culture is still the same. Rather than creating a new culture, they are still following the same culture of Apollo Hospitals, which is hampering the new unit in a small but significant way.

As the future of healthcare is shifting toward telehealth, some changes are required in Apollo Reach. Apollo Reach, first of all, needs to acquire new technological resources (both front end and back end), which can be utilized to make the telehealth service better. Since Apollo Reach is targeting semi-urban and rural areas of India, the new acquisitions should also be cost effective. Secondly, Apollo Reach needs to let go of the culture of its parent company, Apollo Hospitals, because that culture is making it difficult for new innovations to take pace. They need to hire a new management that is different from that of Apollo Hospitals. Hiring new management can lead to a change in the processes and ultimately create a new culture that accepts disruptive innovation and allows it to grow.

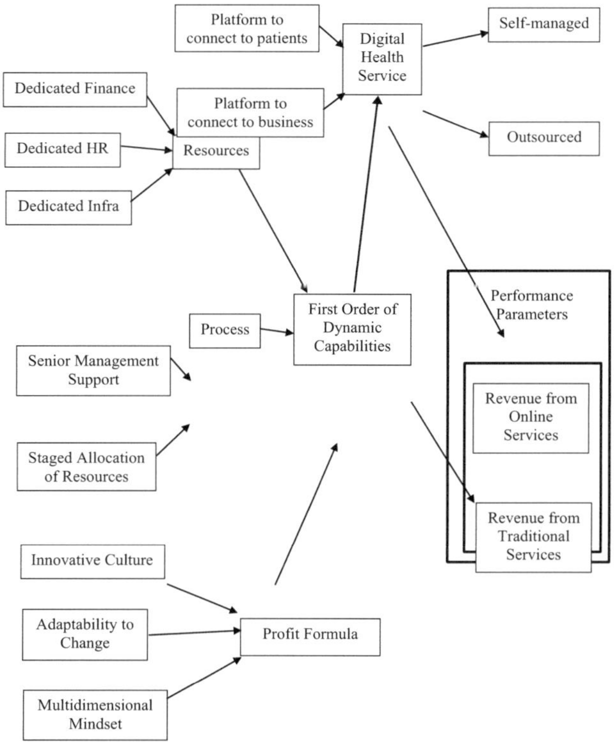


**Fig. (1). Digital Disruption in Healthcare Framework (The** right combination of resources, processes, and values generates the FODCAP of a company).
Source: Suggested by the authors.

## RPP FRAMEWORK

The Resource-Processes-Profit formula (RPP) framework, suggested below, can help companies in the healthcare sector to determine which course of action they should take when faced with such dilemmas. To become responsive to the regular and emerging changes taking place in the healthcare sector, a company first needs to know what it can and cannot do. They cannot just blindly incorporate a digital transformation into their organization. They first need to know whether the transformation will help the core to grow or whether the core will kill the transformation, ultimately hampering it. If organizations do not have the capability to fold the changes into their core, then they need to set up a new unit, such as through mergers, let them run on their own or create a new business unit that runs independently of the core. Also, they need to keep in mind that, for the new unit to succeed, the new unit can use the core for its resources but not vice versa. The resources, processes, and profit formulas, identified by the company as key components in order to address the digital avenue, will be crucial to address the change.

There has been an exhaustive analysis of the forces of transformation within the healthcare sector of India by looking at the various stakeholders such as the life science companies, technology companies and startups The digital offerings and strategies of these companies have been examined, and those that are more disruptive in nature have been identified. Strategies that can enable and fast-track disruption in the healthcare sector have also been suggested (Fig. **1**).

## METHODOLOGY

Systematic analysis was done to look for different life sciences and technology companies with regards to their digital initiatives and ventures in the healthcare sector of India using various online databases like Inc. 42 start-up watch list for health tech in India for 2019, Database of medicastart-ups.org and biopharmguy.com. The keywords "tele-medicines", "e-health", "digital health", and "healthcare India" were used to identify the top 70 companies working in the digital domain. The initiatives taken up by these companies were defined as 'ventures'. Some of the companies had taken up multiple ventures. Such ventures have been considered individually.

**Analysis of identified projects**: Value to customers, Business Models and Mode of Solutions.

The selected ventures were evaluated on the following criteria:

- Customer needs addressed
- Medium of the solution provided
- Presence of a sustainable business model

In total, 70 ventures were identified. To judge the customer needs addressed, the ventures were further evaluated on the basis of adherence, diagnosis, lifestyle, patient engagement, quality management, prevention, and treatment. These categories were identified by looking at the similarities between the different ventures and grouping them by which needs they addressed. The solutions provided were identified on the basis of software, device, service, and platform. The geographical location of the headquarters of the startups was also taken into consideration to evaluate the regions that enabled the startups with an environment to grow, even though the operational area of these startups ranged from urban, semi-urban, and rural areas. The business models were evaluated on the basis of the information available on online channels.

## RESULTS

### Regional Distribution

Out of the 32 startups evaluated, it was found that approximately 40% of the startups were located in Bangalore and Karnataka, 34% in the Delhi-NCR region, 12.5% in Mumbai and Pune in the state of Maharashtra, 6.25% in Kolkata and West Bengal, and 6.25% in other regions of India (Fig. **2**).

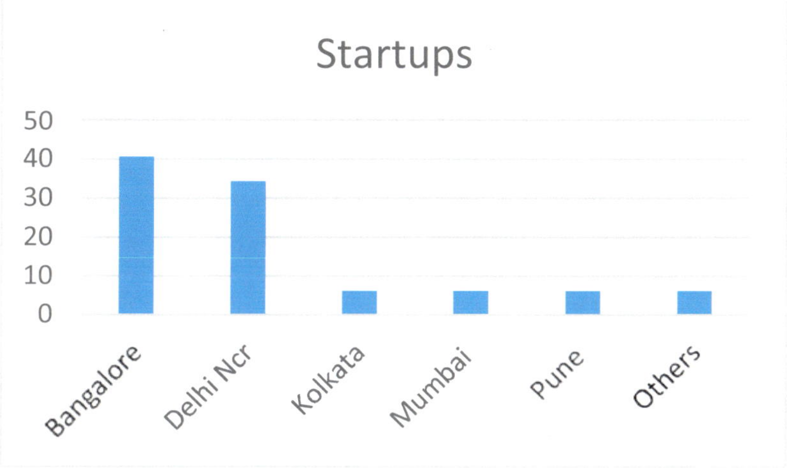


**Fig. (2).** Geographical distribution of startups in India.
*Source:* Analyzed by the authors.

### Value to Customers, Business Models and Mode of Solutions

Within the grouping of startups, services and platform-developing companies are present in larger numbers, and most of the startups address the patient engagement and diagnostic needs of the customer. Whereas in the group of life science and technology companies, the majority are in the platform and software developing category and primarily address the quality management needs of the customer.

### Provided Solutions

The evaluation led to four prominent types of solutions that could be identified: Software, Device, Platform and Service (Fig. **3**).

All three players are involved in ventures that are represented through the classification of the solutions mentioned above. While device solution seems to be evenly distributed, ventures on services appear to be undertaken more prominently by startups. The analysis found a strong involvement of technology companies in providing software solutions.

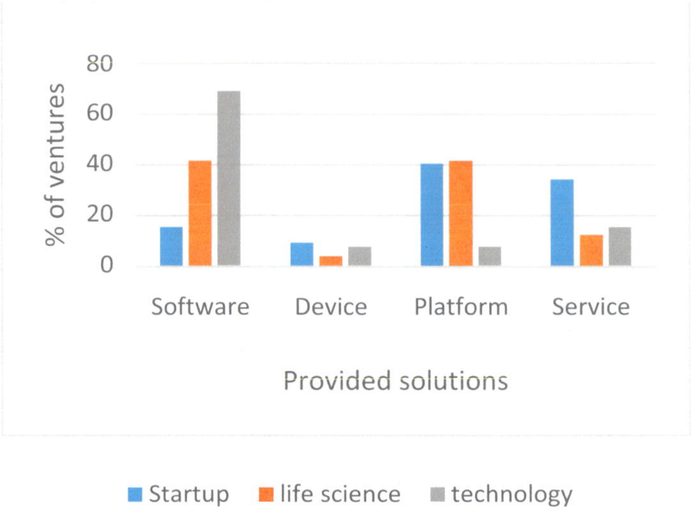


**Fig. (3).** Distribution of identified solutions across the three players.
*Source:* Analyzed by the authors.

## Customer Needs Addressed

To see whether these ventures cater to same or different needs, the focus was made on seven customer needs, namely adherence, diagnosis, lifestyle, patient engagement, quality management, prevention, and treatment (Fig. **4**).

It can be observed that the startup ventures focus on all customer needs while leading in diagnostic and prevention needs and having a prominent presence in lifestyle needs. Ventures from life sciences companies seem to be more driven toward quality management and patient engagement with minor involvement in lifestyle, diagnosis, and prevention. Whereas technology companies primarily focus on quality management, while no ventures were found in lifestyle, prevention and treatment.

## Inter-categorical View

Gathering the information from the previous analyses, it can be seen that patient engagement and quality management ventures are more preferred by companies in the life science and technology sectors while ignoring lifestyle and prevention ventures. On the other hand, technology companies have no presence in lifestyle, prevention and treatment ventures digitally.

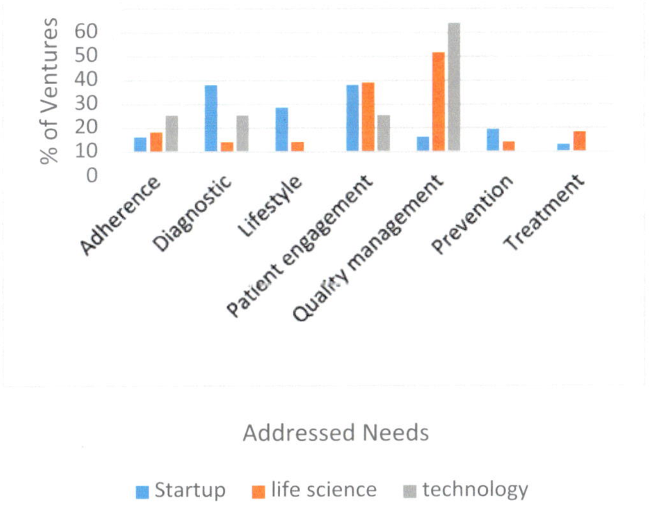


**Fig. (4).** Distribution of customer needs addressed among the three players.
*Source:* Analyzed by the authors.

## DISCUSSION

The aim of the study was to provide an exhaustive analysis of the forces of transformation within the healthcare sector of India by looking at the various stakeholders. The data shows a significant presence of startups in Bangalore and Delhi-NCR region. One reason could be that these regions, being metro cities, attract entrepreneurial talents and create an environment that provides the highest potential for disruptive innovation.

The distributions of the business models provided by different ventures show three main areas that differentiate the incumbents (life sciences and technology) from startups. The new entrants appear to be working in a more solo effort instead of joint ventures, and pursue those ventures which are not pursued by others. While exploring further into solutions provided and needs addressed, it can be seen that startups show a wider approach toward the digitization of the healthcare sector. In contradiction, incumbent life sciences and technology companies focus more on patient engagement and quality management.

With regards to the customer needs addressed, an interesting trend was noticed. Life science and technology companies cater to similar needs. This means that either the technology companies have not been versatile enough or were versatile in the past, but the life sciences companies have caught up to them with regard to providing digital solutions. The startup ventures differed significantly from the others, which means that the wave of disruption in healthcare will be coming from the startups as they are playing in a different domain than the incumbents who have been in the game for a long time. With respect to that, they show strong differentiation and gain competitive advantage in both the supply and the demand side through the lens of disruptive innovation. On these lines, incumbent companies in the life science sector (*e.g.*, pharmaceutical corporations) tend to move toward developing more effective drugs. Still they lack the ability for direct interaction with the patient and hence enhance their competitive position by additional (termed as "beyond the pill") offerings. With regard to the expectations, it was identified that their ventures tend to provide digital outputs, but such efforts are more on the lines of sustainable innovation that stick to their preexisting business model and strategies.

Generally, startups use their flexible business structure to go after entirely new avenues through the use of newer technology, business models, and value networks that give disruptive solutions to a wide range of customer and patient challenges. In the sample selected, incumbents target their offerings to address challenges in relation to patient engagement and quality management dimensions of customer value. Hence, they seem to be absent in the other avenues of customer value. This provides evidence that their focus contradicts the multifariousness of the startups.

## LIMITATIONS

The current study, which looks at disruptive innovation in the healthcare sector of India, has a few limitations. The analysis is based on the information present in the public domain, which might not show comprehensive pictures to startups, and they may tend to overestimate themselves to attract funding. Many have not made their presence felt in the public domain since they might be at their early stage. Simultaneously, incumbents may try to underestimate themselves on their digital initiatives for privacy reasons and to maintain ambiguity.

The majority of the markets in the healthcare sector in India are still in an interdependent phase with a performance gap even though modular components are present. Digital changes can help these modules grow, and companies can gain specialization in these modules. What companies in the healthcare sector need to do is look for these performance gaps, see where the customer needs will reach in the future, and be mindful of the technologies (such as wearable, health apps, data analytics, home diagnostics kits, *etc.*) that can fulfill those gaps and keep skating to the new performance defining components. In order to do so, they should organize themselves around the jobs to be done rather than the product itself. They should realize that even if you are a startup today or an incumbent tomorrow, a new company or technology will come in the future to disrupt you, and in order to survive them, you should be ahead of them and utilize the strategy that can yield the maximum at that moment.

## CONCLUSION

In the healthcare sector, looking at the various components on the basis of processes, there has been a growing trend of E-health wherein doctors can provide diagnoses of some of the major chronic diseases like diabetes and heart diseases. In the future, after the growth of this disruptive trend, many hospitals will be required to disintegrate from the diagnosis part and be more specialized, but right now, it does not seem neccessary. Secondly, if we look at the various components on the basis of different fields, then there are already some hospitals that have disintegrated and have become specialized in specific fields, such as specialists in cancer treatment, orthopedic, pediatric, gynecology, cardiac, *etc.* In the healthcare industry, there are many examples of commoditization, like wearables and at-home diagnostic kits such as BP monitoring and blood sugar checking machines, which are now widely being used, for which earlier you would be required to go to a clinic or hospital. The performance-defining component in the healthcare sector will be the consultation from doctors because the majority of the customers value it the most, and it is not yet good enough in India because the needs of rural India are still not satisfied properly. Hence, they come to the urban cities to get a consultation, and as a result, attractive profits are only available to a few competitors.

The following are some important points to keep in mind while facing disruption:

- It is important to understand the jobs to be done and the requirements of the market. The market does not always need high-end innovation but also needs low-end disruption to grow.
- It is easier to disrupt a market if you have a modular approach and a specialized strategy.
- Once disruption occurs, the barriers to entry can be significantly reduced, and new players can emerge with the help of the disruption.

First of all, organizations should advance through developments in wearable products and technologies that can utilize the health data of the customer and suggest remedies to lead a healthy lifestyle. Secondly, at-home diagnostic kits can also prove extremely crucial in the future. Third, E-health can also gain significant traction in the future. There might come a time when companies need to change their business models according to future needs and the available technology, and in order to do that, they need to keep their organization structured around the job to be done.

In the healthcare industry, new startups must adopt an emergent strategy and see what works for them the best. After learning the right strategy, they should focus on that particular strategy, make it deliberate, and look for good money (investments by investors who let them grow in their own way) with respect to the position they are in. For the incumbents in the industry, it is important that they should not get too strict with their dominant strategy and always be on the lookout for emergent opportunities. For startups and incumbents, it is necessary to focus on the jobs to be done. As the performance-defining component changes from diagnosis and cure to the prevention of diseases, health will be defined holistically as a state of well-being of the body. So, data will play a major role in this. Many companies that help gather this data are slowly harnessing this module. Companies like Samsung, Google, Fitbit, and Apple are developing wearables that act as data gatherers, and through these health data, better services can be provided to customers. This component in the market will help make the market more modular. By harnessing the data gathered from these devices, doctors can track their patients' health and provide assistance whenever required; companies can provide better plans that fit the customer. This constant monitoring will help ensure that health conditions and risks are identified and taken care of early. The data collection module will help grow the market to provide customers with more personalized care. Who knows, maybe in 40-50 years, we might have health pods in our homes that work as mini hospitals just for us.

## BIBLIOGRAPHY

Agarwal, N., Biswas, B. (2020). Doctor Consultation through Mobile Applications in India: An Overview, Challenges and the Way Forward. *Healthc. Inform. Res., 26*(2), 153-158. [http://dx.doi.org/10.4258/hir.2020.26.2.153] [PMID: 32547812]

Arora, P., Suri, D. (2020). Redefining, relooking, redesigning, and reincorporating HRD in the post Covid 19 context and thereafter. *Hum. Resour. Dev. Int., 23*(4), 438-451. [http://dx.doi.org/10.1080/13678868.2020.1780077]

Banerjee, M. (2019). Development of Omnichannel in India: Retail Landscape, Drivers and Challenges. In: Piotrowicz In: Cuthbertson, R., (Ed.), *Exploring Omnichannel Retailing: Common Expectations and Diverse Realities* (pp. 115-137). Springer..

Botwood, S.E., Chinomona, R., Govender, K.K. (2019). Industry Performance and Digital Disruption: Unleashing Possibilities for the African Farmer. *JAEF., 4*(3), 98-108. [http://dx.doi.org/10.22606/jaef.2019.43002]

Christensen, C.M., Grant, A., Govindarajan, V., Davenport, T.H. (2016). *The Definitive Management Ideas of the Year from Harvard Business Review (with bonus article "What is Disruptive Innovation?").* Harvard Business Review Press.

Chanchaichujit, J., Tan, A., Meng, F., Eaimkhong, S. (2019). *Innovative Health Technologies and Start-Ups Process in Healthcare Industry. Healthcare 4.0: Next Generation Processes with the Latest Technologies.* Palgrave Pivot.

Christensen, C.M. (2013). *The Innovator's Dilemma: When New Technologies Cause Great Firms to Fail..* Harvard Business Review Press.

Dash, L., Patnaik, S. (2021). Artificial Intelligence in Covid-19: Application and Legal Conundrums. In:

Mohanty, S.N., Saxena, S.K., Satpathy, S., Chatterjee, J.M., (Eds.), *Add space and App. AI COVID-19.* Springer.
[http://dx.doi.org/10.1007/978-981-15-7317-0_31]

Dillon, A., Timulak, L., Greenberg, L.S. (2018). Transforming core emotional pain in a course of emotion-focused therapy for depression: A case study. *Psychother. Res., 28*(3), 406-422.
[http://dx.doi.org/10.1080/10503307.2016.1233364] [PMID: 27728998]

Ebert, C., Duarte, C.H.C. (2018). Digital Transformation. *IEEE Softw., 35*(4), 16-21.
[http://dx.doi.org/10.1109/MS.2018.2801537]

Edwards, B. (2020). Emerging Technologies, Market Segments, and MarkeTrak 10 Insights in Hearing Health Technology. *Semin. Hear., 41*(1), 037 054.
[http://dx.doi.org/10.1055/s-0040-1701244] [PMID: 32047347]

Funk, D.C., Pizzo, A.D., Baker, B.J. (2018). eSport management: Embracing eSport education and research opportunities. *Sport Manage. Rev., 21*(1), 7-13.
[http://dx.doi.org/10.1016/j.smr.2017.07.008]

Hannah, D.P., Eisenhardt, K.M. (2018). How firms navigate cooperation and competition in nascent ecosystems. *Strateg. Manage. J., 39*(12), 3163-3192.
[http://dx.doi.org/10.1002/smj.2750]

Hastings, G., Angus, K., Eadie, D., Hunt, K. (2020). Selling second best: how infant formula marketing works. *Global. Health, 16*(1), 77.
[http://dx.doi.org/10.1186/s12992-020-00597-w] [PMID: 32859218]

Karimi, J., Walter, Z. (2015). The Role of Dynamic Capabilities in Responding to Digital Disruption: A Factor-Based Study of the Newspaper Industry. *J. Manage. Inf. Syst., 32*(1), 39-81.
[http://dx.doi.org/10.1080/07421222.2015.1029380]

Lubis, A.N. (2018). Evaluating the Customer Preferences of Online Shopping: Demographic Factors and Online Shop Application Issue. *ASMJ., 17*(2), 1-13.

Mazumdar-Shaw, K. (2018). Leveraging affordable innovation to tackle India's healthcare challenge. *IIMB Manag. Rev., 30*(1), 37-50.
[http://dx.doi.org/10.1016/j.iimb.2017.11.003]

Michaud, K., Wipfler, K., Shaw, Y., Simon, T.A., Cornish, A., England, B.R., Ogdie, A., Katz, P. (2020). Experiences of Patients With Rheumatic Diseases in the United States During Early Days of the COVID-19 Pandemic. *ACR Open Rheumatol., 2*(6), 335-343.
[http://dx.doi.org/10.1002/acr2.11148] [PMID: 32311836]

Moldoveanu, M., Narayandas, D. (2019). The Future of Leadership Development. *Harv. Bus. Rev., 97*(2), 40-48.

Odor, H.O. (2018). A Literature Review on Organizational Learning and Learning Organizations. *Int. J. Econs & Mgmt., 7*(1), 1-6.
[http://dx.doi.org/10.4172/2162-6359.1000494]

Patnaik, R., Patra, S. K., Mahapatra, D. M., Baral, S. K. (2022). Adoption and Challenges Underlying OTT Platform in India During Pandemic: A Critical Study of Socio-Economic and Technological Issues. *FIIB Business Review.*

Prinja, S., Bahuguna, P., Gupta, I., Chowdhury, S., Trivedi, M. (2019). Role of insurance in determining utilization of healthcare and financial risk protection in India. *PLoS One, 14*(2)e0211793
[http://dx.doi.org/10.1371/journal.pone.0211793] [PMID: 30721253]

Ramírez-Macías, J.A., Vásquez, R.E., Sørensen, A.J., Sævik, S. (2021). Motion Feasibility Framework for Remotely Operated Vehicles Based on Dynamic Positioning Capability. *J. Offshore Mech. Arctic Eng., 143*(1)011201
[http://dx.doi.org/10.1115/1.4047200]

Salmon, J.W., Thompson, S.L., Salmon, J.W., Thompson, S.L. (2021). Medical Practice: From Cottage Industry to Corporate Practice. *The Corporatization of American Health Care.* Springer. [http://dx.doi.org/10.1007/978-3-030-60667-1_3]

Sapovadia, V. (2018). Financial Inclusion, Digital Currency, And Mobile Technology. In: Chuen, D.L.K., Deng, R., (Eds.), *Handbook of Blockchain, Digital Finance, and Inclusion, 2, 361-385.*. Academic Press. [http://dx.doi.org/10.1016/B978-0-12-812282-2.00014-0]

Singh, A.K., Lv, Z., Ko, H. (2021). Introduction to the Special Issue on Recent Trends in Medical Data Security for e-Health Applications. *ACM Trans. Multimed. Comput. Commun. Appl., 17*(2s), 1-3. [http://dx.doi.org/10.1145/3459601]

Suess, C., Mody, M. (2018). The influence of hospitable design and service on patient responses. *Serv. Ind. J., 38*(1-2), 127-147. [http://dx.doi.org/10.1080/02642069.2017.1385773]

Viswanadham, N. (2018). Performance analysis and design of competitive business models. *Int. J. Prod. Res., 56*(1-2), 983-999. [http://dx.doi.org/10.1080/00207543.2017.1406171]

Weber, F., Lehmann, J., Graf-Vlachy, L., König, A. (2019). Institution-Infused Sensemaking of Discontinuous Innovations: The Case of the Sharing Economy. *J. Prod. Innov. Manage., 36*(5), 632-660. [http://dx.doi.org/10.1111/jpim.12499]

Wojcik, G., Ring, N., McCulloch, C., Willis, D.S., Williams, B., Kydonaki, K. (2021). Understanding the complexities of antibiotic prescribing behaviour in acute hospitals: a systematic review and meta-ethnography. *Arch. Public Health, 79*(1), 134. [http://dx.doi.org/10.1186/s13690-021-00624-1] [PMID: 34301332]

Younossi, Z.M. (2018). Patient-Reported Outcomes and the Economic Effects of Nonalcoholic Fatty Liver Disease and Nonalcoholic Steatohepatitis: The Value Proposition. *Hepatology, 68*(6), 2405-2412. [http://dx.doi.org/10.1002/hep.30125] [PMID: 30070714]

Zakowska, I., Godycki-Cwirko, M. (2020). Data envelopment analysis applications in primary health care: a systematic review. *Fam. Pract., 37*(2), 147-153. [PMID: 31605609]

Zhang, Y., Khan, U., Lee, S., Salik, M. (2019). The Influence of Management Innovation and Technological Innovation on Organization Performance. A Mediating Role of Sustainability. *Sustainability (Basel), 11*(2), 495. [http://dx.doi.org/10.3390/su11020495]

# CHAPTER 6

# A Study on Digital Transformation Empowering Human Resource Management

**Chitra Krishnan**[1,*], **Richa Goel**[1], **Supriya Lamba Sahdev**[2] and **Jasmine Mariappan**[3]

[1] *Symbiosis Centre for Management Studies, Noida, Symbiosis International Deemed University, Pune, India*

[2] *ISBR Business School, Bangalore, India*

[3] *UTAS, Ibra, Oman*

**Abstract:** Due to rapid globalization and spread of digital technology, businesses and employees are under pressure to adapt to them. The term "digitalization" in the business world currently refers to the requirement for businesses to adopt it if they wish to stay current. Previous research has concentrated on how digitalization affects marketing and organizational effectiveness, including consumer preferences, buying trends, and customer relationship management. However, academic research, especially that on HRM, tends to place less emphasis on how it influences internal business. Therefore, the objective of this study is to gain more knowledge about Human Resource Management in the digital era. This study seeks to demonstrate how digital HRM can enhance organizational performance.

This study relied on secondary data from various sources such as business reports, real-world examples, websites, professional blogs, and research papers. The aim was to examine the advantages and challenges of implementing digital transformation in human resource management, using illustrative cases of organizations with innovative business practices. The findings of this research are of great importance for corporate organizations looking to adopt digital human resource management and enhance overall organizational performance.

**Keywords:** Artificial intelligence, Big data, Digitalization, Human resource management, Organisation performance.

## INTRODUCTION

The impact of the industrial and digital revolutions on society, businesses, employment, and daily life is widely acknowledged (Krishnan, 2009). These

* **Corresponding author Chitra Krishnan:** Symbiosis Centre for Management Studies, Noida, Symbiosis International Deemed University, Pune, India E-mail: ananya.chitra@gmail.com

**Sukanta Kumar Baral, Richa Goel, Tilottama Singh, Erdener Kaynak & Vishal Jain (Eds.)**

revolutions have greatly enhanced communication capabilities, enabling interactions with larger audiences. The integration of human resources (HR) and information technology (IT) has been ongoing for some time. HR has incorporated various technologies such as data mining, the Internet of Things, HR analytics, human resource information systems (HRIS), and more recently, artificial intelligence (Bondarouk, Harms & Lepak, 2017; Strohmeier & Piazza, 2017; Stone & Dulebohn, 2013). The advancement of technology has played a significant role in the growth and development of companies. Various industries, including HR, have recognized the advantages of leveraging technology to streamline operations and address complex organizational challenges. To remain competitive and embrace comprehensive digital transformation, HR professionals must adapt and keep pace with the latest advancements in HR technology in today's rapidly evolving technological landscape.

In the rapidly evolving global workplace, future HR professionals will need to acquire new and diverse technical skills to adapt to unexpected shifts and advancements. It is crucial for HR specialists to assess the implications of transitioning to a decentralized economy, which, if managed effectively, can bring about increased freedom and flexibility. This emerging era calls for a novel organizational structure that combines the dedication of independent individuals in a socially sustainable manner. Consequently, there is a growing demand for HR management systems that can navigate these changes proficiently, and new HR managers should be prepared to embrace and lead in this evolving landscape (Anyim, 2011).

According to Indermun (2014), the dynamic competitive market environment and the recognition of the strategic significance of HRM have significantly transformed the role of human resource managers in contemporary times. Furthermore, the advent of artificial intelligence (AI) has automated non-repetitive cognitive tasks that previously relied on extensive access to vast amounts of data, commonly referred to as "Big data". As a result, HR managers now have the opportunity to focus on more strategic and value-added initiatives within their organizations (Makridakis, 2017).

In the current environment, business is conducted to satisfy the demands of international trade. Additionally, services, management skills, and technological transfer, as well as the transfer of goods across nations, all occur. The world has become smaller due to globalization in terms of communication methods. With further innovation, the financial and economic systems around the world have been merged. Digital technology helps the association become more successful by enhancing one of its most valuable resources—its employees. Digital HRM can be defined as an overarching concept that encompasses various integration mechanisms and elements between HRM and IT, aimed at creating value within and across organizations for both employees and management. It serves as a framework for effectively implementing strategies, policies, and practices. With the outsourcing of numerous HR-related tasks, organizations now require HR professionals with new skill sets. It is crucial for the HR management division to understand and explore the interplay between human resources and information technology in an internet-centric society, as this knowledge can greatly benefit their operations. To enhance HR performance and leverage the potential of IT, it is essential to translate the analysis into practical implementation. By embracing digital technology, organizations can achieve a balance between efficiency and innovation. Collaboration between HR management and IT is crucial, as HRM plays a central role in shaping the organizational structure of many companies. By effectively integrating HR practices with IT solutions, organizations can optimize their overall performance and ensure that their HR functions align with strategic goals.

Previous research has primarily examined the impact of digitalization on marketing, overall behavior, and customer relationship management. However, academic research, especially in the field of HRM, has devoted comparatively less attention to understanding the internal implications of digitalization on businesses. Hence, the aim of this study is to fill this research gap and gain a deeper understanding of HRM in the digital era. The objective is to explore the HRM digital research landscape and its relationship with organizational performance, thereby contributing to a more comprehensive understanding of the topic.

## Literature Review

Digital transformation, or digitalization, is a business model that leverages digital technology across various sectors of society (Stolterman & Fors, 2004). It involves converting existing products or services into digital forms, providing advantages over physical counterparts (Gassmann *et al.*, 2014). In this process, technology and human resources collaborate to achieve remarkable outcomes. While computers excel in efficiency and speed, digital transformation allows humans to focus on their unique capabilities. The concept of digital transformation was first mentioned by Patel and McCarthy (2000), although they did not coin the term. Although research specifically focusing on digital transformation is limited, Westerman *et al.* (2011) conducted a notable study titled "Research on Digital Transformation", defining it as the use of technology to significantly enhance company performance or reach. Stolterman and Croon Fors (2006) provided a similar definition, emphasizing the changes brought about by digital technology in all aspects of human life. Digital transformation involves radical and fundamental changes driven by digital technologies rather than incremental improvements. Lucas *et al.* (2013) classified technology-driven transitions based on seven characteristics, considering a change transformational when it significantly influences at least three out of the four criteria. Consumer awareness has significantly increased as a result of the growing accessibility of goods and services *via* digital goods and services offered, their costs, and attributes, leading to the consumers changing the products they buy (Clemons, 2008; Kauffman, Li, & Heck, 2010). With increased digital literacy, customers are better able to evaluate and buy goods and services online without the help of middlemen (Granados & Gupta, 2013; Lucas *et al.*, 2013).

The integration of AI into HR operations often sparks debates about potential job losses as intelligent software replaces human workers. However, it is more likely to result in a significant re-classification and re-sdesigning of jobs at all levels. While certain industries may experience significant employment reductions, new jobs requiring a high level of digital intelligence are also likely to emerge (PWC, "A Report on Artificial Intelligence in HR: A No-brainer"). HR departments in organizations possess a wealth of information pertaining to human resources. Regular examination, analysis, and evaluation of this data assist in making important organizational decisions. The use of artificial intelligence (AI) is employed in such cases as it can process extensive and detailed data more efficiently than humans (Jain, 2016). AI facilitates the management of individual competencies, continuous monitoring, and competency evaluation across different levels of the HR department (Robinson & Sparrow, 2007).

The availability of large datasets has become pervasive, and in today's modern world, numerous activities rely on access to vast amounts of data. While this notion may sound fanciful, it holds true that data has become an essential component of many operations. Both small and large enterprises have embraced cloud computing and its diverse functionalities. The capability of new software to enhance performance, maintain high standards, and enable efficient talent management, all while being cost-effective, has been a driving force behind its adoption.

## Research Objectives

- To examine digital transformation in the context of HRM.
- To comprehend the current function of digitalization in firms' HRM.
- Research numerous difficulties HR may encounter when implementing digital transformation.

## Research Methodology

This study highlights how digital HRM can improve organizational performance. Secondary data was used to perform this study from a variety of sources, including corporate reports, examples, websites, expert blogs, and research publications. In order to discuss the advantages and difficulties of implementing digital transformation in human resource management, examples of well-known organizations and their cutting-edge business practices are given.

## HR and Digital Transformation

The term "digital transformation" refers to the process of transitioning a business from one that heavily relies on manual processes to one where technology plays a central role in all internal, external, and operational tasks (Mariappan & Krishnan, 2022). Transformation occurs as a result of digitization. It is important to note that the challenge lies not in the process of digitizing itself but in the necessary change in culture and mindset when a firm adopts digitalization and a technology-driven business model. Traditional HR practices often revolve around in-person interactions, physical filing cabinets, and paperwork. Numerous HR-related activities, such as candidate management, onboarding, attendance tracking, payroll, and performance measurement, involve extensive documentation. As part of HR digital transformation, these processes need to be converted into technology-based solutions. However, technology is not the sole factor at play. Effective completion of an HR digital transformation also relies on leadership, organizational culture, and employee productivity, which serve as the foundational elements for successful implementation.

The advancement of technology and improved process efficiency have played a crucial role in enabling significant changes in the workplace (Krishnan *et al.*, 2022). Digital transformation in HR brings numerous benefits, including better decision-making based on data, an enhanced employee experience, and various other advantages. Adopting digital solutions allows businesses to improve communication, increase productivity, attract top talent, enable remote work, and provide data that can inform important business decisions. When HR takes the lead in driving digital transformation, involving leadership and engaging every employee throughout the process, it ensures that technology and practices prioritize people and culture, fostering a welcoming environment for advancements.

In today's era of technological advancement, digital transformation is vital for HR, just like it is for every other aspect of an organization. According to Deloitte's analysis, there is a projected 25% increase in spending on digital transformation in the coming year. HR departments that still rely on manual data collection and analysis using Excel sheets must soon embrace automation to keep up with the growth of technologies like artificial intelligence (AI), blockchain, machine learning, and automated performance management, among others. Through the utilization of data, HR is undergoing a digital revolution, leveraging it in various aspects of the field, including payroll, benefits administration, performance management, learning and development, rewards and recognition, and hiring processes. The digital transformation of HR allows for improved efficiency, accuracy, and strategic decision-making within the department.

The digital transformation of HR brings numerous advantages, such as enhanced data-driven decision-making and improved employee experiences. Businesses can leverage digital solutions to enhance communication, increase productivity, attract top talent, enable remote work, and share information that can influence corporate decisions. Additionally, digital transformation in HR can lead to time and cost savings. By taking the initiative to lead the digital transformation movement and involving leadership and every employee throughout the process, HR can ensure that the chosen technology and practices prioritize people and culture. This inclusive approach helps to foster acceptance and adoption of innovations within the organization.

### *Digitalization in Recruitment*

The impact of digitalization is particularly evident in the employment process, bringing about significant changes. In their essay, Mr. Eshan and Dr. Binoy highlight the importance of including relevant information on resumes, such as name, email address, experience, credentials, and skills. Candidates can submit their completed resumes for consideration. Nowadays, many companies utilize video conferencing services like Skype, Facebook, and LinkedIn for recruitment purposes. The rapid advancement of technology has led to the emergence of various alternative platforms for recruiting, and it is worth emphasizing that digitization has greatly improved the efficiency of the hiring process. There is a divergence of opinions among experts regarding the impact of innovative methods on the significance of human resources. Some argue that automation and artificial intelligence (AI) might diminish the role of HR, while others believe that these technologies are not yet capable of fully replicating human qualities such as creativity, empathy, and a humanistic problem-solving approach. Alan Stukalsky, the chief digital officer of Randstad US, suggests that the use of chatbots in the hiring process is still in its early stages of development.

### *Digitalization in Training and Development*

Digitalization has had a positive impact on training and development, leading to advancements in the human resources division. Eshan and Binoy conducted research on the effects of digitalization on training and development in the hotel sector and found that modern technology has brought about changes in instructional methodologies. Examples of these changes include utilizing relevant films, enrolling in online courses, adopting computer-based learning strategies, and accessing digital versions of educational materials. In the past, training and development in hotels primarily relied on lectures, demonstrations, and book references. However, with digitalization, managers can now address specific issues through online platforms and have training materials stored in their accounts for future reference.

## In the Digital Transformation Process, HR Departments have Two Responsibilities to Play

- Through automation and digital, data-driven operations, it is in charge of driving its own transformation, together with the IT department
- HR is now expected to assist businesses with their digital transformation and support their ongoing digital progress. To improve productivity and optimize workplace operations, employees must be given the tools they need to adopt a digital mindset. To transform their HR staff, many firms employ various tactics. However, businesses typically employ these answers:

### *Automation*

Indeed, digitalization reduces the requirement for HR staff to engage in repetitive tasks such as data entry and form filling. As a result, they can allocate their time and efforts towards more pressing matters, leveraging their critical thinking skills and creativity to produce innovative and valuable work. By streamlining routine administrative tasks through digital tools and automation, HR professionals can shift their focus to strategic initiatives, problem-solving, and fostering a more resourceful and inspiring work environment. This allows them to add greater value to the organization and contribute to its overall success.

### *Digital Onboarding*

Digitalization in HR makes it easier for HR professionals to manage various tasks, including the onboarding process. By leveraging digital tools and technologies, HR can streamline and automate the onboarding process, ensuring that new hires and visitors have a smoother and more efficient experience in getting acclimated to the office environment. It is worth noting that despite the potential benefits of effective onboarding, a relatively low percentage (12%) of employees report having a wonderful onboarding experience with their new employers. However, research indicates that exceptional onboarding experiences can significantly impact new recruit retention (up to 82%) and productivity (up to 70%). This highlights the importance of optimizing the onboarding process through digitalization to enhance employee satisfaction, engagement, and long-term success within the organization.

### *Employee Self-Service Portals*

In response to the challenge of employees spending significant time searching for company information, self-service portals known as Human Capital Management (HCM) systems can be implemented. These systems allow employees and their managers to access and review essential information related to various HR areas. Some of the information that can be accessed through these portals includes:

- NPS (Net Promoter Score) ratings, which measure customer satisfaction and loyalty.
- Performance management information, including self-evaluations, objectives, training, and development progress.
- Updates on business news and work policies.
- Job openings within the organization.
- Health surveys for employee wellness programs.
- Updates to the knowledge base and meeting minutes.
- Opportunities for employee upskilling and development.

By implementing a self-service employee portal, organizations can provide a centralized and accessible platform for employees to retrieve relevant documents and information. This reduces the need for employees to search through various channels such as email, memos, or post-it notes. It also minimizes the time and effort required from the HR team to address individual queries, allowing them to focus on other strategic initiatives such as talent acquisition and fostering a positive workplace culture.

### *HR Chatbots*

Instead of relying on an HR staff member to idle away hours answering frequently asked questions, chatbots assist with typical problems. In the event that a specific HR staff member is not readily available, chatbots can assist employees.

### *AI-Based Recruitment*

Reviewing hundreds of resumes and portfolios can be time-consuming and challenging. However, most businesses today employ some sort of AI-based hiring strategy to read resumes and exclude those with erroneous formatting, false information, and similar issues. As a result, HR will have less work to do and will have more time for secondary screening.

## *People Analytics*

People analytics, also known as HR analytics or workforce analytics, is the practice of utilizing data-driven decision-making to enhance HR activities and improve employee performance, engagement, and productivity. Organizations use people analytics to make informed decisions related to various HR processes, including hiring, succession planning, employee retention, and talent management. While the term "analytics" may not immediately evoke thoughts of humanity and culture, they are indeed fundamental to the HR digital transformation powered by people analytics. The data collected and analyzed through people analytics is aimed at assisting employees in succeeding and finding greater satisfaction in their jobs. By leveraging this information, organizations can gain insights into employee needs, preferences, and performance drivers, allowing them to tailor HR initiatives and create a more supportive and engaging work environment. Ultimately, people analytics plays a vital role in aligning HR strategies with the well-being and success of employees.

## Big Data, AI and HR

The impact of big data in various corporate domains, including HR, is significant. Big data and HR data analytics have transformed the way HR functions, such as hiring, training, career development, performance evaluation, and compensation management. By leveraging big data, HR managers can make more informed decisions, leading to improved outcomes for the organization. Traditionally, HR had access to employee salary and benefits information. However, with the introduction of big data in HR, organizations can now collect and analyze data throughout the employee lifecycle, from pre-hiring to post-hiring stages. This data-driven approach enables HR managers to make data-informed decisions during the hiring process, resulting in a more successful and productive workforce.

The utilization of big data analytics in HR provides valuable insights into patterns, trends, and correlations within employee data. This information can be used to identify top talent, predict performance outcomes, design targeted training and career development programs, and create more effective compensation structures. By integrating big data into HR processes, HR professionals have powerful tools at their disposal to optimize decision-making and align HR strategies with organizational goals. In the rapidly changing external environment and highly competitive landscape, enterprises need to develop their core competitiveness through their human resources' differentiated knowledge, skills, and capabilities. Sharing knowledge and collaborating through a shared thinking mode allows employees to outperform rivals in work tasks. Additionally, the fast-changing external environment and intensified competition require enterprises to have shorter strategy cycles, which also raises the bar for effective human resource management.

Big data facilitates the Data Mining process, which then develops appropriate algorithms. The algorithms then assist in the training of computers through the use of Machine Learning techniques and Artificial Intelligence, which in turn generates new Big Data. To put it simply, Data Mining, Machine Learning, and Artificial Intelligence facilitate the production of Big Data. Importantly, Big Data is being adopted by every sector of society today, from manufacturing to agriculture, education and healthcare. Corporate enterprises are under intense pressure to integrate people analytics technologies into their HRM systems. It is high time for businesses to utilize Big Data to power HRM initiatives.

## Benefits of Big Data In HR

A communication gap has historically been a problem for HR. Despite being isolated from the rest of the corporation, it had immediate access to its information. There have frequently been communication breakdowns, and access to information and reporting has not always been immediate. However, with the advent of the cloud and big data, the organization's information has become centralized. Without requiring actual presence in the HR department, it may be accessed from anywhere. Data is now flowing instantly, which has greatly simplified its analysis. This might aid the department in improving judgments and its retention and recruitment tactics.

A poor hire results in several financial losses for the business. Many businesses invest time and resources in training new staff. If they turned out to be lousy hires, the resources invested in them would be wasted. Not to mention how losing them would impact how the company operated and how much it would cost to get a replacement. A bad hire will hurt any company. The use of analytics by HR managers to assist in making the best applicant choice may be due to this. The company can avoid hiring costs, lost productivity, training costs, client losses due to unfavorable experiences and reviews about the employee, *etc.*, if they are prepared to hunt for the simplest candidates.

Big data assists in predicting an employee's performance at the time of hire or even before. HR professionals, for instance, must assess if the applicant can contribute to the company's culture and perform at a level that is acceptable to other employees. It is unreliable in situations like this to rely solely on intuition. Additionally, it would be an additional effort to check each candidate for the group of top performers or employees against the job criterion. As an alternative,

HR departments can employ analytics to build high-performance profiles using worker records. In turn, headhunting for particular targets may become simple.

Big data privacy is a major problem that you can never completely eliminate, and for good reason. People have a real concern about the possibility of utilizing big data against them in a discriminatory manner. Massive data processing must be viewed as a risk management strategy by the Human Resources division.

## Examples of Well-Known Business Organizations Using Digital HR

The important topic of digitalization has attracted a lot of interest from business organizations, numerous entrepreneurs, organizations, and industries. This section will go into detail on how Digital HR is used by various top organizations throughout the world, its advantages, and how crucial it is to the organization. These examples highlight the use of digital HR by well-known organizations.

- **Johnson & Johnson:** Johnson & Johnson, a prominent player in the health and well-being industry, faced a challenge in updating its job descriptions to attract a broader range of candidates for approximately 25,000 positions it fills worldwide each year. Upon comparing job descriptions from the 1970s to the present, it became apparent that little had changed. To address this issue, Johnson & Johnson adopted a digital hiring revolution strategy. The company implemented a tool called Textio, an enhanced writing tool that not only improves language but also identifies potentially biased or misogynistic content. By using Textio, Johnson & Johnson was able to modify its job descriptions to be more gender-neutral and appealing to a wider pool of candidates. The company discovered that many of its job descriptions had unintentionally favored male applicants. The implementation of digital transformation in job descriptions had a significant impact on Johnson & Johnson's recruitment efforts. As a result, the company experienced a substantial increase in qualified female applicants, with an additional 90,000 women applying for science and technology roles annually. This example illustrates how leveraging digital transformation in job descriptions can enhance their appeal to the desired candidate pool. By embracing digital tools and technologies, organizations can ensure their job descriptions are inclusive, attractive, and aligned with their diversity and inclusion goals, thereby attracting a more diverse range of qualified candidates.
- **Royal Dutch Shell:** Shell, a prominent player in the oil industry, recognized a skill gap within its workforce even before the pandemic. Despite the industry's increasing adoption of technologies such as artificial intelligence, machine learning, and other digital tools, Shell's personnel lacked the necessary skills to fully leverage these advancements. To address this gap and ensure the company

remains competitive, Shell implemented a digital learning platform. By embracing a digital learning platform, Shell provided its employees with an opportunity to acquire the skills required to effectively utilize new technologies and stay ahead in the industry. This platform offered various online courses, training materials, and resources to help employees upskill and reskill themselves in areas related to digital technologies. The adoption of the digital learning platform by Shell showcases the importance of continuous learning and development in the digital era. By providing employees with access to digital learning opportunities, organizations can bridge skill gaps, foster a culture of innovation, and ensure their workforce is equipped with the knowledge and competencies necessary to thrive in a rapidly evolving digital landscape.

- **Hero Motor Cop:** Hero Motor Corp, a leading manufacturer of motorcycles and scooters, has implemented a software-as-a-service (SaaS)-based talent management platform. This platform encompasses both internal and external talent pools and aims to recognize and understand the internal talent within the organization. By leveraging a SaaS-based talent management platform, Hero Motor Corp is able to streamline and optimize its talent management processes. The platform includes features such as recruitment management, performance management, learning and development, succession planning, and employee engagement. Through the platform, Hero Motor Corp can effectively manage its talent acquisition efforts, including both internal promotions and external hires. The organization can identify and evaluate internal talent, recognizing individuals who possess the skills, potential, and aspirations to take on higher roles within the company. This holistic approach to talent management enables Hero Motor Corp to make informed decisions about talent deployment, development, and succession planning. By implementing a SaaS-based talent management platform, Hero Motor Corp demonstrates its commitment to strategic talent management practices. The platform enhances HR processes, improves talent visibility, and supports the organization in nurturing and retaining top talent. By effectively leveraging both internal and external talent pools, Hero Motor Corp can drive innovation, build a high-performing workforce, and maintain a competitive role in the automotive industry.
- **AI recruitment at IBM:** IBM, a renowned technology company, has implemented AI-powered recruitment practices to enhance the efficiency and effectiveness of its hiring process. Recognizing the need for thorough applicant vetting and prioritizing job requirements, IBM developed a solution called IBM Watson Recruitment (IWR). IWR utilizes AI technology to leverage data from the labor market and past hiring experiences. It enables recruiters to forecast the time required to fill a position and select candidates who have the highest potential for success. By automating certain aspects of the recruitment process, AI frees up time for recruiters to focus on crucial aspects such as building

connections with applicants and prioritizing candidate suitability. One of the key features of IWR is its ability to generate a match score between the skills listed in a candidate's resume and the skills required for the job. This match score is based on job requisitions, ensuring a better alignment between candidate qualifications and job requirements. Additionally, the solution can predict future job performance based on additional biographical information available in the resume, such as leadership experience. To ensure fairness and eliminate bias in the hiring process, IWR actively monitors the hiring processes to identify and mitigate any potential biases that may arise. In summary, the implementation of AI in the recruitment process at IBM through IWR has resulted in several benefits. It improves the candidate experience by matching their skills with job requirements more accurately, provides recruiters with valuable insights to make informed decisions, and enables faster and more accurate hiring. Additionally, the AI-powered solution helps ensure fairness and reduce biases in the recruitment process.

- **RBC (Royal Bank of Canada):** RBC uses digitalization to re-invent the work experience. In addition to information technology, they established a new digital human resource management team for infrastructure and security reasons. They developed an application called Embard so that employees could learn more about their jobs, understand the company culture, and interact with the team online. RBC has intended to establish a digital platform for a Compelling Careers application as well as a digital system for learning, career development, and employment transactions.
- **Sapphire Ventures:** Technology can improve the candidate side of hiring as well as make life simpler for HR personnel. The venture capital firm Sapphire Ventures is a fantastic illustration of this. The executive talent team at Sapphire Ventures is in charge of creating a talent network to meet the demands of Sapphire's numerous firms as soon as opportunities become available. Previously, the company tracked prospective candidates using spreadsheets and Google Docs. Finding pertinent names and information was difficult and time-consuming because there was no established platform for the talent team to use. Additionally, the unchanging style made it more difficult to track prospective candidates over time. The answer? The Thrive talent relationship management (TRM) platform was implemented by Sapphire. Information on executive searches can be stored and organized in one place thanks to Thrive. Talent managers may easily tag prospects for simple searching, and it features a Chrome extension to add new contact information quickly. Sapphire's digital transformation recruitment helped its clients hire more quickly by building a talent database that is constantly updated. TRM systems enable you to create a network of possible candidates that can be quickly accessed as needed while keeping your talent information organized.

- **Walmart:** Walmart, a prominent retail giant, has always prioritized innovation in its operations. The company consistently seeks out new and creative approaches to engage both customers and employees. In line with this commitment, Walmart has implemented an automation system that enables its employees to directly communicate with customers. This automation system has had a significant impact on the shopping experience, particularly in the fast-growing self-checkout area. By allowing customers to utilize self-checkout options, Walmart has reduced the demand for traditional cashiers. In addition to this, Walmart has invested in training its employees to excel as personal shoppers, providing personalized assistance, and enhancing customer satisfaction. To ensure that its staff is well-prepared for any situation, Walmart has developed a virtual platform for education and training. This platform equips employees with the necessary knowledge and skills to handle various customer interactions and address their needs effectively. By leveraging technology for education and preparation, Walmart ensures that its employees are equipped with the tools and information they need to provide excellent customer service. Walmart's approach to automation and employee training demonstrates its commitment to enhancing the customer experience and optimizing its workforce. By integrating automation systems and providing comprehensive training, Walmart creates a seamless shopping experience and empowers its employees to deliver exceptional service. This focus on innovation and employee development contributes to Walmart's position as a leading retailer in the industry.
- **Deloitte:** Deloitte's initiative to “Make learning a game” serves as an excellent example of how gamification can enhance a digital platform and its overall learning environment. Deloitte recognized the need to enhance its Deloitte Leadership Academy (DLA) training programs, particularly in terms of participant engagement and comprehension. To address this challenge, Deloitte incorporated various game elements into the training program, creating an exciting and immersive learning experience. By designing a gaming world where participants could engage, play, and compete, Deloitte made the training program more interactive and enjoyable. The gamified training program included embedded missions, video lectures, assessments, and quizzes, which helped facilitate communication and interaction between the users and the learning content. Participants were able to navigate through the gaming world, complete missions, and track their progress, creating a sense of achievement and motivation. The impact of this gamified approach to training was significant. The results showed that approximately 38% of users engaged with the Deloitte Leadership Academy on a weekly basis. This high level of user engagement demonstrated the success of the gamification strategy in capturing and maintaining participants' interest in the training program. Deloitte's initiative

highlights the effectiveness of gamification in enhancing learning experiences and driving engagement. By leveraging game features and creating an interactive learning environment, organizations can make training programs more enjoyable, immersive, and effective in conveying knowledge and skills.

- **Leading International Hotel Group:** A leading international hotel group faced the challenges of high turnover, transient roles, and complex personnel management in the hospitality sector. To address these challenges, the company implemented an annual talent program aimed at identifying and developing top talent within their organization. This program aimed to maximize the potential of high-performing individuals and retain them in the company. To identify the best candidates for this talent program, the hotel group organized two-day assessment centers, inviting hundreds of applicants from all over Europe. These assessment centers were held in lucrative conference centers within their properties, even though it impacted revenue from bookings. The hotel group partnered with Cognisess, an intelligent benchmarking company, to identify the profile of the highest-performing candidates. Cognisess used machine learning and data science to create an accurate and unbiased profile of the company's best employees. Using the data from previous successful cohorts, Cognisess developed a prediction model that ranked interview performance and expected performance during a business simulation. Computer vision scores were utilized to rank interview performance. The accuracy of the model allowed the hotel group to rely entirely on the predicted values, eliminating the need for a case study component during the assessment process. This resulted in significant time savings, as the business simulation previously took up a substantial portion of the assessment center's second day.

  The hotel chain could hire applicants based on these improved standards after it had a better knowledge of the attitudes, motivations, and strengths of the new generation of prospective leaders. The new AI-focused hiring procedure cut the review period for candidates from two days to one, saving £250,000 annually. The area directors and HR managers who provided feedback indicated that the time savings and enhanced hiring results made the investment in this AI-driven procedure justifiable. The hotel chain attracted top candidates, learned insightful information about its potential leaders, and saved money and time through its revised hiring procedure.

## CONCLUSION

The study conducted a thorough analysis of recent literature on the application and scope of digital HRM in use today. Supporting new work forms and facilitating more effective communication and cooperation through technology tools underscored the revolutionary potential of digitization. Significant technology breakthroughs, automation, and digitalization have completely transformed the field of human resource management. The use of artificial intelligence (AI) in HRM operations has also become common, helping with problem-solving and automating tasks. With the rise of digital platforms, increased worldwide connectedness, and social networks, among other considerations, the recruitment and selection process has experienced major changes. In the digital age, HRM processes have changed and are still changing.

However, it is crucial to not only discuss the successes of digitalization but also put them into practice. Organizations need to embrace and allocate resources for technological advancements, utilizing every invention and method available. The advancement of AI technologies, driven by increasing computational power, growing data volumes, and enhanced theoretical understanding, necessitates a deeper understanding of its implications. The study emphasized that the interaction between humans and technology at work is highly context-specific, highlighting the importance of adapting to the environment to maximize the positive potential of AI while mitigating any negative impacts. Big data analytics emerged as a prominent trend in the digital era, and HR is no exception to its potential benefits. Leveraging big data and AI can significantly enhance human resource management and contribute to increased operational effectiveness within organizations.

## BIBLIOGRAPHY

Anyim, F.C., Ikemefuna, C.O., Mbah, S.E. (2011). Human Resource Management Challenges in Nigeria Under a Globalized Economy. *Int. J. Econs & Mgmt., 1*(4), 1-11.

Bharadwaj, A., El Sawy, O.A., Pavlou, P.A., Venkatraman, N. (2013). Digital Business Strategy: Toward a Next Generation of Insights. *Manage. Inf. Syst. Q., 37*(2), 471-482. [http://dx.doi.org/10.25300/MISQ/2013/37:2.3]

Bondarouk, T., Harms, R., Lepak, D. (2017). Does e-HRM lead to better HRM service? *Int. J. Hum. Resour. Manage., 28*(9), 1332-1362. [http://dx.doi.org/10.1080/09585192.2015.1118139]

Clemons, E.K. (2008). How Information Changes Consumer Behavior and How Consumer Behavior Determines Corporate Strategy. *J. Manage. Inf. Syst., 25*(2), 13-40. [http://dx.doi.org/10.2753/MIS0742-1222250202]

Cöster, M., Iveroth, E., Olve, N.G., Petri, C.J., Westelius, A. (2019). Conceptualising innovative price models: the RITE framework. *Balt. J. Manag., 14*(4), 540-558. [http://dx.doi.org/10.1108/BJM-06-2018-0216]

Eshan, M.R., Binoy, T.A. (2018). The Role of Digitalization in Human Resource Management in Star Category Hotels: A Review. *J. Emerg. Technol. Innov. Res., 5*(12), 203-211.

Fichman, R.G., Dos Santos, B.L., Zheng, Z.E. (2014). Digital Innovation as a Fundamental and Powerful Concept in the Information Systems Curriculum. *Manage. Inf. Syst. Q., 38*(2), 329-343. [http://dx.doi.org/10.25300/MISQ/2014/38.2.01]

Fitzgerald, M., Kruschwitz, N., Bonnet, D., Welch, M. (2014). Embracing Digital Technology: A New Strategic Imperative. *MIT Sloan Manag. Rev., 55*(2), 1-12.

Granados, N., Gupta, A. (2013). Transparency Strategy: Competing with Information in a Digital World.

*Manage. Inf. Syst. Q., 37*(2), 637-641.

Hennig-Thurau, T., Malthouse, E.C., Friege, C., Gensler, S., Lobschat, L., Rangaswamy, A., Skiera, B. (2010). The Impact of New Media on Customer Relationships. *J. Serv. Res., 13*(3), 311-330. [http://dx.doi.org/10.1177/1094670510375460]

Indermun, V. (2014). Importance of Human Resource Management Practices and the Impact Companies Face in Relation to Competitive Challenges. *SJBEMS., 2*(11), 125-135. [http://dx.doi.org/10.12816/0006786]

Kauffman, R.J., Li, T., van Heck, E. (2010). Business Network-Based Value Creation in Electronic Commerce. *Int. J. Electron. Commerce, 15*(1), 113-144. [http://dx.doi.org/10.2753/JEC1086-4415150105]

Knobel, M., Lankshear, C. (2008). Digital Literacy and Participation in Online Social Networking Spaces. *Digital Literacies: Concepts. Policies and Practices, 11*, 249-278.

Krishnan, C. (2009). Globalization and its impact on business environment. *IndianMBA. com, July.*

Krishnan, C., Gupta, A., Gupta, A., Singh, G. (2022). Impact of Artificial Intelligence-Based Chatbots on Customer Engagement and Business Growth. [http://dx.doi.org/10.1007/978-3-031-10869-3_11]

Lucas, H.C., Jr, Agarwal, R., Clemons, E.K., El Sawy, O.A., Weber, B. (2013). Impactful Research on Transformational Information Technology: An Opportunity to Inform New Audiences. *Manage. Inf. Syst. Q., 37*(2), 371-382. [http://dx.doi.org/10.25300/MISQ/2013/37.2.03]

Makridakis, S. (2017). The forthcoming Artificial Intelligence (AI) revolution: Its impact on society and firms. *Futures, 90*, 46-60. [http://dx.doi.org/10.1016/j.futures.2017.03.006]

Mariappan, J., Krishnan, C. (2022). Integration of AI in Learning: A Paradigm Shift in Education.*Technology Training for Educators from Past to Present.* IGI Global. [http://dx.doi.org/10.4018/978-1-6684-4083-4.ch014]

Mariappan, J., Krishnan, C., Shankaralingam, K., Abbas, S.M. (2022). Theoretical Perspective of Role of Technology on Business Environment.*Integrating New Technologies in International Business.* Apple Academic Press. [http://dx.doi.org/10.1201/9781003130352-16]

Patel, K., McCarthy, M.P. (2000). *Digital Transformation: The Essentials of E-Business Leadership.* Mcgraw-Hill Professional.

Piccinini, E., Gregory, R.W., Kolbe, L.M. (2015). Changes in the Producer-Consumer Relationship-Towards Digital Transformation. *Proceedings of the 12th International Conference on Wirtshaftinformatik,* 1634-1648.

Robinson, M.A., Sparrow, P.R., Clegg, C., Birdi, K. (2007). Forecasting future competency requirements: a three-phase methodology. *Person. Rev., 36*(1), 65-90. [http://dx.doi.org/10.1108/00483480710716722]

Stolterman, E., Fors, A.C. (2004). Information Technology and the Good Life.*Information Systems Research: Relevant Theory and Informed Practice.* Springer. [http://dx.doi.org/10.1007/1-4020-8095-6_45]

Stone, D.L., Dulebohn, J.H. (2013). Emerging issues in theory and research on electronic human resource management (eHRM). *Hum. Resour. Manage. Rev., 23*(1), 1-5. [http://dx.doi.org/10.1016/j.hrmr.2012.06.001]

Strohmeier, S., Piazza, F. (2013). Domain driven data mining in human resource management: A review of current research. *Expert Syst. Appl., 40*(7), 2410-2420. [http://dx.doi.org/10.1016/j.eswa.2012.10.059]

## CHAPTER 7

# An Investigation of Industry 4.0 with Client Value Added in the Business Industry

**Ravi Kumar Gupta**[1,*], **Udit Maheshwari**[1], **Ashutosh Priya**[2] and **Debendra Nath Das**[3]

[1] *Department of Humanities and Management Science, Madan Mohan Malaviya University of Technology, Gorakhpur, India*

[2] *Department of Applied and Regional Economics, Mahatma Jyotiba Phule Rohilkhand University, Bareilly, Uttar Pradesh, India*

[3] *Mahatma Gandhi National Council of Rural Education, Hyderabad, India*

**Abstract:** Industry 4.0 has transformed the way businesses operate and deliver value to their clients. This research aims to investigate the influence of Industry 4.0 on client value added. The study reviews the literature on Industry 4.0 and client value added and conducts a survey to gather data from companies that have acquired technologies of Industry 4.0. The findings of the study suggest that Industry 4.0 has a remarkable and positive influence on client value added. The adoption of Industry 4.0 technologies results in improved efficiency, enhanced quality, increased customization, and greater customer engagement, all of which contribute to a better client experience and increased client value added. The paper concludes by highlighting the importance of Industry 4.0 for businesses seeking to improve their client value added and remain competitive in the marketplace.

**Keywords:** Business, Client, Industry 4.0, Technological Revolution, Value Added.

## INTRODUCTION

Industry 4.0, also synonymous with the 4$^{th}$ Industrial Revolution, is a new phase of the Industrial Revolution that has metamorphosed the way businesses operate and deliver value to their clients. It is distinguished by the amalgamation of various kinds of digital technologies into the production/manufacturing process,

* **Corresponding author Ravi Kumar Gupta:** Department of Humanities and Management Science, Madan Mohan Malaviya University of Technology, Gorakhpur, India; E-mail: raviguptaeco@gmail.com

**Sukanta Kumar Baral, Richa Goel, Tilottama Singh, Erdener Kaynak & Vishal Jain (Eds.)**

including the use of automation, artificial intelligence, the Internet of Things (IoT), and supplementary technologies. The adoption of Industry 4.0 has significant implications for businesses, including the potential to enhance client value added (Chen, 2019).

Client value added is a key component of business success. It refers to the additional value that a business provides to its clients beyond the core product or service. Client value added can take many forms, such as improved quality, increased customization, better customer service, and more. By providing additional value to clients, businesses can improve client satisfaction, increase loyalty, and ultimately drive revenue growth (Demir *et al.*, 2019).

The paper investigates the impact of Industry 4.0 on client value added. The paper reviews the literature on Industry 4.0 and client value added and conducts a survey to gather data from companies that have acquired technologies of Industry 4.0. The findings of the study are intended to provide insights into the impact of Industry 4.0 on client value added and highlight the significance of Industry 4.0 for businesses seeking to improve their client value added and remain competitive in the marketplace.

## LITERATURE REVIEW

The literature on Industry 4.0 and client value added suggests that the usage of technologies of Industry 4.0 has significant potential to enhance client value added. One key way in which Industry 4.0 can improve client value added is through increased efficiency. By automating processes and using real-time data to optimize production, businesses can reduce waste, minimize downtime, and improve overall productivity. This can result in cost savings for clients, as well as faster turnaround times and more reliable delivery of products and services (Drath & Horch, 2014).

Another way in which Industry 4.0 can enhance client value added is through improved quality. The use of sensors and other advanced technologies can help businesses monitor and control the quality of their products and services in real time. This can result in fewer defects, fewer product recalls, and overall higher quality products and services. Clients are likely to value this improved quality, as it can help them avoid costly downtime, rework, and other negative outcomes (Fernandez-Carames & Fraga-Lamas, 2019).

Industry 4.0 can also increase customization, which can enhance client value added. Collecting and analyzing data on client preferences and behavior help businesses tailor their different products and services to satisfy the preferences of individual clients and provide adequate and required value to them. This can result in more personalized products and services, which can lead to higher levels of satisfaction and loyalty (Foidl & Felderer, 2015).

Finally, Industry 4.0 can improve customer engagement, which is another key component of client value added (Ivanov, & Dolgui, 2019). The use of digital technologies can permit businesses to interact with clients in more innovative and creative ways, like through social media, mobile apps, and other channels (Janowski & Bak, 2020).

## EVOLUTION AND DEVELOPMENT OF INDUSTRY 4.0

Industry 4.0 is the fourth Industrial Revolution that builds on the previous three industrial revolutions and involves the integration of advanced digital technologies into the manufacturing process. The following is a brief overview of how Industry 4.0 has developed over time:

### Industry 1.0

The 1st Industrial Revolution started in the late 18th and early 19th centuries with the advent of mechanized production through the use of water and steam power. This led to the creation of large factories and mass production of goods (Kagermann *et. al.*, 2013).

### Industry 2.0

The 2nd Industrial Revolution took place in the late 19th and early 20th centuries with the introduction of electricity and assembly line production. This enabled the mass production of goods on a larger scale and led to the development of the consumer society (Lasi *et. al.*, 2014).

### Industry 3.0

The 3rd Industrial Revolution, also called the Digital Revolution, started in the 1960s with the introduction of computer technology and automation. This led to the development of computer-aided design and manufacturing, as well as the automation of many production processes (Lee & Kao, 2019).

### Industry 4.0

The 4th Industrial Revolution, or Industry 4.0, began in the late 2000s with the integration of advanced digital technologies into the manufacturing process. This includes the use of the Internet of Things (IoT), robotics, artificial intelligence and data analytics to optimize processes of production and create more efficient, flexible, and customized manufacturing systems (Schneider, 2018).

The development of Industry 4.0 has been driven by a range of technological advancements, including the increasing availability of sensors and data analytics, the proliferation of mobile and cloud-based computing, and the growing use of artificial intelligence and machine learning. These advancements have enabled businesses to collect, analyze, and utilize vast amounts of data to optimize their production processes, improve product quality, and enhance client experience (Sony & Naik, 2019).

Overall, the development of Industry 4.0 has been driven by the need for businesses to remain competitive in a rapidly changing global marketplace. By integrating advanced digital technologies into their operations, businesses can improve efficiency, reduce costs, and enhance client value added, ultimately driving revenue growth and profitability.

## BASIC STRUCTURE OF INDUSTRY 4.0/ WHAT INDUSTRY 4.0 CONSISTS OF?

The basic structure of Industry 4.0 is centered around the integration of advanced digital technologies into the process of manufacturing to create more efficient, flexible, and customized manufacturing systems. This involves the usage of technologies such as robotics, artificial intelligence, the Internet of Things (IoT), and data analytics to optimize production processes and enhance client experience. The following is a detailed explanation of the basic structure of Industry 4.0:

### Cyber-Physical Systems (CPSs)

The foundation of Industry 4.0 is the usage of Cyber-Physical Systems (CPSs), which refer to the integration of physical and digital systems in a networked environment. CPS includes the use of sensors, actuators, and controllers to monitor and control physical processes, while digital systems are used to collect, analyze, and utilize data to optimize production processes (Ustundag & Cevikcan, 2017).

### Internet of Things (IoT)

The Internet of Things (IoT) is a network of interconnected physical devices, sensors, and software that are used to collect and exchange data. In the context of Industry 4.0, IoT is used to connect and control a wide range of devices, from manufacturing equipment to logistics and supply chain systems (Varghese & Tandur, 2014).

### Big Data Analytics

Its usage is a key aspect of Industry 4.0, as it permits businesses to collect and analyze huge amounts of data to optimize production processes and enhance client experience. Data analytics is used to identify patterns, trends, and insights used to improve product quality, reduce costs, and enhance overall client experience (Yavari & Pilevari, 2020).

### Artificial Intelligence (AI)

It is used in Industry 4.0 to enhance automation and decision-making processes. AI is used to analyze data and make predictions and recommendations, as well as to automate tasks that would normally require human intervention (Yan *et al.*, 2017).

### Cloud Computing

Cloud computing is used to store and process data in Industry 4.0. Cloud-based computing enables businesses to store large amounts of data in a secure and scalable environment while also providing access to powerful processing capabilities that can be used to analyze and utilize the data (Xu *et al.*, 2021).

### Robotics

Robotics is used in Industry 4.0 to automate many processes of production, from assembly line production to logistics and supply chain management. Robots are used to execute tasks repetitively, hence allowing the human workforce to focus on complex and creative tasks (Xu *et al.*, 2018).

### Additive Manufacturing

It is also called 3D printing and is a key technology in Industry 4.0. It enables businesses to create complex parts and components using digital designs and additive processes, reducing waste and increasing efficiency in the manufacturing process (Schumacher *et al.*, 2016).

### Augmented Reality (AR)

AR is used in Industry 4.0 to enhance workers' productivity and training processes. AR can be used to provide workers with real-time information and instructions, enabling them to perform tasks more efficiently and effectively (Tjahjono *et al.*, 2017).

Overall, Industry 4.0 consists of various technologies and systems that are integrated into the manufacturing and industrial sectors to create more efficient, flexible, and customized manufacturing systems.

Overall, the basic structure of Industry 4.0 is centered around the integration of advanced digital technologies into the manufacturing process to optimize production processes and enhance client experience. This involves the use of CPS, the IoT, big data analytics, AI, cloud computing, robotics, additive manufacturing, and augmented reality to create more efficient, flexible, and customized manufacturing systems.

## ROLE OF INDUSTRY 4.0 IN CLIENT VALUE ADDED

Industry 4.0 has a remarkable impact on client value added (CVA) by enabling companies to deliver products and services that meet their clients' needs more effectively and efficiently. CVA means the value that a company adds to a product or service that goes beyond its basic features and functions. This added value can include things such as personalized services, customization options, and enhanced user experiences. The following are some of the ways in which Industry 4.0 contributes to the enhancement of CVA:

### Customization

One of the crucial benefits of Industry 4.0 is its ability to support mass customization. With the help of advanced digital technologies such as 3D printing and AI, companies can produce customized products and services that meet the specific needs of individual clients. This level of customization is a significant contributor to CVA, as it enables clients to receive products and services that are tailored to their unique requirements.

### Quality

Industry 4.0 technologies such as sensors and big data analytics enable companies to monitor and improve product quality continuously. By collecting and analyzing data in real time, businesses can identify and resolve issues more quickly, reducing the risk of product defects or recalls. This level of quality assurance contributes to CVA by ensuring that clients receive high-quality products and services that meet their expectations.

### Speed

Industry 4.0 enables companies to respond to client needs more quickly and efficiently. With the help of digital technologies such as IoT, cloud computing, and robotics, businesses can optimize their production processes, reducing lead times and increasing production efficiency. This level of speed contributes to CVA by ensuring that clients receive products and services in a timely and efficient manner.

### Communication

Industry 4.0 also enables companies to improve their communication with clients. With the help of digital technologies such as social media, companies can interact with their clients in real time, responding to queries and concerns promptly. This level of communication contributes to CVA by enhancing the client experience and building stronger relationships with clients.

### Innovation

Industry 4.0 technologies are also a significant driver of innovation. With the help of advanced digital technologies such as AI and big data analytics, businesses can identify new opportunities and accordingly work toward developing new customized products and services that meet emerging client needs. This level of innovation contributes to CVA by enabling businesses to deliver products and services that meet the dynamic needs of different clients.

In conclusion, Industry 4.0 has a significant role in enhancing CVA by enabling companies to deliver products and services that meet the unique needs of individual clients more effectively and efficiently. By leveraging advanced digital technologies, businesses can customize their products and services, improve product quality, respond to client needs more quickly, improve communication, and drive innovation, all of which contribute to the enhancement of CVA (Tantawi *et al.*, 2019).

## DISADVANTAGES OF INDUSTRY 4.0 TO CLIENT VALUE ADDED:

While Industry 4.0 has several advantages that contribute to the enhancement of client value added (CVA), there are also some disadvantages that need to be considered. These include:

### Cost

One of the primary disadvantages of Industry 4.0 is its high cost of implementation. The adoption of advanced digital technologies such as AI, robotics, and IoT requires significant investments in hardware, software, and training. These costs can be prohibitive for small and medium-sized businesses, which can limit their ability to enhance CVA through Industry 4.0.

### Security

Technologies of Industry 4.0 are vulnerable to cybersecurity threats, which can compromise client data and undermine trust. As companies collect and analyze more data in real time, they become more attractive targets for hackers and cyber-criminals. This vulnerability can be a significant risk to client data privacy and can negatively impact CVA.

### Dependence on Technology

Industry 4.0 relies heavily on advanced digital technologies such as AI, IoT, and automation. Over-reliance on these technologies can be problematic in cases of system failure, technical glitches, or cyberattacks. These failures can impact the ability of businesses to deliver products and services effectively and, in turn, negatively affect CVA.

### Resistance to Change

Industry 4.0 requires significant changes to business processes, organizational structures, and employee roles. The resistance to change from employees and management can be a significant barrier to the adoption of Industry 4.0, limiting the ability of companies to enhance CVA.

### Ethical Issues

Industry 4.0 technologies can raise ethical issues around the use of client data, automation of jobs, and privacy concerns. The improper use of data or automation of jobs can negatively impact CVA, as clients may perceive these actions as unethical and choose to disengage from the company.

### Digital Divide

The adoption of Industry 4.0 technologies can also create a digital divide, as businesses that can afford to invest in these technologies can gain a competitive advantage over those that cannot. This divide can limit the ability of smaller businesses to enhance their CVA, leading to a reduction in competition and innovation in the market (Vaidya *et al.*, 2018; Liao *et al.*, 2017).

## MAJOR FACTORS CONTRIBUTING TO THE INEFFECTIVE AND EFFECTIVE IMPLEMENTATION OF INDUSTRY 4.0 IN CLIENT VALUE ADDED

The successful implementation of Industry 4.0 can significantly contribute to the enhancement of client value added (CVA), but there are several factors that can impact its effectiveness. Some of the major factors contributing to the effective and ineffective implementation of Industry 4.0 in CVA are as follows:

## Effective Implementation

### *Visionary Leadership*

A clear and compelling vision of how Industry 4.0 can enhance CVA is essential for successful implementation. Leaders who understand the potential benefits of Industry 4.0 and can effectively communicate this to their employees can create a sense of urgency and commitment to the implementation process.

### *Strategic Planning*

Successful implementation of Industry 4.0 requires a strategic plan that aligns with the overall business goals and objectives. A well-defined plan that identifies the key technologies, processes, and resources required for successful implementation can ensure that the CVA benefits of Industry 4.0 are realized.

### *Skilled Workforce*

The implementation of Industry 4.0 effectively requires a skilled and knowledgeable workforce. Training and upskilling employees on the new technologies, tools, and processes can ensure that they can work effectively with Industry 4.0 technologies and leverage them to enhance CVA (Wu *et al.*, 2016).

### *Data Management*

The effective management of data is essential for the successful implementation of Industry 4.0. An effective data management strategy that ensures the collection, storage, and analysis of relevant data can enable businesses to identify trends, insights, and opportunities to enhance CVA.

### *Collaborative Culture*

A collaborative culture that fosters communication, collaboration, and experimentation can enable businesses to effectively implement Industry 4.0. A culture that values innovation and continuous improvement can ensure that businesses can adapt and evolve to meet the changing needs of clients and enhance CVA.

## Ineffective Implementation

### *Lack of Visionary Leadership*

The lack of clear and compelling leadership can hinder the implementation of Industry 4.0 in an efficient manner. A leadership team that is not aligned with the benefits of Industry 4.0 or lacks the ability to effectively communicate this to employees can create resistance to change and hinder successful implementation.

### *Inadequate Planning*

Inadequate planning can also hinder the effective implementation of Industry 4.0. A poorly defined plan that does not align with the overall business goals and objectives can lead to the selection of the wrong technologies, processes, and resources, limiting the ability of Industry 4.0 to enhance CVA.

### *Skill Gaps*

The lack of skilled and knowledgeable employees can also hinder the effective implementation of Industry 4.0. Inadequate training and upskilling of employees can limit their ability to work with Industry 4.0 technologies and leverage them to enhance CVA.

### *Poor Data Management*

Ineffective data management can also hinder the effective implementation of Industry 4.0. A lack of relevant data or poor data quality can limit the ability of businesses to identify trends, insights, and opportunities to enhance CVA.

### *Siloed Culture*

A siloed culture that values individual goals over collaboration can also hinder the implementation of Industry 4.0 in an effective manner. A lack of communication and collaboration between different departments or teams can limit the ability of businesses to effectively implement Industry 4.0 technologies and enhance CVA.

In conclusion, the effective implementation of Industry 4.0 requires visionary leadership, strategic planning, a skilled workforce, effective data management, and a collaborative culture. On the other hand, ineffective implementation can be caused by a lack of visionary leadership, inadequate planning, skill gaps, poor data management, and a siloed culture. Businesses that adopt Industry 4.0 technologies need to address these factors to ensure that they can effectively enhance CVA and attain a distinct competitive advantage in the market (Saucedo-Martínez *et al.*, 2018).

## CONCLUSION

Industry 4.0 is an advanced technological revolution that is transforming the manufacturing industry. It involves the amalgamation of various digital technologies, like the IoT, AI, big data, and robotics, to make factories more advanced, smart, highly efficient, flexible, and connected. Industry 4.0 enables companies to achieve significant improvements in productivity, quality, and cost-effectiveness, which ultimately lead to enhanced customer satisfaction.

One of the crucial advantages of Industry 4.0 is its ability to create value-added services for clients. With the use of real-time data and analytics, manufacturers can personalize their products and services to meet the specific needs of each customer. This not only increases customer satisfaction but also allows manufacturers to differentiate themselves in the market and increase their competitiveness.

Furthermore, Industry 4.0 enables manufacturers to provide after-sales services that were not possible before, such as predictive maintenance and remote monitoring. This helps to reduce downtime, minimize repair costs, and improve overall equipment efficiency, all of which contribute to a better customer experience.

## BIBLIOGRAPHY

Chen, Y. (2019). Industry 4.0 and its impact on customer value creation. *J. Bus. Res., 98*, 365-380.

Demir, K.A., Döven, G., Sezen, B. (2019). Industry 5.0 and human-robot co-working. *Procedia Comput. Sci., 158*, 688-695.
[http://dx.doi.org/10.1016/j.procs.2019.09.104]

Drath, R., Horch, A. (2014). Industrie 4.0: Hit or hype? *IEEE Ind. Electron. Mag., 8*(2), 56-58. [industry forum].
[http://dx.doi.org/10.1109/MIE.2014.2312079]

Fernandez-Carames, T.M., Fraga-Lamas, P. (2019). A review on the application of blockchain to the next generation of cybersecure industry 4.0 smart factories. *IEEE Access, 7*, 45201-45218.
[http://dx.doi.org/10.1109/ACCESS.2019.2908780]

Foidl, H., Felderer, M. (2016). Research challenges of industry 4.0 for quality management. *Innovations in Enterprise Information Systems Management and Engineering, 4*, 121-137.

Ivanov, D., Dolgui, A., Sokolov, B. (2019). The impact of digital technology and Industry 4.0 on the ripple effect and supply chain risk analytics. *Int. J. Prod. Res., 57*(3), 829-846.
[http://dx.doi.org/10.1080/00207543.2018.1488086]

Janowski, P., Bak, M. (2020). Industry 4.0 and customer value creation: A systematic review. *J. Bus. Res., 112*, 1-12.

Kagermann, H., Wahlster, W., Helbig, J. (2013). Recommendations for implementing the strategic initiative Industry 4.0. *Acatech Study, 20*, 1-76.

Lasi, H., Fettke, P., Kemper, H.G., Feld, T., Hoffmann, M. (2014). Industry 4.0. *Bus. Inf. Syst. Eng., 6*(4), 239-242.

[http://dx.doi.org/10.1007/s12599-014-0334-4]

Lee, J., Kao, H.A. (2019). Industry 4.0: A bibliometric analysis and research agenda. *Int. J. Prod. Res., 57*(7), 2157-2179.

Liao, Y., Deschamps, F., Loures, E.F.R., Ramos, L.F.P. (2017). Past, present and future of Industry 4.0 - a systematic literature review and research agenda proposal. *Int. J. Prod. Res., 55*(12), 3609-3629. [http://dx.doi.org/10.1080/00207543.2017.1308576]

Saucedo-Martínez, J.A., Pérez-Lara, M., Marmolejo-Saucedo, J.A., Salais-Fierro, T.E., Vasant, P. (2018). Industry 4.0 framework for management and operations: a review. *J. Ambient Intell. Humaniz. Comput., 9*(3), 789-801.
[http://dx.doi.org/10.1007/s12652-017-0533-1]

Schneider, P. (2018). Managerial challenges of Industry 4.0: an empirically backed research agenda for a nascent field. *Rev. Manag. Sci., 12*(3), 803-848.
[http://dx.doi.org/10.1007/s11846-018-0283-2]

Schumacher, A., Erol, S., Sihn, W. (2016). A maturity model for assessing Industry 4.0 readiness and maturity of manufacturing enterprises. *Procedia CIRP, 52*, 161-166.
[http://dx.doi.org/10.1016/j.procir.2016.07.040]

Sony, M., Naik, S. (2019). Key ingredients for evaluating Industry 4.0 readiness for organizations: a literature review. *Benchmarking (Bradf.), 27*(7), 2213-2232.
[http://dx.doi.org/10.1108/BIJ-09-2018-0284]

Tantawi, K.H., Sokolov, A., Tantawi, O. (2019). Advances in industrial robotics: From industry 3.0 automation to industry 4.0 collaboration. *In 2019 4th Technology Innovation Management and Engineering Science International Conference,* 1-4.

Tjahjono, B., Esplugues, C., Ares, E., Pelaez, G. (2017). What does industry 4.0 mean to supply chain? *Procedia Manuf., 13*, 1175-1182.
[http://dx.doi.org/10.1016/j.promfg.2017.09.191]

Ustundag, A., Cevikcan, E. (2017). *Industry 4.0: managing the digital transformation.* Springer.

Vaidya, S., Ambad, P., Bhosle, S. (2018). Industry 4.0–a glimpse. *Procedia Manuf., 20*, 233-238.
[http://dx.doi.org/10.1016/j.promfg.2018.02.034]

Varghese, A., Tandur, D. (2014). *Wireless requirements and challenges in Industry 4.0. In 2014 international conference on contemporary computing and informatics, 634-638.*

Wu, D., Rosen, D.W., Wang, L. (2016). A framework for supply chain 4.0: A conceptual paper. *Int. J. Prod. Res., 54*(23), 1-16.

Xu, L.D., Xu, E.L., Li, L. (2018). Industry 4.0: state of the art and future trends. *Int. J. Prod. Res., 56*(8), 2941-2962.
[http://dx.doi.org/10.1080/00207543.2018.1444806]

Xu, X., Lu, Y., Vogel-Heuser, B., Wang, L. (2021). Industry 4.0 and Industry 5.0—Inception, conception and perception. *J. Manuf. Syst., 61*, 530-535.
[http://dx.doi.org/10.1016/j.jmsy.2021.10.006]

Yan, J., Meng, Y., Lu, L., Li, L. (2017). Industrial big data in an industry 4.0 environment: Challenges, schemes, and applications for predictive maintenance. *IEEE Access, 5*, 23484-23491.
[http://dx.doi.org/10.1109/ACCESS.2017.2765544]

Yavari, F., Pilevari, N. (2020). Industry revolutions development from Industry 1.0 to Industry 5.0 in manufacturing. *J. Ind. Strateg. Manag., 5*(2), 44-63.

## CHAPTER 8

# Innovations in Environment and Science: A Study on Models of Sustainable Environment across the World to Achieve SDG-9

**Navita Mahajan**[1,*]

[1] *Amity University, Uttar Pradesh, India*

**Abstract:** Digitalization in the modern world opens us to new options like information without any time constraints with continuous education, but it is also a means of survival. In order to effectively satisfy consumer expectations, a firm must integrate data and find methods to enhance its core business processes. The whole industry is working on innovative models that are eco-friendly and operate on a sustainable foundation for a better future. In order to demonstrate the fundamentals of sustainability with its application in contemporary society, the present study explores the distinctive ideas, real-world examples, and models that have been adopted globally as disruptive technologies. With regard to the success of these technical processes and the present change, the research has critically examined the advantages and difficulties. In the study, the issue of SDG-9 of the UN has also been connected to how the present technologies are contributing to the digitization of industry to achieve this objective of the United Nations. The study's foundation is secondary research, which includes data on many sustainable approaches to reaching technology in diverse modes. The research offers a few well-known ideas toward the conclusion to increase this transformation's visibility and usability. The study's implications indicate that everyone participating in the appropriate transition would gain, whether it be at the level of institutional, corporate, or public entities, for policy frameworks, model designs, and distribution through such digital and sustainable models.

**Keywords:** Digitalization, Innovation, Sustainable development, SDGs, Technology.

## INTRODUCTION

The idea of sustainable innovation is a conceptual one. It draws attention to the notion that sustainable innovation entails making adjustments to a company's philosophy, beliefs, products, processes, and practices in order to innovate in a

* **Corresponding author Navita Mahajan:** Amity University, Uttar Pradesh, India;
E-mail: Navitamahajan07@gmail.com

**Sukanta Kumar Baral, Richa Goel, Tilottama Singh, Erdener Kaynak & Vishal Jain (Eds.)**

way that creates environmental, social, and economic benefits (such as through effectively commercializing new ideas).

Sustainable product development and sustaining long-term corporate success are not incompatible goals. Businesses that prioritize sustainable production and consumption are increasingly benefiting from consumers' changing purchasing patterns, loyalty, and objectives.

The Global Sustainability Study (GSS), which Simon-Kucher & Partners performed in 2021, assessed more than 10,000 consumers from 17 different countries and offered insights into how consumers see sustainability and their willingness to pay for sustainable products.

It is significant to note that 80% of the respondents agreed that environmental sustainability is crucial and 63% of those respondents had already altered their purchase patterns to be more sustainable.

This shows that consumers are becoming more aware of the environmental effect of their purchase patterns, concerned about it, and ready to take action to lessen it. It also emphasizes the opportunity for businesses to generate profit *via* the creation and marketing of sustainable goods and services that cater to the demands of these environmentally concerned customers.

## Sustainable Innovation and Traditional Innovation

Three critical traits set sustainable innovation apart from other types of innovation.

• Through the incorporation of environmental, social, and economic factors into their innovation processes, sustainable innovations assist companies in becoming more sustainable. By actively incorporating issues like human rights and climate change into their innovation processes, businesses can develop solutions that not only bring economic value but also have a positive impact on society and the environment. According to the definition of sustainable innovation, the goal is to "meet the needs of current generations without jeopardizing the needs of future generations." Instead of concentrating just on immediate earnings, businesses that practice sustainable innovation search for methods that will have long-term benefits. They are more inclined to make investments in people and technology that will benefit the future.

• Sustainable innovation requires systemic thinking. Sustainable innovation involves companies looking outside of their own structure. They concentrate on the bigger system, which includes other businesses, the environment, stakeholders, and communities to which they contribute. They are aware of the system's dependencies and links, as well as how their actions may have an impact on other businesses and vice versa.

• When long-term sustainable innovations are firmly embedded in a company's culture, they are more likely to be successful. Sustainable innovations are more likely to be successful when they are fully integrated into a company's culture and strategy, as opposed to being considered as an afterthought or a distinct endeavor, unlike traditional innovations, which are often carried out within a separate R&D department or unit. Sustainable-oriented creative ideas will be extinguished before they have a chance to develop when sustainability is not ingrained in a company's culture.

**SDG 9**

**Goal:** Establishing a robust infrastructure, promoting inclusive and sustainable industrialization, and supporting innovation are the objectives.

**Motive:** The primary objectives of the SDGs are societal development, environmental conservation, and economic success. These goals all depend on one another, reinforce one another, and call for action in areas like infrastructure expenditure, industrial expansion, and technology development. The global economy's dynamic structure and the rise in inequality make industrialization crucial for sustaining development. Providing everyone with high-quality opportunities is supported by resilient and creative infrastructure. Recognizing the interconnectedness of the economic, social, and environmental difficulties, SDG 9 places a strong emphasis on the value of cooperation and communication in overcoming these issues. We may increase our understanding of business and technology by cooperating and communicating clearly.

Outcome Targets:

Target 9.1: Develop sustainable, resilient and inclusive infrastructures.

Target 9.2: Promote inclusive and sustainable industrialization.

Target 9.3: Increase access to financial services and markets.

Target 9.4: Upgrade all industries and infrastructures for sustainability.

Target 9.5: Enhance research and upgrade industrial technologies.

The Sustainable Development Goal 9 (SDG 9) calls for the development of resilient infrastructure, the advancement of inclusive and sustainable industrialization, and the promotion of innovation. This SDG addresses three essential components of sustainable development: infrastructure, industry, and innovation. Infrastructure offers the essential physical systems and buildings needed for a neighborhood or commercial firm to operate. When inclusive and sustainable, industrialization fosters economic growth, generates job opportunities, and reduces poverty, especially among low-income and excluded communities. The development of fresh talent and the improvement of the technological capabilities of the industrial sectors are both significantly influenced by innovation. People's living standards might improve rapidly due to inclusive and sustainable industrial growth, which also provides the technological tools necessary for industrialization that is ecologically benign.

## India's Development and SDG-9

India has made good progress in building vital infrastructure aimed at fostering growth. More national highways and roads were constructed that increased from 4,410 km in 2014–15 to 10,824 km in 2018–19. The cargo handling capacity of the 12 major ports was 1,477.22 million tonnes in 2018–19, which increased by 84% from 801 million tonnes in 2014–15. One of the greatest infrastructure projects in the world, the industrial corridor in India, is expected to cost US$90 billion. The objective is to create a high-tech industrial zone encompassing six states that will function as a hub for trade and commerce and inspire industrial hotspots around the nation.

Additionally, more than 7,000 modifications were made in 36 different states and union territories as part of the State Level Business Reforms Action Plan in order to strengthen the business climate. These efforts have started to pay off; in the World Bank's ranking of the ease of doing business, India has risen 79 spots in the last five years, from 142 in 2014 to 63 in 2019. India has been in the top 10 improvers list three years in a row. The next major accomplishment will be for the country to rank among the top 50 nations in the World Bank rankings as it works to realize its aim to establish a USD 5 trillion GDP by 2025.

## Sustainable Innovations: Objectives

Below, we introduce the personal, social, economic, and environmental aspects of sustainability.

• Human Sustainability: The strategy for preserving and strengthening society's human resources is known as human sustainability. In order to help preserve human capital, programs concentrating on human sustainability work to provide access to resources like healthcare and education, as well as services that promote wellbeing, skill development, and education. Finding a balance between future development and increasing everyone's health and prosperity while taking into account the effects on economic and ecological systems is crucial since natural resources and available space are limited. Organizations in the business world prioritize ideas like the development of human capital because they see themselves as an essential element of society. Human sustainability emphasizes the welfare and growth of all those involved in the creation of goods or the delivery of services, including those who are impacted indirectly, as well as other groups that may be impacted by the organization's activities, such as shareholders, the community, and the environment.

• Social Sustainability: Through investments in and the provision of services that support the wellbeing and development of communities and individuals, social sustainability aims to preserve and strengthen the components that make up the fabric of our society, such as values, norms, and shared interests. It considers a wide range of viewpoints, including the effects on various communities and cultures, and how various global processes affect society as a whole. It involves protecting the welfare of future generations and realizing the impact our activities have on other people and the environment. By placing a strong emphasis on ideas like cohesiveness, reciprocity, and honesty, as well as the value of interpersonal connections, it aims to preserve and improve social quality.

• Economic Sustainability: Maintaining capital is the goal of economic sustainability. While improving living conditions is the aim of economic sustainability, increasing social equality is the aim of social sustainability. Economic sustainability in the context of business refers to the effective use of assets to produce long-term financial stability and profitability for the company.

• Environmental Sustainability: By protecting natural resources, including land, air, water, minerals, *etc.*, environmental sustainability attempts to improve human wellbeing. Environmentally sustainable activities and programs are created to address the requirements of the current population without compromising the capacity of future generations to address their own demands. According to Dunphy, Benveniste, Griffiths, and Sutton (2000), environmental sustainability focuses on how enterprises may provide favorable economic results while posing no immediate or long-term environmental risks.

Adopting sustainable lifestyles enhances our quality of life while protecting the environment and natural resources for use by future generations. In the context of business, sustainability is incorporated into an organization's overarching strategy and applies to every facet of the firm's operations, from customer service to production and logistics.

Better air and water quality, fewer landfills, and more renewable energy sources have all benefited our civilization over time. We may contribute to constructive social change by incorporating sustainability into our daily lives. Adopting a sustainable lifestyle can assist in lowering the quantity of pollutants and carbon emissions released into the environment, enhancing its general safety and wellbeing. The entire world benefits from a focus on sustainability since it creates cleaner and healthier living circumstances for everyone.

## Research Gap

As it is currently understood, the study of entrepreneurship, social entrepreneurship, and everything else connected to the issue is a brand-new, alluring academic discipline. This claim is supported by the large number of explanations, frameworks, and descriptions that have been created in recent years.

Entrepreneurship is a complex mix of human ingenuity, organizational development, and trends. According to Kerlin, entrepreneurship is fundamentally social in nature and has a significant impact on society, particularly in terms of employment. The importance of entrepreneurship is primarily theorized as three interconnected dimensions that take into account the "environment", "social" and "economic" aspects. During the economic crisis that hit the European Union and drastically increased unemployment rate, entrepreneurs were primarily responsible for the rise in job creation and opportunities to revive the economy.

Numerous experts assert that entrepreneurship is a topic that is becoming more popular, and recent publications include a large number of articles and periodicals. However, there is still a great deal of controversy among experts regarding the precise definition of entrepreneurship. Given that entrepreneurship might be connected to any aspect of the company, it is possible that we will need to break the idea down into distinct components in order to properly characterize this phenomenon. According to Gibbs, entrepreneurship is the process of locating, assessing, and taking advantage of possibilities. Gartner asserts that the definition of entrepreneurship must go beyond this limited understanding and incorporate the pre-existing conceptual and explanatory frameworks. This idea cannot be defined by merely connecting words together, according to researchers.

Other academics have used a variety of terms to describe the practice of sustainable entrepreneurship, including "sustainable entrepreneurship", "values-oriented entrepreneurs", "sustainability-motivated entrepreneurs" and "sustainability-driven enterprise".

Wagner argues that sustainable entrepreneurship can be viewed as a strategic approach that prioritizes the survival of the natural world, life support in the pursuit of opportunities to bring about future success, process and service for gain, as well as including economic and non-economic achievements of entities and society.

## Approaches to Sustainability

• Green design: At its heart, green design strives to enhance certain product design components, such as by replacing virgin polymers with recycled ones.

• Eco-Design: Eco-design goes beyond green design by considering the entire life cycle of a product, as opposed to just individual materials. Examples include the selection of low-impact materials, optimized manufacturing, effective distribution, and optimized product lifetime.

• Sustainable Product Design: This strategy targets the triple bottom line and may be regarded as an all-encompassing sustainable design when social factors are taken into account throughout the design phase.

• Design for sustainability includes more than just product design; it takes a systemic approach and falls into four categories: design for symbolic and visual communications, design for material objects, design for activities and organized services, and design for complex systems or environments for living, working, playing, and learning. It also addresses issues like democracy and justice as it takes the big picture into account.

• Transformative Design: All of the aforementioned are included in it, as well as the design for entirely new perspectives on the experience of people in the future. This is frequently achieved by creating solutions that emphasize future ways of existence.

## Sustainable Innovations Around the World: A Compilation of Models across the World

### *Smog Free Project: Air Pollution can now be Transformed into Jewellery*

Dutch artist and inventor Daan Roosegaarde is renowned for developing the first smog vacuum cleaner. Ionization is the method used by the Smog Free Tower, a sizable air purification device that has a height of nearly 23 feet (7 meters). The tower can clean up to 30,000 $m^3$ of water each hour.

Smog Free Rings are made as part of Daan Roosegaarde's Smog Free Project using compressed smog particles that are gathered by the Smog Free Tower. According to the initiative, a person may help create roughly 10,700 square feet (1000 square meters) of pure air by purchasing and wearing one of these rings.

The initiative is well-known and has been highlighted in a number of media sites. Many cities throughout the world, including Poland, the Netherlands, China, South Korea, and China, have made attempts to install the towers. The idea aims to increase public awareness of the issue of smog and pollution in metropolitan areas and to inspire individuals to take action to address the issue.

On September 4, in Rotterdam, the Netherlands, Roosegaarde and his Studio Roosegaarde team made the official debut of this project. It consists of two parts: the world's biggest smog vacuum tower and a manufacturing process that transforms smog remnants into lovely jewelry.

The tower's top draws contaminated air in, which is cleaned before being released through vents on its six sides. The tower, according to the researchers, employs patented technology that is safe and tried-and-true, similar to the hospital air purification systems. In a public park known as Vierhavensstraat 52, a seven-meters high modular system with unique ionization technology, lightweight construction, and LEDs is installed. The tower can handle 30,000 cubic meters of air each hour and filter out ultra-fine pollutants. Fig. (**1**) depicts the smog free project.

**Fig. (1).** The Smog Free Project.
(Source: Architect Magazine).

## *The Green Building Initiative*

The Green Building Initiative (GBI), a global movement, strives to create durable, resource-conserving buildings. They provide a certification scheme for commercial buildings that adhere to their environmental goal. Their goal is to establish a global standard for the finest green building practices and to provide impartial evaluation tools for sustainability standards.

Sustainable building is the practice of constructing your home or other structures using sustainable design and construction techniques. Waste reduction, decreased carbon emissions, and the adoption of ecologically friendly products and procedures are all common ways to attain sustainability.

When it comes to environmentally friendly buildings, architects and designers consider how the completed product will impact the environment during its entire existence, not only when it is being built.

As people strive to construct a better future without damaging the environment, green building is becoming more and more common in commercial structures as well as residential houses, flats, and landed properties.

The idea of biophilic urbanism, or the desire to include elements of nature and natural processes into the planning and building of our cities, is adhered to by sustainable construction. These are typically achieved by including efficient natural waterway and energy systems, vegetation, and air-purifying plants for better and cleaner air circulation.

The green construction may be observed in biomimicry, or how we model natural processes in our architecture, as in the case of Melbourne's Council House 2, which was modeled by termite mounds in terms of aesthetics and temperature management. Fig. (**2**) explains a green construction.

**Fig. (2).** Green Construction.
(Source: Architect Magazine).

***Groasis Waterboxx: Now, it is Possible to Grow Trees in the Desert Region.***

The Groasis Waterboxx, a planting device that enables crop growth in deserts with little water, was created by Dutch flower exporter Pieter Hoff. A recycled paper "intelligent bucket" that can irrigate plants, incubate saplings, and germinate seeds makes up the Waterboxx irrigation system. It may be used in some of the most arid places on earth as it requires 90% less water than traditional growth methods.

The Waterboxx is a circular, 20-inch-wide polypropylene box. The box's chamber serves as a condensation and rainfall collecting point, holding water in place. A wick that is buried in the ground underneath the box drips water to the plant's roots gradually each day. As the plant develops, its size increases, causing its roots to eventually find their own water source. After this is done, the box may be taken out.

Although the Waterboxx seems to operate on a fairly simple basis, it has achieved astounding results. Hoff tested the gadget for three years in the Moroccan Sahara Desert. 90% of the trees that were planted survived when the Waterboxx was removed. Conversely, just 10% of the trees planted without the box survived despite being watered.

The Waterboxx would subsequently be put to the test in 25 locations across eight countries, including the United States, according to Hoff.

Hoff also made a biodegradable version of the box that distributes nutrients into the soil as it decomposes. According to Hoff and his company, AquaPro, the Waterboxx will eventually be made accessible to every manufacturer as a non-exclusive, free license. Fig. (**3**) shows Groasis Waterboxx as a device to grow trees in dry places.

**Fig. (3).** Groasis Waterboxx. (Source: Inhabitat.com).

### *Supermarket Herb Gardens: Less Waste, Better Taste*

In order to cut waste and provide consumers with the freshest product possible, the Dutch grocery store company Albert Heijn planted indoor herb gardens in all of its locations in 2017. Together with the design company Studiomfd, the project was created. The herbs are aged off-site before being delivered to retail outlets to guarantee maximum freshness.

Albert Heijn allows clients to cut and take the required amount of herbs, avoiding the usage of plastic packaging. Indoor herb gardens have been installed in all of its stores. An example of a simple, sustainable invention with widespread beneficial consequences is this kind of initiative. Another choice is to try growing your own herbs at home.

It is a new, useful idea that minimizes waste and satisfies customer desires by keeping fresh herbs available whenever required.

The environment will benefit from this approach as well since plants require fewer plastic bags to pack and pesticides to grow.

The concept is relatively new, but because it is accessible and innovative, it is growing in popularity.

The plan was well received, and everyone wanted to move forward. Despite the fact that there are other concepts, we will just examine one here.

People may grow mint and many other plants by soaking their roots in water prior to planting. It is true that not everyone has a green thumb. Additionally, time is equally as significant as talent. If you want a healthy herb garden in your yard, you need to put some effort into it in addition to worrying about bugs, kids stepping on it, and other issues.

Growing plants from seed is certainly the least costly way to generate plants for your garden, provided you have the room to sow and pot them . But if you are an urban gardener, your sole area for producing your own food can be a balcony or window ledge. Fig. (**4**) is an example of a supermarket herb garden.

### *AirCarbon: A Sustainable Plastic for the Future*

The business that developed the substance known as AirCarbon, which has won several awards for its unique and sustainable qualities, is called Newlight Technologies. It is created from carbon emissions that would otherwise be dumped into the environment and has several uses. The whole production and use process has been shown to have a net-negative carbon footprint, making it ecologically beneficial and sustainable. As it is not created from oil like other plastics, it is less expensive than other synthetic materials.

**Fig. (4).** Supermarket Herb Garden.
(Source: www.bbeb.com).

After 10 years of research, Mark Herrema and his business partner and childhood friend Kenton Kimmel found Newlight Technologies in California in 2003. With a revolutionary chemical called AirCarbon that is made from methane using an innovative, practical, and environmentally friendly production process, they thought they had found THE solution to replacing conventional plastic.

The first step in this procedure involves capturing methane emissions from energy plants, landfills, and dairy farms. Methane is a quick-acting greenhouse gas with a greater capacity for warming than $CO_2$. The Newlight reactor's efficiency, according to its designers, is its yield ratio, which is supposedly nine times greater than that of conventional reactors. The gas and air are combined within a reactor to make liquid polymer, which is subsequently turned into plastic pellets.

This significantly alters the cost structure of the greenhouse gas to the plastic conversion process, allowing AirCarbon to produce compounds that are more cost-competitive with polymers derived from crude oil, such as polypropylene and polyethylene. With Sprint for the hulls of Smartphones, Dell for some of its laptops' packaging, and a furniture maker for a number of chairs, some scientists are still skeptical regarding its importance (Is the method commercially viable? Does AirCarbon actually uphold its carbon negative nature, and if so, is it not only a drop in the ocean?). Fig. (**5**) demonstrates Aircarbon.

**Fig. (5).** Aircarbon.
(Source: www.newlight.com).

### *Solar Glass Might Cover our House in the Future*

The development of solar glass by the researchers of the University of Michigan as part of a sustainable engineering program has the potential to completely alter how we construct homes and businesses. As its name suggests, this device has the ability to catch and store solar energy. This technology has drawn a lot of interest because of the possible changes it may make to the landscape of renewable energy.

Between 5 and 7 billion square meters of window space is thought to be accessible, according to research. According to some estimations, solar glass technology has a huge potential to provide up to 40% of the United States' whole energy consumption. This implies a tremendous potential for the technology. Organic solar cells are non-toxic, light, and semi-transparent, and they offer the potential for reduced production costs. However, they frequently perform poorly, and their lifespan has not been found to be great.

The transparent solar coating, according to Ubiquitous Energy, the firm developing this technology, can transform ultraviolet and near-infrared light into power while still allowing visible light to flow through. This is accomplished by using common glass coating equipment to add organic layers directly on the glass. With the use of this technology, energy may be generated while maintaining glass's transparency. The firm was established by a small team of MIT researchers and professors who produced a very basic proof of concept about eight years ago.

In addition to conducting research and developing the technology, the firm has moved to Redwood City in Northern California and now employs a staff of more than 20 people who are committed to building, testing, and investigating various uses of solar glass. The business has a number of patents covering both graded solar cell technology and organic solar cell technology as a consequence of their work. They were acknowledged for their ingenuity and creativity in this sector and were therefore shown to be the forerunners in this technology.

Despite vast variances, passive curtain wall construction costs—technical jargon for a standard glass exterior—are frequently $100 per square foot, claims Hardev. IIis calculations indicatc that thc cost of an activc (solar ccll) curtain wall would likely be 30% more, or $130 per square foot, with wiring. Fig. (**6**) demonstrates a solar glass.

**Fig. (6).** Solar Glass.
(Source: Forbes.com).

### *Demetra: Reducing Food Waste Organically is Easier than you Think*

A natural food preservation system named Demetra was created by an Italian start-up business called Green Code. Demetra, which is comprised completely of plant extracts, extends the shelf life of fresh products, making it a sustainable and environmentally beneficial method of food preservation.

It would be unnecessary to keep produce frozen throughout transportation, which would result in significant energy savings. The method aids grocery stores and supermarkets in reducing food wastage in addition to increasing the freshness and maturity of vegetables.

Green Code Srl is a cutting-edge start-up from Trentino-Alto Adige (Italy) that specializes in cleantech and sustainable technology. By combining traditional techniques with biotechnologies and environmental engineering, Green Code creates novel solutions to reduce the negative environmental consequences of human activities. We provide modern, eco-friendly methods for reducing waste, enhancing output, and utilizing less natural resources.

Green Code is tackling the issue of food waste in the supply chain for fruits and vegetables, as well as its impacts on the environment and society, through Demetra. The economics and sustainability of how these commodities are stored are also improved. Demetra is a natural post-harvest solution for fruit preservation that helps to decrease food waste and lengthen the shelf life of fresh goods.

Fruit ripening is inhibited by Demetra, strengthening the fruit's natural defenses against viruses and stresses. It instantly lowers food waste while also enhancing fruit quality, lowering the ecological footprint and energy expenses related to cold storage. Demetra, which draws its inspiration from nature, is entirely composed of plant extracts and gives users control over the fruit in a way that is akin to how plants do it. All of its parts are suited for organic farming and safe for both humans and the environment. Fig. (7) depicts Demetra.

**Fig. (7).** Demetra.
(Source: ITU Hub).

### *The Seabin: Cleaning the Oceans Safely with Trash Bins*

Two surfers, Andrew Turton and Pete Ceglinski, created the Seabin with the intention of assisting in the cleanup of rubbish from the world's oceans. Clean water can flow out of the Seabin after a catch bag filters out and collects garbage, detergents, and oil.

A submersible water pump is used to pump the water out of the bin once it has been thoroughly cleaned. It just has to be emptied once a month, but it might greatly reduce water pollution in ports and harbors all around the world. Engineering that is sustainable triumphs!

There is a plastic problem in Montenegro's Bay of Kotor.

The beachfront region is where the Adriatic Sea's sparkling waves crash into the mountains, making it a UNESCO World Heritage Site. According to research by the Institute of Marine Biology in Montenegro, the local shoreline is more polluted with plastic than the average beach in Europe.

However, Porto Montenegro, a marina in the midst of the Bay of Kotor, received a 5 Gold Anchor Platinum accreditation in 2017 from The Yacht Harbour Association (TYHA) and the Marina Industries Association (MIA) for exceptional marina operations, including high standards of environmental management.

A submersible water pump that can move 25.000 liters of water per hour is immediately plugged into a 110/230 volt outlet and draws water from the surface, passing it *via* a catch bag inside the Seabin. Litter and other debris are then captured in the catch bag and the water is pushed back into the marina. Depending on the weather, an interior sleeve that slides up and down may be added. Fig. (**8**) demonstrates the Seabin project.

**Fig. (8).** The Seabin Project.
(Source: www.forbes.com).

### *Sundrop Farms: Energy-Efficient Agriculture*

Water is taken from the Spencer Gulf, which is desalinated before being used to irrigate farms in Port Augusta, South Australia. All activities on the farm, including the desalination process, are run entirely on solar energy.

Sundrop Farms' sustainable agriculture technology uses fewer limited resources than conventional farming methods. This environmentally friendly farming idea depends on thermal desalination and concentrated solar power.

Sundrop integrates solar power, electricity generation, freshwater conservation, production, and hydroponics to enable the year-round production of premium produce at high yields with consistent quality and deliver a significant reduction in fossil fuel and water use through innovative use of renewable energy/low carbon technologies.

Sundrop establishes long-term collaborations with its clients for each new project it develops, allowing the creation of facilities.

The firm really believes that they should serve more people than simply their shareholders; thus, in addition to maximizing profits, they also aim to improve the environment and the community in which we operate. Fig. (**9**) depicts Sundrop farms.

**Fig. (9).** Sundrop Farms.
(Source: www.sundropfarms.com).

### *The Veganbottle: An all-natural Alternative to Plastic Bottles*

The Veganbottle is a bio-plastic bottle developed by LYSPACKAGING made entirely of biodegradable materials, including the cap and wrapping. The raw material used to make the Veganbottle is extracted from sugarcane, which is a renewable and sustainable resource. The production of the bottle itself utilizes less energy than traditional manufacturing, and sugar cane requires significantly less water than other crops. A variety of containers (bottles, jars, pill boxes, flasks, and caps) known as Veganbottles are manufactured from the leftovers of diverse co-products from the plant or minerals. The products are produced from recycled flax, hemp, reed, bagasse, shells, reeds, seeds, kernels, and wood fibres. These organic components are converted into bio-plastic to create containers that may be blow molded or injection molded in the same manner as conventional plastics. The "organic recycling" towards the end of this bio-plastic's life is different. The retired bottles are crushed to create "a recycled vegetable bio-plastic", which is accepted worldwide.

The first biobased polymers were first made from maize (cob) and intended for food, although they have been accessible for more than 20 years. The Veganbottle has been explained in Fig. (**10**).

**Fig. (10).** The Veganbottle.
(Source: www.veganbottle.com).

### *CloudFisher: Converting fog into Drinking Water*

With the help of CloudFisher, created by Aqualonis, people of coastal or mountainous areas may be able to transform fog into drinkable water that may also be utilized for forestry projects or to irrigate crops.

It is made of a 3D mesh material that can withstand strong winds and still hold water. It comes in various sizes to accommodate the needs of both individual users and large villages. People all across the world are already utilizing the green innovation example to their advantage. After years of study and testing, Peter Trautwein (Aqualonis GmbH) created the CloudFisher for the Water Foundation: a reliable fog collector that efficiently transforms moisture from the air into potable water in locations with heavy fog. The fog collector is the first to be capable of withstanding winds up to 120 km/h. It uses no energy, is incredibly low maintenance, and is quick and simple to install. The CloudFisher's effectiveness ensures that many individuals will have access to low-cost, high-quality drinking water that satisfies WHO criteria. The daily water yield ranges from 6 to 22 liters per square meter, depending on the region and the time of year. However, the meshes are also used to collect water during monsoon seasons, which occur from November to June and following the fog season, as in Eritrea, in addition to horizontally linked polyethylene sheets. The collected rainwater can be utilized for agriculture and livestock irrigation, or it can be used as drinking water, depending on its purity. The CloudFisher ensures that many people will have access to affordable, WHO-standard drinking water of the highest quality. The water that is retrieved can also be used for farming, cattle breeding, reforestation efforts, and commercial endeavors.

Every fog project begins with the first step of collecting meteorological data on the wind speed and direction, temperature, relative humidity, amount of precipitation, and amount of water collected. The results of this evaluation are used to assess the suitability of the location for harvesting water from fog and to determine the best orientation of the collectors with respect to the wind. CloudFisher is depicted in Fig. (**11**).

**Fig. (11).** Cloud Fisher.
(Source: www.wasserstiftung.com).

### *Waitrose Delivery Vans Fuelled by Food Waste*

The use of biomethane-powered vans, like those introduced by the British supermarket chain Waitrose last year, is crucial as delivery trucks are a significant source of carbon emissions.

Even some of its fusilli pasta is packaged in boxes produced partially from recycled food waste, which the company claims decreases the consumption of virgin tree pulp by 15% and cuts greenhouse gas emissions by a fifth. Waitrose, however, wants to go further with the issue—both literally and figuratively. Waitrose, an expensive British grocery store that stopped throwing its leftovers in the trash as early as 2012, has always had a problem with food waste.

Food waste in the UK is an issue that has to be addressed immediately because, despite the fact that 8.4 million people there struggle to put food on the table, food waste generated by homes alone was predicted to exceed 7.3 million metric tonnes in 2015.

The trucks can go up to 500 miles on what is essentially decaying food, which is nearly twice as far as the current standard, according to The Times, which says that Waitrose is collaborating with CNG Fuels to refill 10 of their vehicles using 100% sustainable biomethane.

According to CNG Fuels, switching to biomethane will pay for itself in two to three years because it is 40% less expensive than diesel.

The CEO of CNG Fuels, Philip Field, claims that renewable biomethane has a range of up to 500 miles, which gives it a significant edge over diesel and makes it a lot more affordable and environmentally friendly fuel option. Waitrose delivery is explained below in Fig. (**12**).

**Fig. (12).** Waitrose Delivery.
(Source: The Times).

### *Bakeys: A Delicious way to Replace Plastic Cutlery*

Since plastic cutlery cannot be recycled, it creates a lot of waste each year. Narayana Peesapaty created Bakeys, a brand of sustainable alternative to plastic cutlery. There are three types of edible cutlery under the Bakeys brand: plain, sweet, and savory. They are made entirely of natural ingredients and will biodegrade if not used.

Since 2011, Bakeys has produced over 1.5 million edible spoons in eight flavors: sugar, ginger-cinnamon, ginger-garlic, celery, black pepper, cumin, mint-ginger, and carrot-beet. They are made from a mixture of rice, wheat, and millet flour. A Bakeys spoon can live up to three years if kept in its packaging, but Peesapaty asserts that when left outside, the spoons will decay in four to five days.

Peesapaty is also interested in lowering production costs and establishing a global distribution network. In the Bakeys advertising video, he expresses his hope that raising the firm's output will encourage farmers to concentrate their efforts on cultivating millet rather than rice, which needs 60 times as much water. Three million spoons will be produced using the crowdsourced money, and eventually forks and chopsticks as well.

The production of plastic increased from 15 million tonnes in 1964 to 311 million tonnes in 2014, according to Forbes, which also states that "the figure is anticipated to triple by 2050, unless some type of racial or ethnic conflict occurs." Plastic bag bans have been implemented in cities from Los Angeles to Kathmandu, and algae-based water bottles and biodegradable kitchenware are also available.

It will be interesting to see if they are as tasty as Peesapaty promises. The Bakeys spoon is in the race to become the first edible object to be mass-produced in history; perhaps this crispy cutlery is a component of the fundamental revolution that has to take place. Bakeys cutlery has been shown in Fig. (**13**).

**Fig. (13).** Bakeys Cutlery.
(Source: Bloomberg.com).

## *Outerwall EcoATM: Get Cash for your old Electronics*

The EcoATM is a machine that takes old electronics in exchange for cash. Since electronic items generate a significant quantity of rubbish, recycling efforts are being stepped up to convince people not to throw away their outmoded equipment.

Bring your gadget to an EcoATM kiosk for evaluation and valuation, and you can leave with cash that is transferred directly to your bank account, PayPal, or in the form of vouchers. A compelling argument for going green! There have only been a few alternatives for recycling old cell phones: returning them to the manufacturer, sending them to one of the many websites that pay cash for used gadgets, or taking them to a cell phone retailer in person. The simplest answer to date is EcoATM, an automatic E-cycling facility that has recently been launched in the Nebraska Furniture Mart. The San The first EcoATM was installed that could scan cell phones, estimate their secondary market value, and give payment in the form of cash or in-store credit. The phone is taken to a recycling bin if it is no longer valuable, if it is too old or shows too many indications of wear. Later this year, EcoATM intends to expand the system's distribution to San Diego, Texas, Washington State, and Vermont. Next year, EcoATMs should be available in big-box stores all around the nation. The devices may be able to handle anything in the future, including laptops and MP3 players.

Instead of hurrying to find a method to recycle them, you can bring old electronics to your local WalMart, drop them off, and exchange them for cash, allowing you to continue shopping with a few extra bucks in your pocket. EcoATM has been explained in Fig. (**14**).

**Fig. (14).** EcoATM.
(Source: fastcompany.com).

## *Asking Machines for Help: $CO_2$-reducing Robots*

Many people do not want to deal with the hassle of cooking after a long day at work, which makes perfect sense. If that happens, you can solve the problem by using DoorDash or Uber Eats. However, doing so results in more than 6 million tonnes of emissions being produced by food delivery every year. This six million tonnes of emissions will soon be history as a result of the creation of autonomous robots by Kiwibot, which is a Colombian startup.

Kiwibot has created small autonomous robots. Each Kiwibot robot did roughly 400 deliveries in 2017. Their delivery rates will increase as their technology does. Kiwibot has agreements in place with several nations, even stretching as far as the Middle East. As a result, if you have a need for anything delectable, you may anticipate arobot from Kiwibot knocking on your door. Fig. (**15**) depicts a $CO_2$-reducing robot.

**Fig. (15).** $CO_2$-Reducing Robot.
(Source: www.bbeb.com).

## Sustainability Practices in Corporates

**Biogen:** In terms of the environment, Biogen is a carbon-neutral business, which means it has successfully offset and reduced carbon emissions from its operations. The company also actively participates in community outreach by offering STEM education opportunities and encourages diversity and inclusivity in hiring, particularly in the advancement of women on leadership positions.

**Adidas:** Adidas is a German-based company that manufactures sporting goods under the Adidas and Reebok brands and operates globally. To promote a good work-life balance for its employees, Adidas uses innovative scheduling and time off models, such as the lifetime working time account, which enables employees to save time for paid vacation.

Among the goals of its responsibility program are the enhancement of working conditions, social responsibility, product safety, and the prevention of climate change. In its list of sustainability indicators for 2019, Kesko showed a steadily rising number of community projects such as youth sports, veteran care, scientific research, and environmental organizations.

**BMW:** BMW's environmental initiatives begin on the assembly line as it continuously works to reduce the emissions of the vehicles it produces and offers electric and hybrid options to its customers. BMW, a global German corporation, has been working to lessen its internal environmental impact since it appointed one of the first environmental officers in history in 1973. BMW is rethinking its strategies to engage an aging workforce rather than alienate it because it is committed to giving equal opportunity to all of its employees. In order to help employees strike a balance between work and life, BMW actively pushes women to assume leadership positions and uses flexible scheduling and career opportunities.

## IMPLICATIONS

It is undoubtedly challenging for a country to reach its own goal of having a GDP of $5 trillion by 2024. Nigeria is anticipated to be essential to achieving the Sustainable Development Goals (SDGs), as well as taking part in this global transition. By 2040, India's energy consumption is projected to quadruple, with a potential increase in electricity demand (three times). The best course of action is to use renewable energy to meet this rise in demand.

India wants to produce 175 GW of renewable energy, of which 100 GW will come from solar power, 10 GW from biopower, 60 GW from wind power, and 5 GW from small-scale hydropower.

A youth-friendly education policy, the implementation of skill development programs, pertinent updated educational materials, the availability of qualified teaching staff, and most importantly, exposure of children to the environment are all necessary for providing good and quality education. To modernize the nation's armed forces, the Sustainable Development Goals also seek to encourage opportunities for all people to learn new things throughout their lives.

The Smart Cities Mission of the Indian government seeks to modernize and revitalize 109 cities throughout the country in order to create sustainable, environmentally friendly communities.

A sustainable smart city is yet another result of "innovation that is prompted by sustainability" that employs information technology and modern communication technologies to improve people's quality of life and productivity.

There is still work to be done and to invest in a future with zero carbon emissions. Businesses, industries, and the government must work together to tackle the issue and find innovative solutions to build a sustainable, carbon-neutral economy.

## CONCLUSION

Smart workers gravitate toward sustainable businesses, which are better able to attract talent than their non-sustainable competitors. According to 44% of millennials and 49% of Gen Z respondents to a recent Deloitte survey, personal ethics have had an impact on their professional decisions.

In other words, a focus on sustainability encourages both increased and higher-quality innovation. Businesses engaged in sustainable innovation think more broadly and gain knowledge from other viewpoints. They receive information and solutions from outside sources, such as stakeholders and other sectors. According to research by Caroline Flammer and Aleksandra Kacperczyk, organizations that consider stakeholders issues more significant patents.

A study by Natalia Ortiz-deMandojana and Tima Bansal found that companies with a sustainability focus were more likely to endure crises and price volatility, and produce more revenue over the long term than those without one. Furthermore, businesses that value sustainability are more resilient than their competitors, which is crucial in today's volatile environment.

## BIBLIOGRAPHY

Casallas-Ojeda, M., Soto-Paz, J., Alfonso-Morales, W., Oviedo-Ocaña, E.R., Komilis, D. (2021). Optimization of operational parameters during anaerobic co-digestion of food and garden waste. *Environ. Process., 8*(2), 769-791.
[http://dx.doi.org/10.1007/s40710-021-00506-2]

Goldstein, A.O., Gans, S.P., Ripley-Moffitt, C., Kotsen, C., Bars, M. (2018). Use of expired air carbon monoxide testing in clinical tobacco treatment settings. *Chest, 153*(2), 554-562.
[http://dx.doi.org/10.1016/j.chest.2017.11.002] [PMID: 29137909]

Goratela, R. (2021). *Green Building: The Future of Construction and Architecture. Architectures Ideas.https://architecturesideas.com/green-building/.*

Hipwell, D. (2017). *Retail Editor. (2017, February 9). Waitrose Lorries to be Fuelled by Gas from Rotting Food. The Times. https://www.thetimes.co.uk/article/waitrose-lorries-to-be-fuelled-by-gas-from-rot-ing-food-k0rnw9scn.*

Lundell, C., Thomas, J. (2020). *Proceedings of the AHFE 2020 Virtual Conferences on Design for Inclusion, Affective and Pleasurable Design, Interdisciplinary Practice in Industrial Design, Kansei Engineering, and Human Factors for Apparel and Textile Engineering,* July 16–20, 2020USA248-254. Springer International Publishing..

Sarsour, J., Stegmaier, T., Gresser, G. (2017). 3D textile structures for harvesting water from fog: overview and perspectives. *Textile Finishing: Recent Developments and Future Trends,* 325-343.

Schwartz, W.R., Kembhavi, A., Harwood, D., Davis, L.S. Human detection using partial least squares analysis. In *2009 IEEE 12th international conference on computer vision* (pp. 24-31). IEEE..

Plunkett, E., Negoita, L., Sevilla, C., Velasco, N., & Díaz, P. J. (2023). Enhancing restoration success of rare plants in an arid-tropical climate through water-saving technologies: a case study of Scalesia affinis ssp. brachyloba in the Galapagos Islands.. (2009). *Peer J, 11*, e16367.

Schwarz-Herion, O. (2019). The role of smart cities for the realization of the sustainable development goals.

Shields, K. (2022). *Sustainable Innovation.* Leading Innovation.

Walshe, R., Casey, K., Kernan, J., Fitzpatrick, D. (2020). AI and big data standardization: Contributing to United Nations sustainable development goals. *J. ICT Stand., 8*(2), 77-106. [http://dx.doi.org/10.13052/jicts2245-800X.821]

Xiao, L., Feng, Q., Liang, S., Sonne, S.B., Xia, Z., Qiu, X., Li, X., Long, H., Zhang, J., Zhang, D., Liu, C., Fang, Z., Chou, J., Glanville, J., Hao, Q., Kotowska, D., Colding, C., Licht, T.R., Wu, D., Yu, J., Sung, J.J.Y., Liang, Q., Li, J., Jia, H., Lan, Z., Tremaroli, V., Dworzynski, P., Nielsen, H.B., Bäckhed, F., Doré, J., Le Chatelier, E., Ehrlich, S.D., Lin, J.C., Arumugam, M., Wang, J., Madsen, L., Kristiansen, K. (2015). A catalog of the mouse gut metagenome. *Nat. Biotechnol., 33*(10), 1103-1108. [http://dx.doi.org/10.1038/nbt.3353] [PMID: 26414350]

# CHAPTER 9

# Understanding of General Population toward Global Energy Crisis: A Qualitative Study

**Jaya Bharti**[1,*] and **Hitaishi Singh**[2]

[1] *Department of Psychology ANDNNMM (CSJM University) Kanpur, India*

[2] *Department of Home Science (Extension Education & Communication) ANDNNMM (CSJM University) Kanpur, India*

**Abstract:** If one goes back to the history of world energy requirements with regard to the consumption and sources of energy, the last century was largely dependent on various forms of fossil fuels. These fossil fuel sources of energy have served humanity for a prolonged era and powered the Industrial Revolution in the 17th to 18th century. However, like other natural resources, the reserves of fossil fuels are also depleting fast and are anticipated to finish completely in the coming years. Currently, the world is witnessing the greatest ever energy crisis. In the last few years, major events, especially the lockdown during the COVID-19 pandemic, post-pandemic economic rebound, the recent Russia-Ukraine war and extreme weather conditions occurring due to greenhouse gas emissions and global warming have led to a severe energy crunch in terms of fossil fuels. This has impacted the lives of the general population to a greater extent. In any such crisis, not only does the general population get directly affected, but it also plays a key role in energy conservation if they understand the nuances of the problem. Hence, an attempt has been made to find out the understanding of the general population, both males and females, about various terms related to energy and its sources, and problems resulting from this global energy crisis and their solutions. Responses were analyzed, conclusions were drawn and suggestions were provided to deal with the problem in an orderly manner.

**Keywords:** Alternative Energy, Energy Crisis, Energy Resources, Renewable Energy.

## INTRODUCTION

Energy is the primary source of life on this earth; however, in the form of fuel, energy was the key player in the industrialization of the modern world, which began in Europe. Energy, therefore, is pivotal to attain material prosperity for any

* **Corresponding author Jaya Bharti:** Department of Psychology ANDNNMM (CSJM University) Kanpur, India; E-mail: Jayabharti_kn18@csjmu.ac.in

**Sukanta Kumar Baral, Richa Goel, Tilottama Singh, Erdener Kaynak & Vishal Jain (Eds.)**

nation. This accumulation of material wealth ultimately becomes the medium for the overall development and growth of any nation. It is this reason why today all the countries across the world are desperately making all possible efforts to trap the various sources of energy in the form of fuel to achieve the path of development. "In the last century, there has been a huge exploitation of natural resources of energy for multiple purposes. Especially the industrialized nations took uninterrupted supply of cheap hydrocarbons for granted and exploited it to the extent of exhaustion" (Nashawi *et al.*, 2010).

It is estimated that if the exploitation of these energy resources continues the way it is taking place at present, then there will be a grave shortage of these resources on the earth after 2050. This situation of shortfall or interruption in the supply of energy resources is called an "energy crisis". The energy crisis data shows that the global energy requirement has increased tremendously over the last 200 years. Experts in this field know that the resources are close to exhaustion. It is only a matter of time before conventional energy resources will end, for which we are really not ready right now. "The link between reckless consumption of these fuel energy sources for different activities, greenhouse gas emission and its consequences as global warming has been well proven through research evidence" (Reijnders & Huijbregts, 2007; Nashawi, 2010; Martins, 2018). There will certainly be a question - What are we going to do in the future without the fossil fuels that we have used in the past? The fossil fuels that have served the energy demands of mankind for long. The answer certainly is that our future is bleak as far as the availability of conventional sources of energy is concerned. During COVID-19 and afterward, the crisis became even more serious. "Europe and Asia both have had very strong economic recovery post third wave of COVID-19 pandemic. This raised tremendous demand for energy not only from industry, infrastructure sector and other businesses but also from domestic (homes) front" (Bordoff, 2021). Likewise, "in the first half of 2021, the demand for Liquified Natural Gas (LNG) continued to grow due to switching from coal to gas to fulfill industrial power needs, especially from China" (Froley, 30 June, 2021).

"Also due to obstacles on coal-fired descent, economic rebound, and cold weather, demand for LNG increased in countries like Japan, Korea, and Taiwan." (Elliott, 14 September, 2021)

"The picture seemed horrifying. Power crunch in China has already started leading to the closure of factories", and in "India too, the situation is getting worse due to coal shortage"(Singh and Zhang, 27 September, 2022, S. Sundaria, *et al.*, 05 October, 2022). This is not only hampering the already obstructed and slowed economic growth but also has multiple ill consequences.

Therefore, "many countries of the world have started taking serious measures to deal with this situation by reducing the use of fossil fuels and promoting the use of innovative new energy sources such as solar power, wind power and biodiesel and increasing stocks" (Lazarus and Eselt, 2018; Leonard *et al.*, 2020).

Perhaps this was the reason why 193 countries of the world came together and signed the official document of SDGs 2030, formally named "Transforming Our World: The 2030 Agenda for Sustainable Development" (Pietrocemoli et.ai, 2019; United Nations, 2015; Ahmed T. and D. Zhang, November, 2020). These goals were formulated and articulated by the United Nations after 2015 to set the development agenda for the future.

"A lot of attention and concern has been shown towards energy and its judicious and clean consumption by most countries of the world considering it as the key component for ensuring sustainable and inclusive development across the globe" (Pietrosemoli *et al.*, 2019). "This is confirmed by the fact that the world's energy utilization has increased considerably from 8,588.9 million tons in 1995 to 13,147.3 million tons in 2015", which "further rose to 0.8% in 2020. This was 0.2% higher than the projected worldwide energy consumption by the International Energy Agency (IEA) of 0.6% for 2020 as compared to 2019" (Ahmad *et al.*, 2020; Dong *et al.*, 2020a; IEA, 2020b).

This is a matter of great worry for the whole world community, and this is not where we are going to stop. Despite several attempts to keep a check on the amount and type of energy consumption, the picture is grim. Several international research projects on global energy needs and consumption have been carried out (Cooperation, 2015). "Global energy projects have been taken on radar and investigated by national agencies of various governments and international organizations" (Kohl W.L. Oil, 2019). But as technological advancement and population growth are taking place at a rapid pace, the requirement for energy usage is also rising. "Today's call is making the supply of reliable and clean energy sources available and accessible for better and improved wellbeing of mankind", which seems to be a big challenge (Central Statistics Office, Ministry of Statistics and Programme Implementation, GOI, 2020).

In addition, the "shift in the demand of coal in the power and manufacturing sector is expected to lead to further increased future energy consumption and consequently crisis" (Ahmad T. and D. Zhang, November, 2020). The critical situation that the world is expected to face in the coming years is the constantly increasing demand for energy from all regions across the globe. However, "this demand may vary from country to country and region to region". In this context, IEA (2017) estimates that "out of total projected world energy requirement of 739 billion btu, the non-OECD (Organization of Economic Co-operation and Development) States are expected to have a share of 64%, with Asia emerging as the major player in this field." Recently, India and China saw unanticipated shortfall of coal for their utilities. "India took strong steps restricting coal supplies for other purposes, keeping supplies only for power generation sector because 70% of the total power in the country is generated by burning coal. This was a preferential measure by the Indian Government where non-power users had no access to coal energy" (Cooperation, 2015). Likewise, "The Chinese government implied rationing over power supplies to factories in various provinces of the country to fight with the crisis" (Ozili, September 2022). "So far, oil consumption is a concern; India and China are respectively the fourth and second largest importer in the world"; however, due to rapid population growth, India's energy consumption is also growing at a relatively faster rate (Anandan and Ramaswamy, September 2015). "Global energy crises and rise of around 11% in demand of Liquified Petroleum Gas (LPG), petrol and diesel for fuel for domestic use in August 2021 caused Indian households to suffer due to the rise in the oil price of global oil products" (Edwin, T., 29 September, 2021).

Likewise, "India, for instance, is expected to contribute toward 25% of the total world's energy need by 2040 while China's energy needs are expected to double by 2040". (Ahmad T. and D. Zhang, November, 2020). Another important point is related directly to equal and equitable representation as well as share from all the countries of different regions. Thus, though all the countries have signed the Paris Agreement that sets the goal to keep temperature rises below 2°C, but if the status of increasing global demand for energy continues with varied contexts, this will certainly result in a devastating impact leading to persistent global warming and its related effects" (IEA, 2017; Kona A. *et al.*, 2018).

Under such circumstances, "various renewable energy sources have come up as the most robust solution to deal with the energy crisis when the COVID-19 pandemic hit the world. This, with the current severe coal crisis, has led the world, especially European countries, to think about other renewable and sustainable energy systems, thereby helping in reducing unsustainable negative energy systems" (Martins *et al.*, 2018). "There are versatile sources such as sun, wind, biomass, small hydro and co-generation, bagasse, biogas, ocean, geothermal, *etc.* that have a high potential for generating energy" (Anandan *et al.*, February, 2022). "The most important benefit of renewable energy is that it has no carbon footprints thus, it does not pollute our environment" (Goldemberg, 2006).

"It is presumed that even if the global lockdown continues for an uncertain period during the COVID-19 pandemic, the demand for such renewable energy will not go down; rather, it would be seven times greater than what it was in 2008-2009 even if the lockdown is lifted at a larger scale as a consequent impact in terms of Global Financial Crisis" (The Indian Express, 2020). This rise in demand for these renewable energy sources may be due to many factors, such as lower operating costs and preferred access. It is also important to mention that the general population, which is getting and going to be the most affected by the energy crisis in the near future, can also play a crucial role in providing some solution to the problem by doing their bit. "The energy 'problem' is not only related to science and technology, but it is equally related to culture, social perspective, the will to change our societal energy behavior, and politics" (Kaufman, Gordon, Jonathan King, Stephen J. Lippard, George Verghese, January, 2007). The energy crisis directly and indirectly affects the lives of the general population to a large extent. Therefore, the understanding of the general population about the concept and their contribution towards the solution of the problem of energy crisis may play a very important role. Under such circumstances, the current study becomes very important. Hence, a micro-level study was carried out on 100 respondents comprising 50 females and 50 males from the general population to get wider and versatile perspectives on the issue of global energy crises. This chapter is based on the findings of the same micro-level study. The responses obtained were used to draw inferences under different response categories and provide constructive solutions to meet the challenges of energy requirements and crises.

## GLOBAL ENERGY CRISIS – THE RESPONSES

### *Global Energy Crisis- The Concept*

Energy means property, power or force that enables one to do any work. Energy has different connotations according to its forms and usage. "For example, in science, energy is a key attribute of things that can be transformed into different forms as per the requirement. In nature, energy exists in several different forms, such as mechanical, electrical, chemical, magnetic, gravitational, nuclear, light, and sound energy. We can observe energy in various ways in nature, with potential energy and kinetic energy being prominent because they help maintain objects and life in motion."

The responses obtained on the basic understanding of respondents on the concept of energy, energy crisis and other related terms are given as under:

### What is Energy?

| Categories | Male (50) | Female (50) |
|---|---|---|
| Mineral oil, electricity, fuel, *etc.* | 80% | 5% |
| Capacity of an object to do work | 10% | 60% |

*(Table) cont.....*

| Categories | Male (50) | Female (50) |
|---|---|---|
| Zest, spark, liveliness, *etc.* | 10% | 5% |
| Know the meaning but not able to define in words | - | 30% |

The first question tried to explore the understanding of the word 'Energy' amongst the respondents. For the majority of male respondents (80%), the word energy meant 'the sources of energy used by people such as mineral oil, electricity, fuel, *etc.*' On the other hand, (60%) majority of female respondents considered it in terms of 'capacity of an object to do work'. Thirty percent of the respondents were unable to express the term, though they claimed that they had an understanding of the term.

***Narrative of Males:*** Man gets energy from food to do work. We use scientific instruments in our daily life. We need mineral oil and electricity to run these scientific instruments. In this way, the source of energy for scientific instruments (motor cars, trains, *etc.*) is mineral oil or electricity. The resources from which we get energy are called sources of energy. "There are various sources of energy such as coal, mineral oil, natural gas, sunlight, wind, water, *etc.* Coal, mineral oil, natural gas, *etc.* have been used for centuries and are referred to as traditional sources of energy. These conventional energy sources are limited. They are also known as fossil fuels, which take millions of years to form naturally. Due to the increasing pace of industrialization, it is estimated that these resources will likely be depleted in the next 40 to 60 years."

***Narrative of Females:*** The capacity of an object to perform work is called its 'energy'. Just like work, energy is also a 'scalar' quantity. Its SI unit is the joule. Scientists define energy as the capacity to perform work. Modern civilization has become possible because people have learned to convert energy from one form to another and then use it to perform work. For people to walk, ride bicycles, move cars on roads and boats through water, cook food on stoves, make ice in the freezer, light our homes and offices, or use products, energy is required. Energy is used to build spacecraft and send astronauts to space.

The responses of both groups portray entirely different views in terms of their understanding of the term energy, where male respondents gave more theoretical connotations of the term energy, while female respondents answered more in terms of its application in different spheres of life.

**b). What is Energy Security?**

| Categories | Male (50) | Female (50) |
|---|---|---|
| 3A | 100% | - |

*(Table) cont.....*

| Categories | Male (50) | Female (50) |
|---|---|---|
| Uninterrupted availability of energy | - | 90% |

***Narrative of Males:*** To secure energy, 3A's have been made, which are defined as - Availability, Access and Affordability. The availability of energy resources is essential for the economic development of a nation. Therefore, it is very important to have strong energy security.

***Narrative of Females:*** Energy security is all about easy access to energy everywhere at affordable prices. That is, the availability of energy at an affordable rate to all without any hindrance is the onl way to save energy. India needs to become self-reliant in the field of 'energy security' to convert demographic dividends into returns and become a global superpower.

Again, female respondents showed more concern about affordability and access to all, focusing on a more inclusive perspective.

### a). What is Renewable Energy?

| Categories | Male (50) | Female (50) |
|---|---|---|
| Gathered from renewable resources | 90% | 20% |
| Obtained from natural sources | 10% | 80% |

On asking about their understanding of the term renewable energy, 90% of the males responded it as energy 'gathered from renewable resources', whereas the other side of the coin, *i.e.*, females, stated renewable energy as 'obtained from natural sources.'

***Narrative of Males:*** Renewable energy is energy that is collected from renewable resources. The development of renewable energy by human communities aims to reduce environmental pollution and dependence on non-renewable energy sources. The major renewable resource commonly used is sunlight, which is directly converted into electricity using solar panels. This solar photovoltaic (PV) technology is used to convert solar heat and solar energy into electricity. The kinetic energy of the wind is harnessed using wind turbines, which rotate and generate electricity. Wind energy is an important renewable source in India and many other countries. Rainfall and runoff are collected and used as a supply of water in hydroelectric power plants. This energy is obtained from natural springs, rivers and tidal movements. Energy from ocean waves is converted into electricity through the use of wave energy converters. Wave energy is primarily harnessed in coastal areas that experience significant wave activity.

***<u>Narrative of Females:</u>*** Renewable energy is very important energy derived from natural resources. These inputs may be found in greater quantities on the Earth, for example, from sunlight and air. We can easily convert solar energy into electrical energy. It can be changed and stored in the battery so that it can be used later. It is also used in two different ways. In the first method, we take energy directly from the sun in the form of light, and in the second, we take energy through heat.

## Global Energy Crisis-The Current Status

It is no longer a matter to be hidden that India has new energy resources available in large quantities. The country has initiated worldwide awareness programs to provide better products and systems for new resources that can generate energy. This country has a special ministry for new resources of energy development, which is giving better results in this direction.

### a). *What Do You Think About the Role of Energy?*

| **Categories** | **Male (50)** | **Female (50)** |
|---|---|---|
| Important Building Block | 20% | 70% |
| Contribution to the tempo and stance of economic development | 80% | 30% |

The respondents were very clear about the role energy plays in the life of humans. However, male and female respondents had different views on it. 70% of females considered the role of energy as an 'important building block'. On the other hand, (80%) majority of males considered its role in terms of 'contribution in the tempo and stance of economic development'.

***<u>Narrative of Males:</u>*** The production and consumption of energy play an important role in the tempo and stance of economic and socio-institutional development. On the one hand, the developed countries are increasing their pace of 'industrialization' or mature stage, on the other hand, the developing countries are trying to catch up with the pace of industrialization from the agricultural and pre-industrial stages. Growth and development require a balance between energy demand and economic activity.

***<u>Narrative of Females:</u>*** Energy is considered the most important element in human development, and it plays an important role in the progress of any country. If there is no energy, then the progress of the country is affected. Today, developed countries have new resources available to generate energy, due to which they are making further progress in the right direction. The future of developing countries depends on the use of our energy. If we will not strike a balance between them, then it will have a negative impact on our environmental values, health and society in general.

**b). *What is the Current Status of Renewable Energy Sources?***

| Categories | Male (50) | Female (50) |
|---|---|---|
| Solar Power | - | 70%-21,651 (1,00,000mw target till 2022) |
| Wind Power | 88%-34,046 (60,000 mw target till 2022) | - |

There are three major renewable energy sources. These are solar power, wind power and bioenergy. Therefore, responses were obtained under these categories. 88% of males reported in the category of 'wind power'. On the other hand, (70%) majority of females considered it in terms of 'solar power'.

***Narrative of Males:*** Wind energy is emerging as a very promising alternative energy of the future. If we talk about electricity generation, then its place is first among various sources. Over the years, turbine technologies have increased the amount of energy generated by wind turbines. Although India is still relatively new to the wind industry compared to many countries, domestic policy support for wind power has led India to rank fourth in the world and is now the fourth largest wind power producer.

***Narrative of Females:*** Solar energy does not generate any harmful waste and does not have a negative impact on the environment; it is also seen as a sacred energy according to the Indian tradition. PV cells have been given a place in generating solar energy, in the manufacture of which, semiconductors and energy collectors are used. The total amount of solar energy incident on the Earth is much more than the current and projected energy needs of the world. If harnessed appropriately, this highly diffused source has the potential to meet all future energy needs. Solar energy is expected to become an increasingly significant renewable energy source in the 21st century because of its inexhaustible supply and non-polluting character, in sharp contrast to the limited fossil fuels, such as coal, petroleum and natural gas.

Solar energy and wind energy have come up as the major known sources of alternative and renewable energy that need to be tapped. However, there is a need to generate more awareness among the masses on the use of waste as an alternative source of energy, such as jatropha grown on wasteland in India as a source of biodiesel, animal and kitchen waste as a source of biogas, paddy crop and wheat crop residue oil as a source of biofuel, *etc.*

**c). Renewable Energy- Why increasing the conversion to fresh energy is the way to a happier, healthier and more livable space?**

| Categories | Male (50) | Female (50) |
|---|---|---|
| Surrounded by renewable energy sources in every way | 70% | 20% |
| Renewable energy is reasonably priced | 10% | 80% |
| Renewable energy is salubrious | 10% | - |

Out of the total, 90% of males responded 'Surrounded by renewable energy sources' and 'Renewable energy is salubrious in every way'. The other side of the coin, *i.e.*, females, stated that 'Renewable energy is reasonably priced'.

***Narrative of Males:*** If observed carefully, around 80 percent of our world population is linked to countries that are net importers of fossil fuels – that is, about 6 billion people who depend on fossil fuels from other countries, making them vulnerable to environmental threats. On the contrary, renewable energy sources are found in all countries, and they are still not fully utilized and are present in the same form that nature has given us. IRENA predicts that in the next 25 years, 90 percent of the world's electricity can and should come from renewable energy, which is the need of the hour. Renewable energy ends the country's dependence on imports from other countries. With this, the country will progress meaningfully and people will live a happy life, with inclusive economic development, new jobs and poverty alleviation.

***Narrative of Females:*** Today, renewable energy is the most accessible option for providing electricity all over the world. The prices of technologies associated with renewable energy are coming down rapidly. If we look into the past, then, in the last 12 years, the cost of electricity has come down by 85 percent due to the use of solar energy. While the cost of onshore wind power has come down by 56 percent and the cost of offshore wind power has come down by 48 percent. Falling prices have made renewable energy more attractive, in both developed and developing countries, from where most of the additional demand for electricity will come in the future. With prices coming down, we have an opportunity today to provide new electricity supplies from low-carbon sources in the future. Affordable electricity from renewable sources can provide 65 percent of the world's total electricity supply by 2030 and decarbonize 90 percent of the electricity sector over the next 30 years, massively cutting carbon emissions and halting climate change.

Since environmental concern is key to achieving sustainable development, therefore, practices that harm the environment can only be expected to change if people are aware of their ill effects. However, the data obtained do not reveal an encouraging picture because very few out of the total respondents were aware of the healthier impact of renewable energy sources on life and the environment.

## Global Energy Crisis - The Reasons

We can easily blame anyone for the energy crisis we are facing today, but we cannot turn away from the situation of energy crises. We have to give a real explanation for the reasons for energy crises, only then can we overcome them. Several reasons for the current energy crisis, such as "unprecedented population growth, excessive consumption, poor infrastructural development, low efforts to explore unexplored energy sources, energy wastage, poorly organized distribution system, extreme financial crisis leading to tax hike, delayed completion of powerplant projects and other multiple crisis situations such as political events, strikes, outbreak of pandemic, war, military coup or other conflicting situations, occurrences of any natural calamity, major accident or disaster, and extreme weather conditions such as extremely hot summers or cold winters, *etc*.," have been suggested by Sultan, Z. (June 12, 2016) in his article titled, 'What is the Energy Crisis?' Such conditions can cause a sudden increase in energy demand and supply constraints, especially if such conditions occur in Middle East countries such as Qatar or major oil-supplying countries such as Russia and Belarus. If we recall the Gulf War, a similar situation arose when oil prices skyrocketed, causing huge problems for energy consumers. One of the main reasons for the energy crisis that has arisen today is due to the state of affairs between Russia and Ukraine, which has deeply disturbed the European countries. Natural disasters like volcanoes, floods, and earthquakes can also have an impact on the energy supply. The gap between the supply and demand of energy can increase the prices of essential commodities, leading to inflation. In the third section, an attempt was made to explore the understanding of the reason for the global energy crisis amongst respondent groups.

### *a). Why this Energy Crisis Occurred?*

| Categories | Male (50) | Female (50) |
|---|---|---|
| Non-achievement of the targets of hydroelectricity with the slow pace of development of atomic power. | 50% | 20% |
| Increasing use of petroleum, wastage of energy and lack of coal. | 30% | 70% |
| Protraction in operating power plants. | 20% | 10% |

Majority of the male respondents (50%) responded as 'non-achievement of the targets of hydro-electricity with the slow pace of development of atomic power'. On the other hand, (80%) majority of the females considered it in terms of 'increasing use of petroleum and lack of coal'.

***Narrative of Males:*** Hydropower is the largest and oldest source of energy, but sometimes, due to low levels of water in reservoirs and technical problems, the set targets for generating hydropower are not achieved. This is also an important reason for energy crises in the country. It is true that sufficient reserves of minerals are available in the country for the development of atomic power, but so far, very little use of this power has been done for energy. The specific plan that Dr. Bhabha had prepared for the development of atomic power could not be implemented so quickly due to his untimely death. The establishment of nuclear power stations requires a lot of foreign exchange. Inadequate foreign exchange hinders the development of nuclear power stations.

***Narrative of Females:*** It is easier to generate energy from mineral oil than coal. There has been a steady increase in the use of mineral oil over the years. Dieselization of railway engines, fertilizer factories based on mineral oil, and the use of petrol in various modes of road transport are indicative of the increase in the use of mineral oil. Even after seeing the dire circumstances of today's energy crisis, people do not understand the importance of energy conservation. Energy conservation is still confined to advertisements, symposia, lectures, conferences and seminars. We will not be able to overcome this crisis until we become responsible. If we make small efforts, there can be a revolution in energy conservation. Switch off the power when not in use, switch off the lights, make the most of daylight, take short walks, and use CFLs. On the other hand, the coal reserves in the country have also dwindled, and coal, being a major source of energy, is nearing its end. The lack of coal reserves is creating a situation of energy crisis in the country.

However, none of the respondents reflected any of the human activities like unprecedented population growth or carelessness and overconsumption as the reasons for the current energy crisis. These reasons may be the minor reason for the current crisis but are one of the major contributors if considered in longer duration.

### b). *How Energy Crisis is Affecting Lives?*

| Categories | Male (50) | Female (50) |
|---|---|---|
| Fuel estate price hike. | 80% | 20% |
| Environmental impact. | 5% | 60% |
| Political disturbances. | 10% | 10% |
| The effect on the tourism industry. | 5% | 10% |

As humans increase their level of energy tolerance, conventional sources of energy are being depleted. The real source of energy is the invaluable old fossil fuels. If observed carefully, a certain effect is produced by the use of all these sources. The major impact of the global energy crisis as reported by 80% of male respondents was 'fuel estate price hike', while according to females (60%), it was 'environmental impact'.

***Narrative of Males:*** As we are using fossil fuels to meet our needs, the cost of these resources is also increasing. We should not forget that these fossil fuels are also available in limited quantities on the earth. Their quantity is decreasing due to our indiscriminate use, leading to an increase in their value. Yet supplies are not being met, and economic unrest is being created.

***Narrative of Females:*** When non-renewable fossil fuels are burnt, energy is generated, and today, a large amount of energy is being generated from this. Not only does this affect the available fossil fuel resources, but it also has a negative impact on the environment. Burning fossil fuels releases greenhouse gases like carbon dioxide and others. These greenhouse gases cover the Earth's surface as a blanket, which prevents the sun's heat from escaping at night. Because of this, global warming is increasing.

**How is it Crucial for Future Generations in the form of Economy?**

| Categories | Male (50) | Female (50) |
|---|---|---|
| Effect on the food and agricultural secto.r | 50% | |
| Effect on health and well-being. | - | 60% |
| Impact on cessation of small businesses. | - | 40% |
| Impact on digital finance. | 50% | |

50% of males responded with 'Effect on food and agricultural sector', and the other 50% reported 'Impact on digital finance'. On the other hand, 60% of females reported 'Effect on Health and Well-being' and 40% of females reported in the category of 'Impact on cessation of small businesses'. The male respondents were more worried about the impact on major economic activities such as agriculture and the digital economy that affects the economic growth of the nations, whereas women were more concerned about the lives of people, health and small-scale economic activities.

***Narrative of Males:*** The energy crisis has many side effects, such as food shortage, which can lead to famine. Coal is associated with many needs of human beings today. Rising coal prices can affect fertilizer supply, leading to a hike in food prices. Moreover, power cuts can also create insecurity and unrest among people as people depend on refrigerators to preserve food.

The energy crisis affects every area of human life. Due to a lack of energy in the health sector, the lives of patients can be at risk. All the equipment used in hospitals depends on power supply. Patients most affected are those dependent on life-support equipment, such as adults and children on respirators and ventilator machines.

***Narrative of Females:*** Today, all types of small or big businesses depend on the supply of energy. Due to the energy crisis, there may be a danger of closure of these businesses, especially those businesses which are dependent on electricity. Energy is subsidized by the government to run these businesses, making it easier for businesses to bear the cost. However, if electricity is not available for an extended period of time, small businesses are at risk of being shut down. The resulting economic loss may be intolerable for these business personnel.

If we talk about the digital economy, it is completely dependent on electricity. If there is a power cut for a long time, then the digital economy may end because the digital economic activities are completely dependent on power-operated devices, such as mobile phones, computers, and laptops, which need to be charged using electricity. Therefore, when the power stored in the batteries is depleted, severe power outages can kill the digital economy.

## Global Energy Crisis - The Solutions

The crisis of energy in the country is spreading very fast. The demand for energy is increasing continuously in the economic and non-economic sectors, and the traditional means of supplying energy are almost extinct. This is a problematic situation. An effective solution to this serious problem is very necessary. It is not possible to reduce the increasing demand for energy. Therefore, there is a need that the available energy resources should be consumed responsibly, and new energy sources should be discovered.

## How it Could have been Prevented?

| Categories | Male (50) | Female (50) |
|---|---|---|
| Energy transformation to renewable energy sources. | 80% | 20% |
| Energy efficiency and conservation. | 10% | 50% |
| Do not know. | 10% | 30% |

The most important section, "the solution", tried to explore prevention strategies for the global energy crisis. The majority of males (80%) responded, 'Energy transformation to renewable energy sources.' On the other hand, the majority of females (50%) responded in terms of 'Energy efficiency and conservation'.

***Narrative of Males:*** In contrast to fossil fuels, there are some energy sources that are completely new, and they do not cause any greenhouse gas emissions. Such energy sources include solar energy, hydropower, wind energy, geothermal energy, biomass energy, *etc*. Their maximum use can save human lives from the coming dangers as well as end the energy crisis.

***Narrative of Females:*** Today, if we want to save the human race, we have to stop the energy crisis; for this, we have to improve and modernize the energy infrastructure like smart grid solutions and smart cities, which consume less energy. Along with this, we have to replace old appliances with energy-efficient solutions that will consume less energy, such as replacing traditional light bulbs with LEDs, using solar plants, *etc*.

Thirty percent of females and 10 percent of males were not aware of the reason, which is really crucial. This further shows that despite development and the information revolution, a considerable number of people are either not interested in knowing the reason, least concerned about serious issues like preventing energy crisis or out of reach of information. This is the point where some form of intervention is needed to deal with the problem.

### a). How to Fight with this GEC?

| Categories | Male (50) | Female (50) |
|---|---|---|
| Economical consumption of liquid fuel with expansion of hydroelectric energy. | 60% | 30% |
| Exploration of mineral oil and gas with the use of coal in place of mineral oil. | 30% | 70% |
| Expansion of gobar gas or biogas plants. | 10% | - |

The majority of males (60%) responded as 'Economical Consumption of Liquid Fuel'. On the other hand, the majority of females (70%) considered it in terms of

'Illness, Disorder, Health Problems and Death'.

***Narrative of Males:*** Economical consumption of liquid fuel was suggested by this group of respondents. The increase in the consumption of liquid fuels like petroleum and kerosene has mainly happened in two areas- first in rail and road transport and second in domestic use. The use of liquid fuels can be reduced by creating electricity capacity; apart from this, the energy crisis can also be reduced significantly by using liquid fuels economically. Hydroelectricity is an important form of renewable energy. The supply of energy can be increased by expanding hydroelectric power. According to the Central Water and Power Commission, only 410 lakh kilowatts of hydroelectric power generation capacity exists in India, but at present, only 70 lakh kilowatts of hydroelectricity is generated. Energy supply can be increased by increasing the capacity of hydroelectric power.

***Narrative of Females:*** To reduce the energy crisis, exploration of mineral oil deposits and natural gas should be done because mineral petrol and raw gas are vital forms of renewable energy. With the help of current technology, the production of crude petroleum can be increased by liquefaction of coal. The use of coal gas as an industrial and domestic gas can also be increased. Using coal in place of mineral oil in the generation of power can also reduce the consumption of mineral oil, but before that, it is necessary to increase the production of coal because coal reserves are almost on the verge of extinction.

**What can be Done to Prevent this Situation in the Future?**

| Categories | Male (50) | Female (50) |
|---|---|---|
| Easy grid access and general stance on climate change. | 88% | 15% |
| Energy simulation and buy energy-efficient products. | 12% | 85% |

88% of males responded as 'Easy Grid Access and General Stance on Climate Change'. On the other hand, the majority of females (75%) reported in terms of 'Energy simulation and Buy Energy-Efficient Products'.

***Narrative of Males:*** Today, people are adopting various methods to generate electricity; they should be allowed to plug into the grid and use the electricity generated from it. Today, the power crisis can be overcome to a great extent by using the grid, but the cost of setting up the grid is high, so for this, a ration loan system should be prepared. Apart from this, awareness should also be encouraged to find new options. Subsidies should be provided for solar panels. In our opinion, it is important that both developed and developing countries take a similar stand on climate change. All countries should focus on reducing greenhouse gas emissions and make every possible effort in this direction. The way the population is increasing today and resources are being consumed excessively, the consequences of global warming and climate change cannot be denied. Both developed and developing countries should focus on cutting their emissions to half of the current levels over the next 25 years.

**Narrative of Females:** By using energy simulation software, we can prevent future energy problems as well as reduce business energy costs. For this, we need to start an awareness program so that the people playing the main role in this can understand the problems of the future and make energy-efficient buildings using this design by engineers, architects and designers. With this, we can save energy and also save the future of our children. Make small efforts to replace the bulbs at home with CFL and LED, as they use low-wattage electricity and last longer. If awareness or compulsion is brought across the world, then energy demand can be reduced and the energy crisis can be avoided.

## CONCLUSION

Energy has a vital role in the operation of the ecosystem. In other words, it is energy that operates and controls this system. At the same time, along with the fulfillment of the basic needs of human beings, energy drives huge industries and transport. The use of energy has become a sign of development in the present era, and its lack is a hindrance to development. In this sequence, there is competition for maximum use of energy; as a result, the energy crisis has arisen on the one hand and on the other hand, its excessive exploitation is also affecting the ecology adversely. Today, maximum use of energy is being done in the desire to develop and progress; and the more the energy consumed by the country, the more developed it is considered. For example, in the year 2021, the energy consumption in the United States was 76,634 kWh-hours per capita, while in India, it was 6,922 kWh-hours per capita, and in Bangladesh, only 2,712 kWh-hours per capita energy was consumed (Ritchie, H. and Max Roser. 2021).

The continuous increase in the use of energy in industries, transport and for domestic use has led to the shortage of many energy sources; and today, there is a concern all over the world about the energy crisis. If we look at the statistics of the last 25 years, globally, the consumption of fuel has doubled, the consumption of oil and gas has quadrupled and the consumption of electricity has increased seven times. Mineral oil and coal account for about 44 and 39 percent of the consumption of all sources of energy, respectively. As industrial and technological progress is expanding, the consumption of energy is increasing, while their known sources are limited and are about to be exhausted. It is clear that energy resources are getting depleted at a fast pace. Apart from this, the use of hydropower and nuclear power is increasing day by day, and their impact on the environment can also be seen. The sources of energy are mainly divided into two categories. The energy crisis across the country has become more serious due to a shortage of supply of fuel for power plants. Due to this crisis, the wheels of revival of the world's fastest growing major economy have stalled in the coming days. More than 100 thermal plants in the country (India) had only four days of coal stock till the last day of September, as indicated by government data. According to the rules, it is mandatory to keep a coal stock of 22-25 days in thermal plants (Vanamali *et al.*, October 8, 2021).

The statistical data and information available in government and non-government sources in India proves that the production, distribution and availability of energy is very low in comparison to the energy required for agricultural and industrial development in India.

This situation is at that stage when high priority is given to the creation of various types of energy power during the planning period, and a large amount of capital investment has been made. It is also note worthy in this regard that in addition to internal efforts in the field of energy, significant foreign cooperation and loans have also been obtained. Due to these efforts, the production and distribution of energy has been done sufficiently, but with the increasing population in the country, the consumption of energy is very low in view of the needs, and on the other hand, there is a continuous energy crisis in the country. To meet the domestic shortfall, the option of buying coal from abroad is available, but the increase in worldwide electricity demand post COVID-19 has generated additional interest in securing fuel sources, Which has increased the prices of coal in the world. There has been a big jump in the price of coal (import) in Indonesia. Coal imports have come down as compared to 2019-20 due to rising coal prices. Not only this, the price of Australian non-coking coal was more than $ 200 per ton in July 2021 (Care Ratings, August 12, 2021). Apart from this, extreme weather also has an impact. China's top coal-producing province suspended production at mines, adding further pressure to the country's energy crisis. China is the largest producer and consumer of coal (Global Times, October, 2021). The lack of sufficient growth in renewable energy and skyrocketing natural gas prices are also contributing to the escalation of the global energy crisis (Power Technology, November, 2021). Due to the decision taken by China to secure the fuel, there is a shortage of fuel in the world market, leading to a hike in prices. A power sector analyst stated that the changes happening around the world are now affecting the Indian market as well. Major industrialized states like Maharashtra, Gujarat, and Tamil Nadu have seen a 14-20 percent increase in electricity demand in the last three months (Kentaka *et al.*, 13).

## IMPLICATION AND SUGGESTION

There is a need to consume available energy resources responsibly and discover new energy sources. Following are some important suggestions to solve the energy crisis:

- Increase in the use of tide power and sun power - Natural energy can be used properly by using tide power and sun power in different areas. It is available at a nominal cost. Therefore, by using them in various fields of inventions, not only can energy be saved, but energy sources can be increased.

- Expansion of Gobar-Gas or Biogas Plants - Energy supply can be increased by setting up new gobar gas or biogas plants. Gobar gas or biogas is the best alternative to cooking gas; it can be used not only for cooking but also for lighting, *etc.*
- Use of human power and animal power - Energy can also be saved by making maximum use of human power and animal power.
- New methods of electricity generation - Electricity can be originated by taking energy from the ground temperature and also from the temperature difference of seawater. There is every possibility that the electric potential generated in this way will make an important contribution to the solution of the energy crisis.
- Energy resources obtained from forests - By using wood obtained from forests as fuel, a lot of energy resources like minerals, oil, natural gas, coal, *etc.* can be saved.
- New possibilities of energy production - In the form of the current sources of energy, agricultural produce like sugarcane, sera, cereals *etc.* or the alcoholic organic matter obtained from them has a lot of potential. Biomass-based ethanol can be a replacement for petroleum products. In America and Denmark, the possibilities of producing energy from these methods are being successfully worked out. It can replace liquid fuel and can prove to be a good fuel for automobiles and aircraft in the future. Research work is in progress in this direction in India.
- International Collaboration on research related to environment-friendly, clean and affordable energy. Such initiatives have already started, for instance, China, the United States, France, Spain, and the United Kingdom are a few countries that have emerged as the major contributors in international collaborations for writing research papers during 2015-21 on this issue (Cheung, 2022).
- The example of Norway can also be taken and followed that is poised to reduce greenhouse emissions by 2050. In this process, its extensive hydropower resources that provide 92 percent of the total electricity to the country have a pivotal role to play (Crew, 7 September 2022). These examples can be replicated in countries like India, which still have a scope of using hydropower in many areas.
- Further, to overcome this crisis, it is very important to prepare a long-term energy policy and ensure its effective implementation. The long-term policy should be such that along with the increase in energy resources, everyone should try their best to save energy, otherwise, the day is not far away when the cycle of industrial development will stop. In the absence of energy, machines will get jammed, industries and businesses will start shutting down, terrible unemployment will start spreading in the country, and the economy will be disturbed. In the future, it is very important to pay serious attention to all this to end the energy crisis.

- Other organizations working toward saving energy are regulating and restricting carbon emissions and promoting green construction, and hybrid and sustainable technologies.

## BIBLIOGRAPHY

Anandan, M. (2022). Global energy crisis and its impact on indian economy. *Int. J. Res. Analyt. Rev., 9*(1), 800-900.https://www.researchgate.net/publication/358899309_Global_Energy_Crisis_and_Its_

Aruga, K., Monirul Islama, A.J. (2020). Effects of Covid 19 on indian energy consumption. *Sustainability: Special Issue on Energy, Economics and Sustainability, 12*(14), 5616. https://www.mdpi.com/2071-1050/12/14/5616#B49-sustainability-12-05616
[http://dx.doi.org/10.3390/su12145616]

Anandan, M., Ramaswamy, S. (2015). Global Oil Market: Macro economic scenario. *Global J. Res. Analy., 4*(9), 53-57.

Bec, C. (2022). Solving Energy Crisis- Research Collaboration and a Diversified Approach to Generation could play dividends. *Nature: Index. 2022 Energy* Springer Nature Limited. https://www.nature.com/articles/d41586-022-02830-5
[http://dx.doi.org/10.1038/d41586-022-02830-5]

Causes, Effects and Solutions to the Growing Problem of Global Energy Crisis. https://www.conserve-energy-future.com/causes-and-solutions-to-the-global-energy-crisis.php.

Central Statistics Office. (2020). *Energy Statistics. Central Statistics Office. Ministry of Statistics and Programme Implementation.* New Delhi: Government of India.

Catherine, C. (2021). The National and Institutional Connections Driving Research in Affordable and Clean Energy- A Broad and Narrow Look at the Collaborations in the Field. Nature Index. 609.S5. https://www.nature.com/articles/d41586-022-02832-3

Cooperation, E.M. (2015). *The Outlook for Energy: A view to 2040.*. Exxon Mobil Cooperation.
[http://dx.doi.org/10.1080/01998595.2012.10491656]

Dong, K., Dong, X., Jiang, Q. (2020). How renewable energy consumption lower global $CO_2$ emissions? Evidence from countries with different income levels. *World Econ., 43*(6), 1665-1698.
[http://dx.doi.org/10.1111/twec.12898]

Elliott, S. (14 September, 2021). Infographics: Sky's the limit? Global Gas Prices on Stellar Rally. S & P Platts. https://www.spglobal.com/commodityinsights/ko/market-insights/latest-news/natural-gas/091421-infographic-skys-the-limit-global-gas-prices-stellar-rally-winter-lng-cargoes-storage-russia-power

Froley, A. (30 June, 2021). China Overtakes Japan as World's Largest LNG Importer. ICIS. https://www.icis.com/explore/resources/news/2021/06/30/10658118/china-ov

Global Times. Heavy downpour Kills Four, Shuts Down 27 Coal Mines in N China's Shanxi. October, 2021. https://www.globaltimes.cn/page/202110/1235668.shtml.

Goldemberg, J. (2006). *The promise of clean energy., Energy policy, 34*(15)2185
[http://dx.doi.org/10.1016/j.enpol.2005.03.009]

Global Energy Review 2020: the impacts of the Covid-19 crisis on global energy demand and $CO^2$ emissions. https://www.iea.org/reports/globalenergy-review-2020/electricity#abstract.

IEA. (2017). Report: World energy outlook..

Jason, B. (24 September, 2021). Why This Energy Crisis? https://www.energypolicy.columbia.edu/research/op-ed/why-energy-crisis-.

Kaufman, G., King, J., Lippard, S.J., Verghese, G. (2007). *Human Engineering and the Energy Crisis. XIX:3. Editorial. MIT Faculty News Letter.*. Massachusetts Institute of Technology.

Kohl, W.L. Oil: The arab-israel dispute, and the industrial world. *The International Energy Agency: The Political Context.,* 246-257.

Kona, A., Bertoldi, P. Covenant of mayors signatories leading the way towards 1.5 degree global warming pathway. *Sustain. Cit. Soci., 41*, 568-575.http://web.mit.edu/fnl/volume/193/editorial.html [http://dx.doi.org/10.1016/j.scs.2018.05.017]

Lazarus Michael. and Harro van Asselt. (2018). Fossil Fuel Supply and Climate Policy: Exploring the Road Less Taken. https://link.springer.com/article/10.1007/s10584-018-2266-3

Leonard, M.D., Michaelides, E.E., Michaelides, D.N. (2020). Energy storage needs for the substitution of fossil fuel power plants with renewables. *Renew. Energy, 145*, 951-962. https://ideas.repec.org/a/eee/renene/v145y2020icp951-962.html [http://dx.doi.org/10.1016/j.renene.2019.06.066]

Martins, F., Felgueiras, C., Smitková, M. (2018). Fossil fuel energy consumption in European countries. *Energy Procedia, 153*, 107-111. [http://dx.doi.org/10.1016/j.egypro.2018.10.050]

Nashawi, I.S., Malallah, A., Al-Bisharah, M. https://www.academia.edu/30070551/Forecasting_World_Crude_Oil_Production_Using_Multicyclic_Hubbert_Model Forecasting world crude oil production using multicyclic hubbert model. Energy & Fuels. American Chemical Society. 23:3. 1788-1800, 2018. [http://dx.doi.org/10.1021/ef901240p]

Omer, M.A.B., Noguchi, T. (2020). A conceptual framework for understanding the contribution of building materials in the achievement of Sustainable Development Goals (SDGs). *Sustain Cities Soc., 52*, 101869. [http://dx.doi.org/10.1016/j.scs.2019.101869]

Ozili, K. Global Energy Crisis: Impact on the global economy, 1-2. https://www.researchgate.net/publication/355020759_Global_energy_crisis_impact_on_the_global_economy

PIB, Delhi (Press Information Bureau). (09 October, 2021). Statement of Power Ministry on Coal Stock Situation in Thermal Power Plants. Ministry of Power, GOI. https://pib.gov.in/PressReleseDetailm.aspx?PRID=1762579.

Pietrosemoli, L., Rodríguez-Monroy, C. (2019). The Venezuelan energy crisis: Renewable energies in the transition towards sustainability. *Renew. Sustain. Energy Rev., 105*, 415-426. [http://dx.doi.org/10.1016/j.rser.2019.02.014]

Power Technology. The Global Trickle Down of China's Energy Supply Shortage. (November, 2021). https://www.power-technology.com/features/china-energy-crisis/.

Reijnders, L., Huijbregts, M.A. (2007). Life Cycle Green House Gas Emissions, Fossil Fuel Demand and Solar Energy Conversion Efficiency in European Bioethanol Production for Automotive purposes. *J. Clean. Produc., 15*, 18.1806-1812.

Ratings, C. (12 August, 2021). Sharp Increase in Cooking Coal Prices to Reduce Steel Spreads by Rs. 4,000 per tons,1. https://www.careratings.com/uploads/newsfiles/12082021114644_Sharp_increase_in_coking_coal_prices_to_reduce_steel_spreads_by_Rs_4000_per_tonne.pdf

Renewable Energy in India: Current Status and Future Potential https://www.indiary.org/en/legal-advice/Renewable-Energy-in-India-Current-Status-and-Future-Potential-2-79-429.

Ritchie, H. and Max Roser. (2021). Energy Production and Consumption. Our World in Data. https://ourworldindata.org/energy-production-consumption.

Singh, S., Zhang, M. (27 September, 2022). China Power Crunch Spreads, Shutting Factories and Dimming Growth Outlook. Reuters https://www.reuters.com/world/china/chinas-power-crunch-begins-weigh-economicoutlook

Sundria, S., Singh, R.K., Chakraborty, D. (06 October, 2022). As Coal Stock Shrink, India Faces Growing Energy Shortage Crisis. Aljazeera. https://www.aljazeera.com/economy/2021/10/6/as-coal-stocks-shr-nk-india-facesescalating-power-crisis

Sultan, Z. (June 12, 2016). What is the Energy Crisis? https://www.linkedin.com/pulse/what-energy-cris-s-sultan-zafar-1/

Tanveer, A., Zhang, D. (2020). A critical review of comparative global historical energy consumption and future demand: The story told so far. *Energy Rep.,* *6*, 1973-1991. https://www.sciencedirect.com/science/article/pii/S2352484720312385

Tina, E. (29 September, 2021). Why Europe and China are Facing an Energy Crisis and How it Affects India. https://www.moneycontrol.com/news/business/explained-why-europe-and-china-are-facing-an-ener-y-crisis-and-how-it-affects-india-7523541.html

The Indian Express. (2020). Explained: how COVID-19 lockdowns have impacted the global energy sector. https://indianexpress.com/article/explained/covid19-lockdown-impact-global-energysector d mand-explained-6386515/.

United Nations. Gen. Assembly 70th Sess. A/RES/70/1. 2015. Resolution adopted by General Assembly on 25 September 2015–transforming our world: the 2030 Agenda for Sustainable Development. 1–35..

Vanamali, K.V. (October 8, 2021). Coal Shortage: Will Coal Crisis Derail India's Nascent Economic Recovery? Business Standard. New Delhi. https://www.business-standard.com/podcast/current-affairs/co-l-shortage-will-coal-crisis-derail-india-s-nascent-economic-recovery-121100800284_1.html

# CHAPTER 10

# Changing Competitive Business Dynamics of OTT Platforms' Viewership for Transformational Digital Engagement: Post-Pandemic Entrepreneurship

**Aurodeep Kamal[1,*], Abhiraj Malia[1], Biswajit Das[1], Ipseeta Satpathy[1] and Bhubaneswari Bisoyi[2]**

[1] *KIIT School of Management, KIIT University, Bhubaneswar, Odisha, India*

[2] *Sri Sri University, Cuttack, Odisha, India*

**Abstract:** This research aims to understand possible parameters that influenced the viewership and acceptability with regard to OTT (Over the Top) platforms in the midst of the COVID-19 lockdown. The consumption of content by the general audience and its perception have evolved exponentially over the years. The advent of the internet has made the process more accessible and convenient. The emergence of OTT Platforms has enabled various service providers to deliver digital content like movies, shows, standups and documentaries to consumers *via* an internet connection. Favorable features like a wide catalog of genres and shows, flexible pricing and packaging allow a plethora of devices to deliver content at the sheer convenience of the consumer. There is an ever-expanding demand for such services, leading to substantial adoption rates amongst the masses. The inception of the COVID-19 pandemic has positively enhanced the OTT landscape in terms of consumer viewership, production and distribution of content across OTT platforms and customer engagement from the service provider's end. The growth rate of subscriptions for OTT service providers increased seven times in March 2020 in comparison to preceding years. It can be surmised that OTT platforms have inevitably become a part of the life of the average person. There are a lot of parameters that have affected the inclusion and growth of this service, like intention of use, accessibility, content quality and free time, to name a few.

**Keywords:** Accessibility, Consumer Viewership, Content Consumption, Customer Engagement, Intention of Use, OTT (Over the Top).

[*] **Corresponding author Aurodeep Kamal:** KIIT School of Management, KIIT University, Bhubaneswar, Odisha, India; E-mail: aurodeep.naarm19@gmail.com

**Sukanta Kumar Baral, Richa Goel, Tilottama Singh, Erdener Kaynak & Vishal Jain (Eds.)**

## INTRODUCTION

The materialization of the digital era in the international market has dawned on innumerable big industries, with entertainment market subtleties being noticeable emblems of such phenomenon. The emergence of over-the-top (OTT) platforms such as Netflix and Amazon Prime confronted the practicalities of conventional content watching behaviors of customers on a global scale, as well as in India. In January 2016, Netflix took the industry by surprise, revealing a synchronized introduction in 130 countries, including Korea, in an effort that marked "the birth of a global Internet TV network". OTT Platforms are streaming services designed to let consumers watch video content, online or offline. According to Mordor Intelligence, "The OTT Market was valued at USD 101.42 Billion in 2020 and is expected to reach USD 223.07 Billion by 2026, indicating a CAGR of 13.87%."

2008 saw the introduction of BigFlix, India's first OTT platform, launched by Reliance Corporation. Following 'Renaissance', post-2016 was a significant era for Indians all over. People became increasingly aware of things around the world, thanks to the easy availability of high-speed internet to the masses on a wide scale. Adding to this is the rapidly increasing adoption of smartphones. When people cut the cord of their cable service and switch to watching television online, this is known as cord cutting. The desire to avoid advertising has been noted as one element that encourages cable cord-cutting. Ownership of high-end technology combined with the convenience of internet diffusion has led to people being exposed to multitudes of content. This was highly noticeable during the COVID-19 pandemic, as the most preferred mode of obtaining information during the pandemic while under lockdown was through the internet. The rise of Internet-based, over-the-top (OTT) streaming platforms, which bypass conventional distribution routes, is the main factor driving this change in media consumption. Most relevant sources of infodemiology involve mass social media such as Instagram and Facebook in addition to search engines, health websites, blogs and forums. The crippling effect of COVID-19 has especially impacted the growth of OTT services and the corresponding customer base. Over the course of a few successive years, far-reaching changes will be noticed in how content is consumed. One of them being Over the Top Content Consumption. In India, however, this surge in popularity of such platforms was not seen overnight. Netflix faced challenges in an attempt to acquire five million subscribers. However, in developing nations, consumers are hesitant to spend money on OTT platforms and instead choose to use the free content that is available online. India has also experienced a paradigm change from traditional television to OTT platforms during the last few years. Along with global content that is produced and made available for consumption, the ushering of indigenously-produced content has brought in a lot of rural masses into the mix. This has diversified the visual media-consuming demographic into various categories. As a result, consumers were categorized as "cord loyalists", "non-pay TV" and "cord couplers".

The growth of online streaming services has introduced the culture of "binge-watching", where multiple instances of a show can be watched in a single go. Factors like self-efficacy, attitude, purpose of use, skepticism towards technology, and overall convenience designate a drastic shift. This consequentially led to a rise in overall OTT viewership amongst the general populace, as people relied more on entertainment being delivered to devices of their choice due to the shutting down of theatres and the availability of run-of-the-mill content on cable television. This is true especially as the number of market players is increasing. As people have started watching content on OTT platforms progressively, the fact that OTT platforms have seen substantial inorganic growth by taking up the market share of other platforms has been evident. It is crucial for such services to keep satiating the consumers' demand in an effort to retain their target and, at the same time, keep up a healthy environment that attracts new demographics. Due to the widespread use of the internet during the pandemic for a variety of reasons, people's need for data has skyrocketed. Given the expanding digital divide in contemporary nations, the discussion of zero-rating systems has been revived by the rise in Internet data usage. Businesses can give customers access to data from their websites and services without charging them for the use of the data, thanks to zero-rating programs. Normally, this is not permitted because it violates the principles of net neutrality, which state that all internet traffic must be treated equally in terms of priority and cost.

When it comes to age groups, the competition between YouTube, Netflix, and traditional TV primarily affects the younger generations, for whom these services serve as strong substitutes, whilst older generations continue to be more devoted to TV. Following such a shockwave, the way we perceive entertainment has drastically changed. Production houses find it rather convenient and profitable to opt for an OTT release over a theatrical one. With all the buzz in the appropriate circles, OTTs are quickly persuading those who were on the fence to switch, across different age and demographic groups, since they are viewed as an aspirational medium of content consumption. Acceptance and subscription rates amongst customers have seemingly skyrocketed, owing to interest in the wide ocean of content available on the platform. As far as India is concerned, the playing field is literally booming with potential for more growth, especially with budding OTT players like Zee5 and SonyLIV. The increase in customer base is not just significant in urban areas but will also percolate the rural market as well. Features like cheap data rates, increasing customer base of smartphones and laptops, as well as development and production of domestic content, have cemented the roadmap for fertile progression in the domain.

## REVIEW OF LITERATURE

In reference to the above, the review of literature deliberated on the quintessential nuances of understanding the aspects of consumer engagement, consumption convenience and intention of consumption vividly. The literature review examined 43 research papers from journals and selected 18 for reflecting pertinently in the context of the review below. The observations of authors culled into the context are self-explanatory and interrelated to the factors of the research study, identifying the need and gap.

Bertin *et al.* (2011) observed a strong association between consumer engrossment and customer service experience, which cumulatively impacted consumers' inclination to subscribe for a longer term. However, their study demographics comprised relatively younger respondents alongside a unidimensional assumption of CE and QoSE factors, which limited the study toward a rather broad spectrum.

Nagaraj *et al.* (2021) highlighted the primary indicators that traced consumers' readiness to give in to OTT services, namely recommendation/search algorithm, resolution and variety of viewing preferences. The central factor for Chinese consumers is resolution or overall picture quality, the second being the viewing options. Prices are a significant factor in consumers' inclination toward subscription retention. There exists a significant disparity in the paradigm of convenience between OTT and television.

Moochhala *et al.* (2018) stated that convenience is a multi-faceted factor revolving around five factors, namely acquisition, time, use, place and execution. The mentioned factors mold a significant portion of accessibility in services.

Gershon *et al.* (2016) observed that digital media has demonstrated to be a sea of change in visual content consumption. Consumers are now consuming online content in lieu of traditional television. In the past several years, the way Indians consume video has evolved. Now, either the viewer has more dominance over the content being watched, or they watch it periodically. Over-the-Top platforms have a sizable fan base, especially in rural areas.

Chen (2019) stipulates the adjustments in functions of telecom operators, envisages them continuing to be market leaders and endorses capitalizing in OTT, following which, the content produced to satisfy consumers' customized wants can be proposed. The problem of allowing or disallowing the entry of such services into the business is depicted in the specialized study of the African telecom sector; however, the operators who welcome OTTs have had quicker revenue growth than those who are hesitant to adopt them.

The researcher examined the psycho-sociological impacts of web series and online movies on Indian netizens in her study. The total impact of web series and web movies on viewers, particularly young people, in terms of their psychological and social aspects, is the main topic of this study article. All that is needed is a smartphone, a good network connection, and access to the platform. These services have low subscription costs in India. The way people process online information has changed due to the development of digitalization or technology, which allows users to watch digital content from a variety of locations and on a variety of devices. Because of the development of the Over-the-Top platform, new content, original tales, and audience viewing patterns, the internet has become increasingly widespread. The content of such platforms has altered culture with the aid of technology and a broader audience. The interactive and distinctive nature of the content offered by Over-the-Top platforms sets it apart from television and cinema content and makes it popular with Internet users. (Pal, 2020).

Yi-Ning Katherine Chen (2018) conducted similar research in Taiwan through the Online Survey method and found that because of their content, the OTT platforms have superiority over traditional TV. So, TV should adopt more advanced technologies to catch up with the OTT platforms or it will be difficult for the traditional platforms to compete in the upcoming days. However, this study lacked demographic heterogeneity.

Chung, Y. K. (2014) stated that despite the fact that OTT services have brought about several developments in media and entertainment, there remains a dearth of OTT literature. Other researchers emphasized the significance of said characteristics as well as the expansion of these services. Numerous academics have studied the psychological factors that influence the adoption of VOD. The factors that lead a user to accept VOD services were analyzed utilizing the Technology Acceptance Model (TAM).

Patnaik *et al.* (2021) observed that more than 94% of youth watch online videos, and they mostly prefer to watch them on smartphones. Amongst the top contenders was Netflix, followed by Amazon Prime, which is mostly watched by the young audience. They also found out that most of the audience is addicted to binge-watching because they spend more than 2 hrs a day on OTT platforms.

Patel *et al.* (2020), through the sample survey method, found out that affordable internet connections are among the multitude of factors for the development of online streaming services in India. One of the major reasons for choosing OTT over TV platforms is that no content has been updated on TV platforms in the last 2 years.

Sundaravel *et al.* (2020) observed through secondary data and analytical study that to compete with the paradigm shift brought by the OTT platform during the lockdown, other media platforms like TV should focus more on providing high-quality content as it was found as the main reason of customers choosing OTT over other media platforms.

Steiner *et al.* (2020) used the snowball sampling technique and MTurk and found that all the factors studied *i.e.*, content, suitability, quality, price and features, affected consumers' verdicts inversely, including gender, age, occupation, and education. However, the study is limited to only 5 predictors as the factors responsible for defining one's inclination to subscribe to SVOD services.

McKenzie *et al.* (2019) observed through both quantitative and qualitative data analysis that roughly 87% of respondents realized their screen time had increased during lockdown. Increasing content accessibility on OTTs and deficiency of exclusive entertainment sources were the principal causes. However, the study included participants 18-35 years of age.

Joshi *et al.* (2016) performed a descriptive and analytical study and concluded that the OTT platform has significantly been chosen by the viewers in place of the other entertainment options that require public gatherings like TV because of its content, which TV was not able to provide. However, they did not find any relationship between the income pattern and the M&E consumption pattern during the lockdown.

Menon *et al.* (2022) observed that appropriate explorability is one of the substantial interpreters of retaining a subscription and its prolongation. Two new gamifications emanating from new media are convenient navigability and binge-watching. Their study was prone to methodological bias as they opted for a cross-sectional survey.

Mulla *et al.* (2022) focused their research on the UAE (United Arab Emirates) region and found that OTT approval has skyrocketed over the past decade, especially during the pandemic; price, content, and convenience need to be free from any limitation. Socialization, binge-watching and self-efficacy are some of the influencing factors for its adoption.

Patel *et al.* (2020) observed that the OTT platform is expected to continue to spread due to many reasons like cost effectiveness, access liberty, *etc.* To increase footfall in the cinema hall, customer experience and convenience, as well as cost-effectiveness, need to be given prime importance after COVID-19. However, the research is limited to report analysis and survey methods.

Madani *et al.* (2020) observed that 95% of internet users happen to be millennials and Gen Z. During the lockdown, people used to watch content on the OTT platform for an average of 2-5 hours each day as compared to 0-2h before COVID-19. However, the sample size of the study was small and the obtained data was undifferentiated.

Joshi *et al.* (2015) identified four key performance indicators that lead to substantial enhancement of viewership, or Viewership Enhancement (VE). The said factors include Intention of Use (IoU), Convenience, Customer Engagement (CE), and Knowledge of Consumption. Appealing to these factors would allow OTT service providers to improve the viewers' overall satisfaction with their viewing experience, in turn ensuring customer retention. Fig. (**1**) explains the conceptual model of factors affecting customer viewership enhancement.

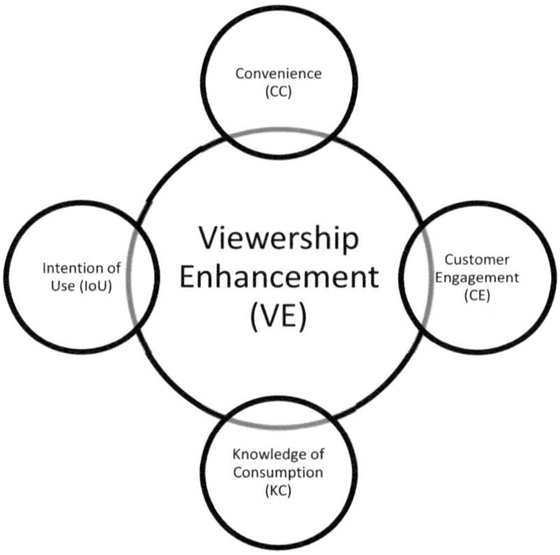


**Fig. (1).** Conceptual Model of Factors Affecting Customer Viewership Enhancement (VE).
Source: Own Compilation, 2022.

In view of the literature above, the scope and need of research have been identified below with the rationales introspecting on the aspects at depth.

## Need of Study

This study intends to pinpoint the latitude of OTT platforms and the degree of their acceptability amongst Indian consumers during the COVID-19 pandemic. Furthermore, the aim of the study is to understand the features that account for the adoption of said services, viewership status, customer engagement and retention in the future. In addition, it will aid in providing a full picture of how OTT has experienced an exponential boom, eventually taking over other mediums of consumable entertainment. The consumer's intention to utilize OTT and what really drives the use of OTT video streaming platforms have not been considered in studies conducted to date. In the assessment, the research gap below was explored with its logical reasoning.

## Research Gaps

Diversified sampling of the consumer's intention to use OTT and what really leads to the use of OTT video streaming platforms have not been taken into account in studies conducted to date. (Sultana, 2021)

Different dimensions of customer engagement other than post-sales service have not been taken into account in the studies conducted in this regard (Garima Gupta, 2021).

Evidence-based research that supports the legitimacy and usefulness of having arbitrary screen-time cutoffs in today's digital world has a number of gaps and methodological shortcomings (Kardfelt-Winther, 2017)

The gaps identified were questioned to explore the objective assessment of the factors and variables that could be subtly deciphered.

## Research Questions

The salient research questions for the objective evaluation of the study are as follows:

1. How many hours does the general consumer dedicate to watching content on a daily basis on OTT platforms before and after the onset of the pandemic lockdown?

2. Which is the preferred OTT platform for the consumer for the consumption of content?

3. How much is the customer willing to pay for a periodic subscription to the said OTT platform?

4. What factors are involved in the rise of viewership during the lockdown period in India?

## Research Objectives

The objectives of the research are mentioned below

- To understand the consumption pattern of OTT content in the COVID-19 pandemic.
- To study the factors impacting the inclination towards OTT platform in the COVID-19 pandemic.
- To determine the association between customer engagement and viewership.

## RESEARCH METHODOLOGY

The research methodology applied different modalities, tools and techniques to validate the findings with justifications. The study was exploratory as well as conclusive in nature, derived from primary and secondary data. The data was collected from primary sources, which consisted of respondents' inputs. It was decided to use the survey method to gather primary data. A questionnaire that was modified to make it acceptable for the current study after taking into account a pre-tested questionnaire was used to conduct the survey. The questionnaire covered various aspects of different factors related to the consumption of content on OTT platforms, *i.e.*, age, gender, income, time spent on consumption of content and number of OTT platforms subscribed.

### Sampling and Coverage

The probability sampling method was involved in the process, more specifically known as random sampling. The structured questionnaire was framed on Google Forms and was circulated to friends and family members in various parts of India. For the purpose of this study, 110 respondents were targeted and 104 responses were collected for data analysis. The data was collected in May 2022.

### Tools for Data Analysis

Data Analysis was carried out using MS Excel and IBM SPSS Version 26. The statistical tools used were descriptive statistics, Chi-Square Test, Correlation, Tables and Factor analysis.

For this purpose, a five-point scale (Likert Scale) was adopted, 5 being "Strongly Agree" and 1 being "Strongly Disagree".

## KMO and Bartlett's Test Indicators

The data analysis below deeply analyzes and evaluates the assessments made through the questionnaires and interviews conducted over a period of time, as mentioned in Table **1**.

**Table 1. KMO and bartlett's test of sphericity.**

| KMO and Bartlett's Test | | |
|---|---|---|
| Kaiser-Meyer-Olkin Measure of Sampling Adequacy. | | .835 |
| Bartlett's Test of Sphericity | Approx. Chi-Square | 858.153 |
| | Df | 136 |
| | Sig. | .000 |

Source: Own Database, 2022.

The Kaiser-Meyer-Olkin Test is a measure to check data suitability, which is further required for factor analysis. The value of Sampling Adequacy here is more than 0.8. Thus establishing that there is a somewhat relevant correlation between all the variables chosen for this study and that the sampling itself is adequate.

## DATA ANALYSIS

The data analysis part of the research paper was considered for informative graphs. Through the analysis, findings, conclusions and recommendations were provided.

### Gender Distribution of Respondents

The majority of respondents happened to be female respondents, constituting 59% of the total sample size, as compared to male respondents who made up 40% of the total sample size.

### Age Distribution of Respondents

Respondents aged between 26 and 30 years, representing 39% of the total sample size, were found to be major consumers of OTT platforms, followed by respondents belonging to the 19-25 years age demographic. However, there were very less respondents below the age of 18 years, representing only 4% of the total sample size.

### Distribution of Income Levels of Respondents

The majority of respondents belonged to the income level group of below 2 Lakhs, while the others belonged to the income level group of 10-15 lakhs.

## Cities Distribution of Respondents

It was found that most of the respondents were from Bhubaneshwar and Kolkata, representing 26% and 14% of the total sample taken, respectively. The remaining respondents happened to be from other cities like Lucknow, Aska, Patna, and Bangalore, to name a few, as mentioned in Fig. (**2**).

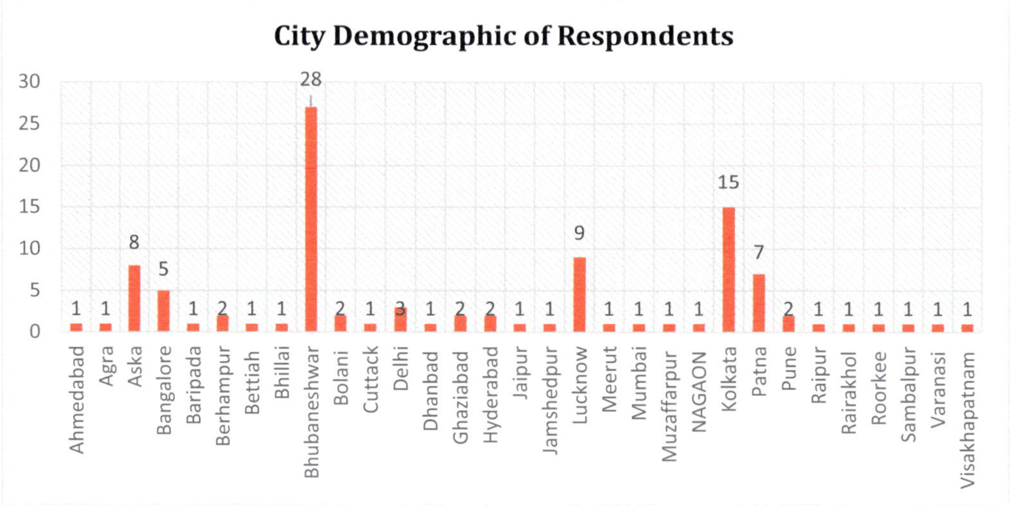


**Fig. (2).** Source: Own database, 2022.
City Demographics of Respondents.

## Distribution of Occupation of Respondents

The above visualization details the occupation of the respondents, where the highest number of OTT viewers belonged to different professionals (51%), followed by students, who comprise 17% of the respondents.

## Distribution of Place of Living of Respondents

The highest number of OTT viewers belong to urban areas, representing 82% of the total sample taken, followed by semi-urban areas. It should also be noted that the majority of respondents belonged to Bhubaneswar and Kolkata.

## Preferred Device for Consumption of OTT

It is noted that a major portion of respondents preferred smartphones over laptops for OTT consumption, mostly because of better portability and battery life. The least chosen device in all the preference groups was a tablet, mostly because of the growing redundancy over the years, as mentioned in Fig. (**3**) above.

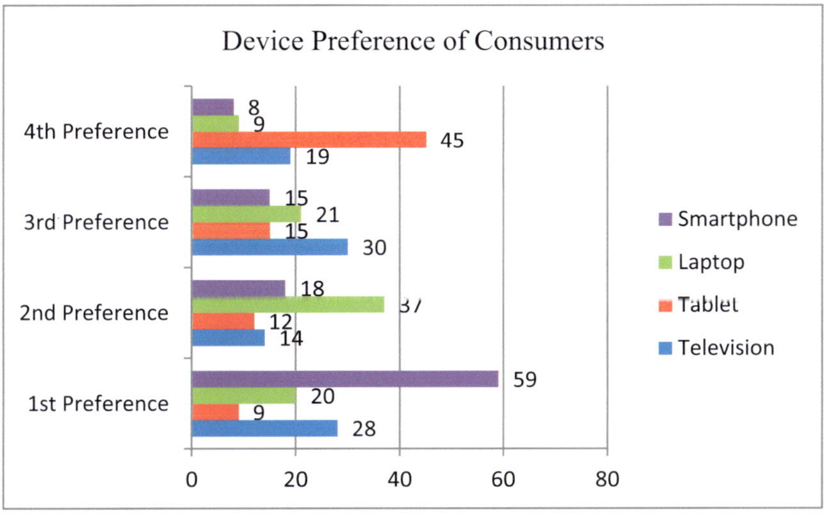


**Fig. (3).** Source: Own database, 2022.
Device Preference of Consumers.

## Language(s) Preferred for Consumption of OTTs

As the first preferred language, the majority of respondents chose English, assumedly for both subtitles and voiceovers. In contrast, foreign language was the least preferred in all of the preferred groups, as mentioned in Fig. (**4**).

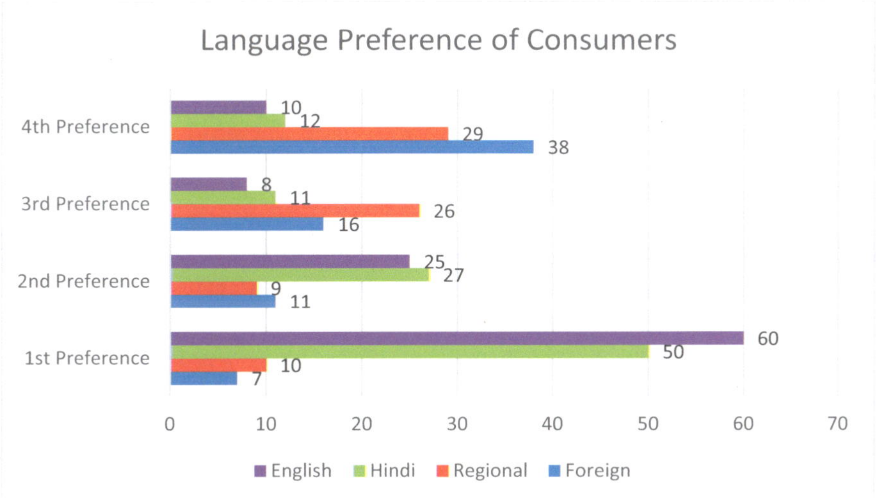


**Fig. (4).** Source: Own database, 2022.
Language Preference of Consumers.

## Preference of Time for Consumption of OTTs

The majority of respondents preferred to consume OTT at night as the first preference, followed by respondents preferring No Fixed Time as the first preference. It should be noted that morning time is chosen as the last preference by respondents, as mentioned in the Fig. (**5**).

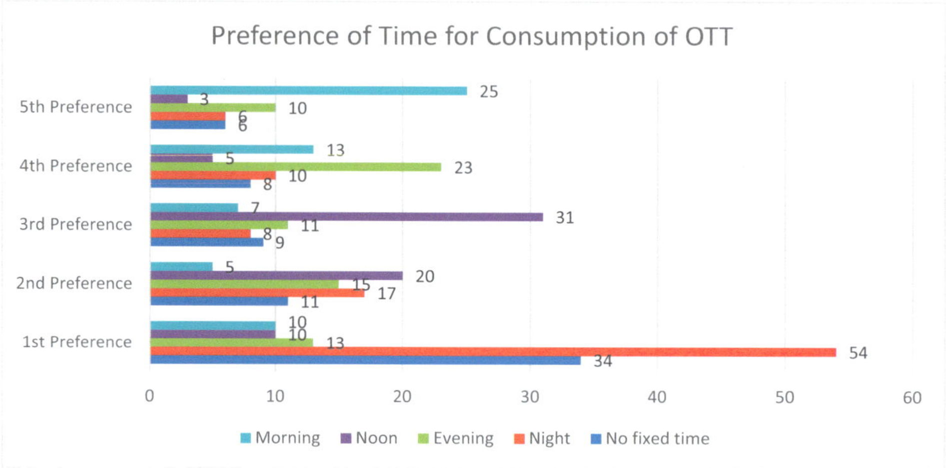


**Fig. (5).** Source: Own database, 2022.
Preference of Time for Consumption of OTTs

## Subscription Plans Opted by Respondents

Annual Plans were the most sought-after subscription plan for OTTs by respondents (75%). It should be mentioned that the daily plan was launched by Netflix very recently, but none of the respondents had opted for a daily plan.

## OTT Platforms Subscribed by Respondents

Amazon Prime was the most popular choice when it comes to choice of OTTs by respondents (80%), followed by Hotstar (74%) and Netflix (68%). It should be noted that subscribing to Amazon Prime not only allows access to OTT services but also to features like fast-delivery services and exclusive deals on their Amazon website, therefore providing more value for money to customers.

## Responses to Intention to Use by Respondents

The respondents strongly agreed with the components that were associated with Consuming OTT within Budget, Future Consumption of OTT and Preferring OTT over Television owing to quality content. Neutrality in collective agreement was observed in Time Constraints for the consumption of OTT, as depicted in Fig. (**6**).

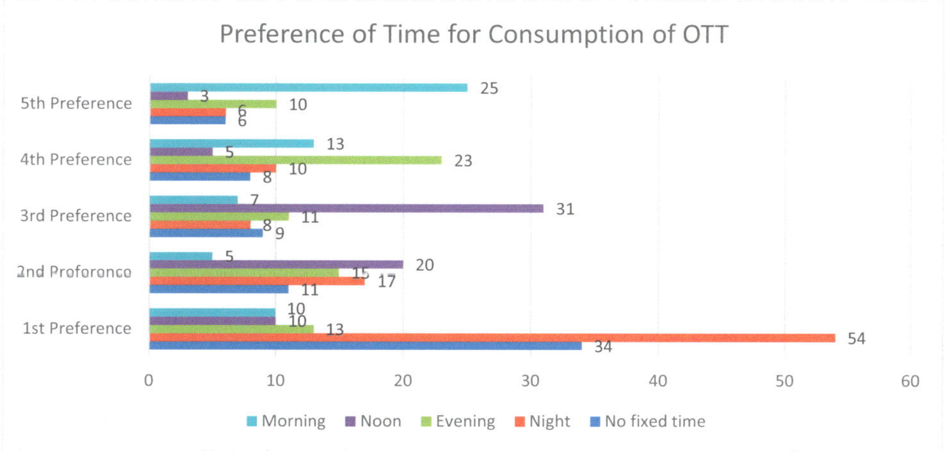


**Fig. (6).** Source: Own database, 2022.
Intention to Use OTT Services

## Responses to Convenience by Respondents

The respondents strongly agreed to components associated with good value for money, watching with friends and family, watching in free time, overall viewing experience and faster browsing compared to television, as mentioned in Fig. (**7**). A neutral response was observed in the case of conditional connectivity viewing.

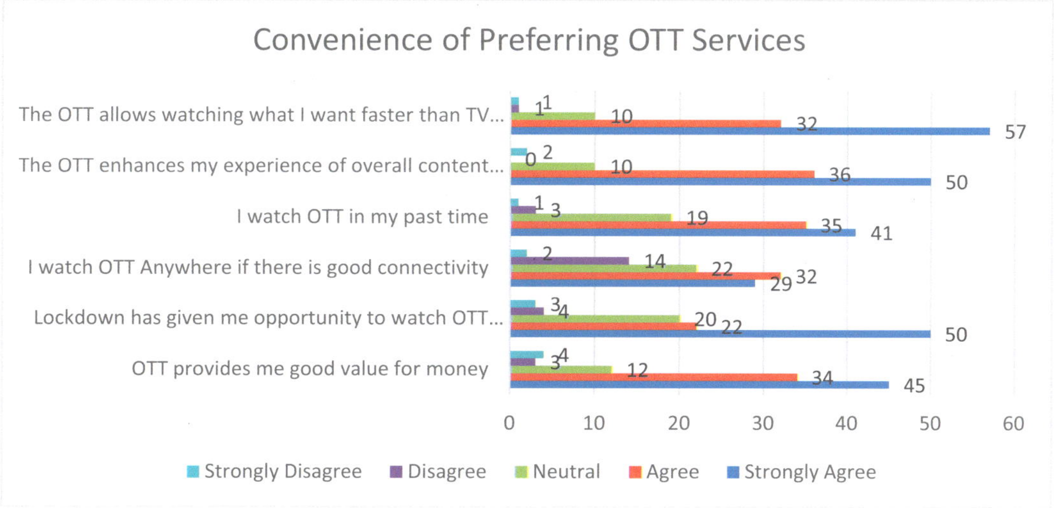


**Fig. (7).** Source: Own database, 2022.
Convenience of Preferring OTT Services

## Responses to Customer Knowledge by Respondents

Respondents mostly agreed, but not strongly, to both the components of consumer knowledge. It should be noted that the viewers could not critique the content available on OTT platforms because of the pandemic. In addition, the viewers are now more knowledgeable because of the viewing experience provided by OTT services, as mentioned in Fig. (**8**).

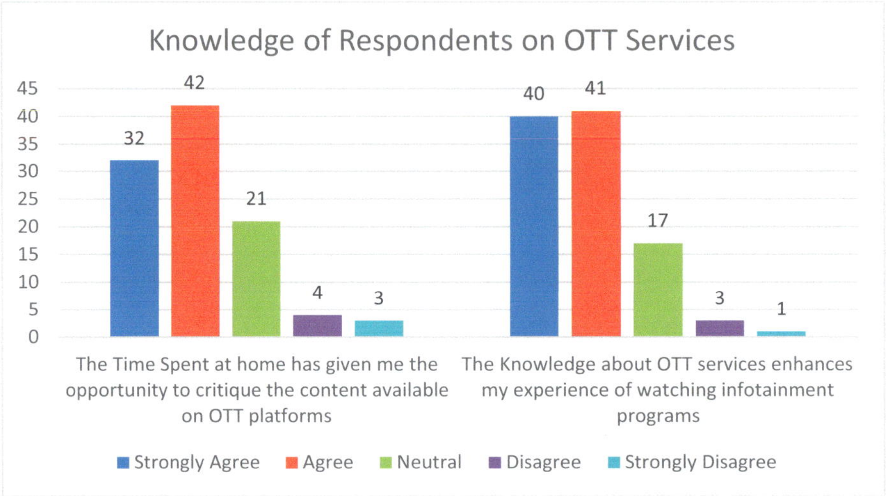


**Fig. (8).** Source: Own database, 2022.
Knowledge of OTT Services.

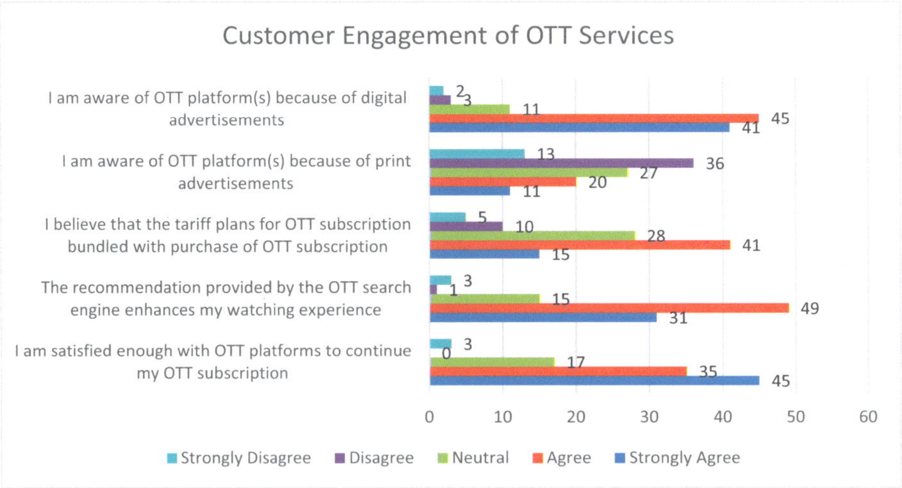


**Fig. (9).** Source: Own database, 2022.
Customer Engagement toward OTT Services

## Responses to Customer Engagement by Respondents

The respondents strongly agreed to components like awareness due to digital media and overall satisfaction factor. Neutral responsivity was observed in the case of awareness due to print media, OTT subscription plans bundling and search engine/algorithm interface, as mentioned in Fig. (**9**).

## Factor Loading

**Table 2. Exploratory factor loading.**

| Communalities | | |
|---|---|---|
| | **Initial** | **Extraction** |
| **INTENT OF CONSUMPTION** | | |
| I consume OTT content within a budget. | 1.000 | .668 |
| I spend more than the required time to consume OTT content. | 1.000 | .622 |
| I plan to use OTT platforms in the future. | 1.000 | .623 |
| I prefer the OTT platform over television because of quality content. | 1.000 | .717 |
| CONVENIENCE | | |
| The OTT allows me to watch what I want faster than TV subscriber services. | 1.000 | .527 |
| The OTT has enhanced my experience of overall content viewing. | 1.000 | .717 |
| I watch OTT in my past time. | 1.000 | .667 |
| I watch OTT anywhere IF there is good connectivity. | 1.000 | .525 |
| Lockdown has given me the opportunity to watch OTT with friends and family. | 1.000 | .545 |
| OTT provides me good value for money. | 1.000 | .742 |
| CUSTOMER KNOWLEDGE | | |
| The time spent at home has given me the opportunity to critique the content available on OTT platforms. | 1.000 | .692 |
| The knowledge about OTT services enhances my experience of watching infotainment programs. | 1.000 | .721 |
| CUSTOMER ENGAGEMENT | | |
| I am aware of OTT platform(s) because of digital advertisements. (YouTube, Social Media) | 1.000 | .485 |

*(Table 2) cont.....*

| Communalities | | |
|---|---|---|
| | **Initial** | **Extraction** |
| **INTENT OF CONSUMPTION** | | |
| I am aware of OTT platform(s) because of print advertisements. | 1.000 | .735 |
| The tariff plans for OTT subscription bundles with the purchase of electronic goods or recharges are satisfactory. | 1.000 | .606 |
| The recommendations provided by the OTT search engine enhances my watching experience. | 1.000 | .686 |
| I am satisfied enough with OTT platforms to continue my OTT subscription in the future. | 1.000 | .728 |

**Source:** Own Database, 2022.

The curve for the Scree Plot determines that at least 4 variables of the study are fit for Exploratory Factor Analysis, as mentioned in Fig. (**10**).

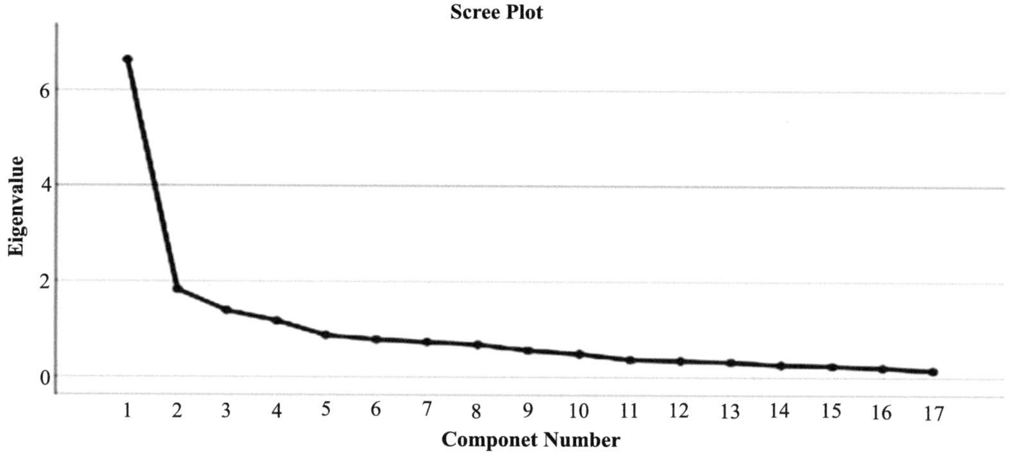


**Fig. (10).** Source: Own Database, 2022.
Scree Plot for Referencing Eigenvalues

## Chi-Square Tables

Bivariate Analysis was done between various variables. Since there are multiple permutations possible, only the findings that had an asymmetric significance of less than 0.05 are presented here.

**Table 3. Chi-Square Test for Various Variables.**

| **a) AGE*HOURS A DAY SPENT ON CONSUMPTION OF OTT CONTENT** | | | |
|---|---|---|---|
| - | **Value** | **Degree of Freedom** | **Asymptomatic Significance (2-Sided)** |
| Pearson Chi-Square | 18.417[a] | 10 | .048 |
| Likelihood Ratio | 23.640 | 10 | .009 |
| Linear-by-Linear Association | 6.022 | 1 | .014 |
| **b) AGE*SUBSCRIPTION PLAN OPTED** | | | |
| - | **Value** | **Degree of Freedom** | **Asymptomatic Significance (2-Sided)** |
| Pearson Chi-Square | 22.197[a] | 15 | .103 |
| Likelihood Ratio | 20.727 | 15 | .146 |
| Linear-by-Linear Association | 1.060 | 1 | .303 |
| **c) AGE*I PLAN TO USE OTT PLATFORMS IN THE FUTURE** | | | |
| - | Value | Degree of Freedom | Asymptomatic Significance (2-Sided) |
| Pearson Chi-Square | 31.803[a] | 20 | .045 |
| Likelihood Ratio | 30.088 | 20 | .068 |
| Linear-by-Linear Association | .892 | 1 | .345 |
| **d) AGE*I AM AWARE OF OTT PLATFORMS BECAUSE OF DIGITAL ADVERTISEMENTS** | | | |
| - | Value | Degree of Freedom | Asymptomatic Significance (2-Sided) |
| Pearson Chi-Square | 43.399[a] | 20 | .002 |
| Likelihood Ratio | 27.913 | 20 | .111 |
| Linear-by-Linear Association | 1.860 | 1 | .173 |
| **e) GENDER*THE TARRIFF PLANS FOR OTT SUBSCRIPTION BUNDLES WITH THE PURCHASE OF ELECTRONIC GOODS/RECHARGES ARE SATISFACTORY** | | | |
| - | Value | Degree of Freedom | Asymptomatic Significance (2-Sided) |
| Pearson Chi-Square | 25.392[a] | 8 | .001 |
| Likelihood Ratio | 12.071 | 8 | .148 |
| Linear-by-Linear Association | .041 | 1 | .839 |
| **f) SUBSCRIPTION PLAN*LOCKDOWN HAS GIVEN ME THE OPPORTUNITY TO WATCH OTT WITH FRIENDS AND FAMILY** | | | |
| - | Value | Degree of Freedom | Asymptomatic Significance (2-Sided) |
| Pearson Chi-Square | 30.172[a] | 12 | .003 |

*(Table 3) cont.....*

| | | | |
|---|---|---|---|
| Likelihood Ratio | 20.167 | 12 | .064 |
| Linear-by-Linear Association | 4.730 | 1 | .030 |
| **g) SUBSCRIPTION PLAN*I AM SATISFIED ENOUGH WITH OTT PLATFORMS TO CONTINUE MY SUBSCRIPTION IN THE FUTURE** | | | |
| - | Value | Degree of Freedom | Asymptomatic Significance (2-Sided) |
| Pearson Chi-Square | 25.460[a] | 9 | .003 |
| Likelihood Ratio | 19.495 | 9 | .021 |
| Linear-by-Linear Association | 11.850 | 1 | .001 |
| **h) SUBSCRIPTION PLAN*I AM AWARE OF OTT PLATFORMS BECAUSE OF DIGITAL ADVERSTISEMENTS** | | | |
| - | Value | Degree of Freedom | Asymptomatic Significance (2-Sided) |
| Pearson Chi-Square | 33.396[a] | 12 | .001 |
| Likelihood Ratio | 13.442 | 12 | .338 |
| Linear-by-Linear Association | 3.108 | 1 | .078 |
| **i) SUBSCRIPTION PLAN*THE OTT ENHANCES MY EXPERIENCE OF OVERALL CONTENT VIEWING** | | | |
| - | Value | Degree of Freedom | Asymptomatic Significance (2-Sided) |
| Pearson Chi-Square | 23.275[a] | 9 | .006 |
| Likelihood Ratio | 14.169 | 9 | .116 |
| Linear-by-Linear Association | 8.374 | 1 | .004 |

**Source:** Own Database, 2022.

A significant association was observed between age and hours spent on the consumption of OTT content. It is noted that opting for a subscription plan is not influenced by age to a significant extent. There is a significant association between the tendency to continue watching OTT in the future and age. There is a relevant association between age and the tendency to watch OTT content if there is good connectivity. Age is significantly influenced by print and digital advertisements. There is a significant association between gender and satisfaction with tariff plans for OTT subscription bundles with electronic and digital goods. There is a significant association between occupation and the tendency to watch OTT with friends and family during the lockdown. There is a significant association between hours spent on a daily basis and the tendency to watch OTT content if there is good connectivity, as well as planning to watch OTT in the future. There is a significant association between the subscription plan opted and having to watch OTT with friends and family in lockdown. There is a significant association between the subscription plan opted and the perception that OTT provided good value for money, the satisfaction of continuing OTT subscription, and awareness due to digital advertisement. There is a significant association between subscription plans and the tendency to watch OTT with good connectivity as well as overall experience enhancement provided by OTT, as explained in Table **3**.

## Findings

The study was conducted to understand the psychology of consumers that enables prolonged viewership and two-way engagement between consumers and service providers; it is safe to conclude that this form of entertainment has carved its way into the everyday life of Indians and is going to remain relevant for a long time. Even though more investments, both in terms of monetary and time resources, are being observed in this domain, it is tough to infer whether such services are completely going to disrupt the conventional network television viewing or theatrical experiences. With increasing internet penetration and technological intervention in India, the long-term viability and longevity of this platform remains a highly bankable domain.

# CONCLUSION

Viewership enhancement is significantly influenced by the Purpose of Consumption, Convenience of Consumption, Knowledge of Content and Customer Engagement. Technology intervention and high Internet penetration provide a foundation for the adoption and acceptability of OTT platforms. Due to locally relevant content, inexpensive prices, and the widespread use of 4G (and, eventually, 5G), OTT platforms have been rising in popularity in India, and this trend is expected to continue. The market is dominated by streaming services like Netflix, Amazon Prime Video, and Hotstar, with others like AltBalaji and Voot also gaining popularity. The novelty and variety of content available on such platforms, compared to the regular Television and theatre content, are what enable higher conversion rates (*i.e.*, The probability of a potential customer converting into an actual customer/consumer of the service or product). Customer engagement is seen mostly *via* digital advertisements and social CRM.

When it comes to entertainment and usability, OTT and traditional TV are very comparable in their own niches. Overall, OTT TV is more advantageous than traditional TV in terms of competition in every way. It should be inferred that good customer engagement and rapport building lead to a higher probability of the customer opting to continue his/her subscription plan, thus ensuring customer retention. Satisfactory customer engagement also cements brand loyalty in the long run. In India, Amazon Prime and Hotstar continue to be the most commonly used when it comes to OTT platforms. As is the case in the Indian market, price sensibility remains latent. The Indian market is large and far from being saturated, so growth in the user base and digital advertising bodes well for all enterprises in the entertainment sector. Thankfully, OTT platforms happen to provide flexible pricing plans suited to customer needs. Customers are mostly not satisfied with the bundling of OTT tariff plans that are available on the purchase of Smart Televisions or mobile recharges. Social Media continues to remain the ideal ground, acting as a mediator of communication between the everyday customer and service provider.

The OTT domain is perceived as extremely marketable, with both new content and an increasing subscriber base on the rise. Understanding that binge-watching cannot be either good or bad, cultural or structural, but rather a developing human experience will help us comprehend its subtleties. This leads to the conclusion that production houses are starting to use this platform for their cinematic ventures, and the average internet user is all for it.

## SUGGESTIONS

Pricing plans should offer more features or perks in addition to just viewing to help customer retention. It could be in the form of adding extra Behind the Scenes footage or Director's Commentary. OTT platforms can integrate social features into their services, which can allow benefits like group watching with friends. Another tactic is service bundling that can be used. Many operators are utilizing this tactic, where they provide group offers so that the promise of financial savings from using OTT services is more alluring.

The gamification of services allows incentivization for customers. It can be a subtle discount voucher for the number of hours/shows watched or an extra free month subscription that comes with the annual subscription plan purchase. New market entrees can collaborate with existing market players, which will help this ecosystem be perceived as a safe space and not a cutthroat competition for newcomers. Since the majority of customers are not satisfied with bundled OTT plans that come with the purchase of electronics or recharges, the bundling scheme remains an area worth revising.

The roadmap to a brilliant OTT platform service initiates with deciphering the customers' psyche and appealing to their demands for content consumption, user experience, or the overall business model. It is crucial to closely monitor big data streaming analytics in order to facilitate achievable decoding of customer behavioral patterns, as it is the "viewer" who lies in the center and forefront of the business. It has been standard practice to deliver syndicated content on apps like JioApps and Airtel Wynk. Partnerships between telcos and OTT providers have significantly increased in India and throughout the world to provide subscribers of specific telcos with free access to exclusive video content in order to enhance earnings.

It should be noted that OTT viewers gravitate towards customized/personalized, pertinent content recommendations that are tailor-made to their viewing experience. Nonetheless, with new streaming services that pop up almost every other day, the ocean of content keeps growing to an overwhelming amount. Therefore, recommendation engines need to be attuned toward customizability in order to deliver apt content to users. This, in turn, will ensure overall customer satisfaction and guarantee customer retention. Massive scale viewer data sets, in conjunction with metadata for analysis, will provide OTT services in improving their recommendation engine.

In addition, deep big data streaming analytics (Average amount of time spent in viewing, amount of pausing time, genre of shows preferred, the time window of viewing and so on) also provides OTT services with deeper insights. It allows them to decode the various whims and wants of the audience. The facilitation of such information helps OTT service providers make improved decisions when it comes to content propagation.

## BIBLIOGRAPHY

Bertin, E., Crespi, N., L'Hostis, M. (2011). A few myths about telco and OTT models. [http://dx.doi.org/10.1109/ICIN.2011.6081106]

Banerjee, A., Alleman, J., Rappoport, P. (2013). Video-viewing behavior in the era of connected devices. *Commun. Strateg.,* (92), 19-42.

Castro, D., Rigby, J.M., Cabral, D., Nisi, V. (2021). The binge-watcher's journey: Investigating motivations, contexts, and affective states surrounding Netflix viewing. *Convergence (London), 27*(1), 3-20. [http://dx.doi.org/10.1177/1354856519890856]

Cebeci, U., Ince, O., Turkcan, H. (2019). Understanding the intention to use Netflix: An extended technology acceptance model approach. *Int. Rev. Manag. Mark., 9*(6), 152-157. [http://dx.doi.org/10.32479/irmm.8771]

Chung, Y.K. (2014). Analysis of Netflix and Hulu for Online Video Content Distributors' Business Model Comparison in N-Screen Era. *J. Korea Content. Assoc., 14*(5), 30-43. [http://dx.doi.org/10.5392/JKCA.2014.14.05.030]

De', R., Pandey, N., Pal, A. (2020). Impact of digital surge during Covid-19 pandemic: A viewpoint on research and practice. *Int. J. Inf. Manage., 55*, 102171. [http://dx.doi.org/10.1016/j.ijinfomgt.2020.102171] [PMID: 32836633]

Das, B., Panda, R.K. (2017). Emerging Innovations in Branding: Paradigms in Social Media Marketing through Digital Platform *Management Practice for the New Economy.,* Hardback, Section-I: India and Global Economic Perspective. Bloomsbury, India: (45), 11.

Das, B., Das, S., Padhy, P. (2019). *Change Management through Enterprise Resource Planning..* New Delhi: City Publication.

Gershon, R.A. (2016). *Digital media and innovation: Management and design strategies in communication..* Sage Publications.

Gupta, G., Singharia, K. (2021). Consumption of OTT media streaming in COVID-19 lockdown: Insights from PLS analysis. *Vision: The Journal of Business Perspective, 25*(1), 36-46. [http://dx.doi.org/10.1177/0972262921989118]

Jog, Y., Joshi, S., Thenuan, P. (2016). Net neutrality and impact of regulation on over the top (OTT) services and study of responses of public and telecom service provider. *International Journal of Management, IT and Engineering, 6*(6), 183-197.

Katherine Chen, Y-N. (2019). Competitions between OTT TV platforms and traditional television in Taiwan: A Niche analysis. *Telecomm. Policy, 43*(9), 101793. [http://dx.doi.org/10.1016/j.telpol.2018.10.006]

Kim, M.S., Kim, E., Hwang, S., Kim, J., Kim, S. (2017). Willingness to pay for over-the-top services in China and Korea. *Telecomm. Policy, 41*(3), 197-207. [http://dx.doi.org/10.1016/j.telpol.2016.12.011]

Leung, L., Wei, R. (2000). More than just talk on the move: Uses and gratifications of the cellular phone. *Journal. Mass Commun. Q., 77*(2), 308-320. [http://dx.doi.org/10.1177/107769900007700206]

Madnani, D., Fernandes, S., Madnani, N. (2020). Analysing the impact of COVID-19 on over-the-top media platforms in India. *Int. J. Pervas. Comput. Commun., 16*(5), 457-475. [http://dx.doi.org/10.1108/IJPCC-07-2020-0083]

Malia, A., Paramita Pradhan, P., Das, B., Bisoyi, B., Satpathy, I. (2023). Impact of Digital Marketing on Customer Perception During Covid -19 (Omicron) Relating to Ease of Banking Transactions. *Parikalpana KIIT J. Manag., 19*(1), 188-199. [http://dx.doi.org/10.23862/kiit-parikalpana/2023/v19/i1/220847]

McKenzie, J., Crosby, P., Cox, J., Collins, A. (2019). Experimental evidence on demand for "on-demand" entertainment. *J. Econ. Behav. Organ., 161*, 98-113. [http://dx.doi.org/10.1016/j.jebo.2019.03.017]

Moochhala, Q. (2018). The future of online OTT entertainment services in India. *Actionesque Consulting, Pune–India, 4*, 2581-5792.

Mulla, T. (2022). Assessing the factors influencing the adoption of over-the-top streaming platforms: A literature review from 2007 to 2021. *Telemat. Inform., 69*, 101797. [http://dx.doi.org/10.1016/j.tele.2022.101797]

Menon, D. (2022). Purchase and continuation intentions of over -the -top (OTT) video streaming platform subscriptions: a uses and gratification theory perspective. *Telematics and Informatics Reports, 5*, 100006. [http://dx.doi.org/10.1016/j.teler.2022.100006]

Nijhawan, G.S., Dahiya, S. (2020). Role of COVID as a Catalyst in increasing adoption of OTTs in India: A Study of evolving consumer consumption patterns and future business scope. *JCCC., 12*(6), 298-311. [http://dx.doi.org/10.31620/JCCC.12.20/28]

Nagaraj, S., Singh, S., Yasa, V.R. (2021). Factors affecting consumers' willingness to subscribe to over-th- -top (OTT) video streaming services in India. *Technol. Soc., 65*, 101534. [http://dx.doi.org/10.1016/j.techsoc.2021.101534]

Parnami, S., Jain, T. (2021). A study on increase in the usage of OTT streaming services. *Int. J. Res. Eng. Sci. Manag., 4*(8), 142-145.

Patel, M.K., Khadia, R., Awasya, G. (2020). A study: OTT viewership in "lockdown" and viewer's dynamic watching experience. *IJTMJMC., 5*(2), 10-22.

Steiner, E., Xu, K. (2020). Binge-watching motivates change: Uses and gratifications of streaming video viewers challenge traditional TV research. *Convergence (London), 26*(1), 82-101. [http://dx.doi.org/10.1177/1354856517750365]

Sundaravel, E., Elangovan, N. (2020). Emergence and future of Over-the-top (OTT) video services in India:

Analytical research. *IJBSR., 8*(2), 489-499.

Tefertiller, A. (2020). Cable cord-cutting and streaming adoption: Advertising avoidance and technology acceptance in television innovation. *Telemat. Inform., 51*, 101416.
[http://dx.doi.org/10.1016/j.tele.2020.101416]

Vaterlaus, J.M., Spruance, L.A., Frantz, K., Kruger, J.S. (2019). College student television binge watching: Conceptualization, gratifications, and perceived consequences. *Soc. Sci. J., 56*(4), 470-479.
[http://dx.doi.org/10.1016/j.soscij.2018.10.004]

Venkatesh, V., Davis, F.D. (2000). A theoretical extension of the technology acceptance model: Four longitudinal field studies. *Manage. Sci., 46*(2), 186-204.
[http://dx.doi.org/10.1287/mnsc.46.2.186.11926]

## CHAPTER 11

# Women-Driven Innovation in Industry 5.0 Post Pandemic

**Neeru Sidana**[1,*] and **Richa Goel**[2]

[1] *Amity School of Economics (ASE) Amity University, Noida, U.P., India*

[2] *SCMS, Noida, U.P. Symbiosis International University, Pune, India*

**Abstract:** The COVID-19 pandemic has affected women disproportionately, with women-led businesses suffering an economic blow and decades of progress that had been made towards gender equality being erased. As per the UN 2030 Agenda, one of the ways to address global challenges like poverty and foster prosperity (SDG 5 & 9) is to put greater focus on catalyzing innovative entrepreneurship among women. The resultant economic empowerment will pave the way for greater gender equity. Recent literature in this field has highlighted a lacuna for additional support for women-based enterprises in order to recover from the impacts of the pandemic and resume their operations. Such support could be provided in the form of stimulus funding or government grants and financing provided by the private sector. Additionally, capital should be provided to innovate and implement modern technologies and skill advancement programs to help these enterprises gain a competitive advantage. Such initiatives are crucial in order to provide active support to nurture the projects that can aid women entrepreneurs in adapting to new technologies, develop digital literacy, and access financial support and capital in order to run their businesses. Particularly from the lens of Industry 5.0, this study takes a hard look at honing down the key factors that can contribute toward fostering an environment of innovation among women entrepreneurs. Additionally, this study provides insights into the relevant literature with a specific focus on future research opportunities using a literature review approach covering 40-50 literature reviews, as well as identifies expository aspects that can promote the revolution navigated by female entrepreneurs.

**Keywords:** Entrepreneurial success, Industry 5.0, Risk-taking, Women entrepreneurs, Women-driven innovation.

## INTRODUCTION

Industry 5.0 is considered to be an antithesis to the vision of Industry 4.0. Sustainability and resilience have become an important issue after the COVID-19

* **Corresponding authors Neeru Sidana:** Amity School of Economics (ASE) Amity University, Noida, U.P., India; E-mail: nsidana@amity.edu

pandemic. Because of this, policymakers and organizations increasingly pay attention to Industry 5.0 with an aim to place human workers at the midpoint of innovation, exploiting the impact of technology on our society. This is aligned with the objectives of the United Nations Sustainable Development Goals (Huang *et al.*, 2022; Carayannis *et al.*, 2022). The crucial role of women will be experienced in Industry 5.0 in the workplace. The empowerment of womens worldwide is the most important SDGs.

It has been recognized as a statistically proven and accepted fact that women entrepreneurs have a significant role to play in the country's economic development (Hassan *et al.*, 2020). Job creation can be witnessed as a result of the participation of women in the labor force. Electronic manufacturing is an industry where more than 50% of the employees are women. Businesses that have women at the helm are considered to bring creativity into the operations (Balhara and Singh, 2015).

As per a report prepared by (GEM) Global Entrepreneurship Monitor in 2015, the participation of women in areas of innovation like entrepreneurship does not only contribute in favor of the development of a nation. If we look at the MSME owner's portfolio, then 20.37% of women hold ownership, comprising around 23.3% of Indian Labour Force positions. Indian women are also heading startup businesses, as 45% of startups are in the name of women. Some major startups run by women include Nykaa (USD 12.5 billion), MobiKwik (USD 750 million), and Byju's (USD 18 Billion). As per McKinsey Global (2022), India provides an added US$ 700 billion to global GDP by increasing female participation. The manufacturing and agriculture sectors have witnessed a visible participation of women. Women can help their families come out of poverty and contribute to household income. Bright prospects for the country can be seen through an increased literacy rate of 8.8% in FY 2021.

Societies can be transformed with the development of women entrepreneurship. This opportunity is still unachievable because of less participation of women in entrepreneurial activities India's performance in the female entrepreneur index is very low. It is believed that uncertainties of characteristics give new dimensions to women innovators (Abd *et al.*, 2019). Presently, there is a need to study some factors such as a drive for achievement, risk-taking abilities, self-confidence and creativity because these characteristics are often cited as compared to others based on previous studies (Mendryk & Dylon, 2014 Hassan *et al.*, 2014; Ummah & Gunapalan, 2012; Hoe *et al.*, 2012; Lai *et al.*, 2010). Tulus (2009) stressed that women innovators need to understand the abilities and personality characteristics that are needed in order to bring success to their ventures. Evidently, timely identification of the factors will help them to grow their business. The purpose of the present study is to know the functional relationship between entrepreneurial characteristics, experience of work, and women-driven innovation.

## Research Objectives

The following research objectives are evaluated:

- To know expository aspects that can promote revolution navigated by female founders.
- To understand the relationship between identified critical factors and sustained growth.
- To identify the many implications and strategies that could aid policymakers in building a sustainable women-driven infrastructure.

RQ1: What are the major barriers restraining women from moving towards innovation post pandemic?

RQ2: Which research gaps and further research areas are suggested?

The research is organized as follows: Section 2 is 'Literature review', which provides a comprehensive overview of research already existing in this field. In this section, a detailed analysis of the factors behind women-led innovation and their role with regard to Industry 5.0 has been presented. In section 3 of the paper, the relationship between factors of women-driven innovation and sustainable development goals has been highlighted. Section 4 of the study provides suggested strategies for policymakers to drive innovation among women workforce for Industry 5.0. Finally, Section 6 discusses the conclusion of the present study.

## Methodology/Strategy

This study will be conducted in four phases:

Phase 1: Reviewing past and current research conducted by the researchers using the LR approach to identify the research gap and investigate the critical factors fostering innovation driven by women entrepreneurs.

Phase 2: Developing a robust framework/model for conceptualizing and encouraging women-driven innovation. The authors then identify the broad challenges to encourage it and use the model thus created to develop directions for future research.

Phase 3: Evaluating the relation between identified critical factors and sustained growth

Phase 4: Results and discussions are mentioned

Phase 5: Conclusion is summarized along with future implications and scope for further research.

## Literature Review

In the current section, a comprehensive review of relevant literature in this field has been presented in a structure following the chronology of research questions as provided in the introduction of this paper.

## Innovation in Industry 5.0

Industry 5.0 is on the verge of harnessing extreme automation and using Big Data with safety, policy for technology innovation, and principles of responsible implementation enabled by 3D-symmetry in innovation design (Ozdemir and Hekim, 2018). It aims to re-evaluate the impact of technology on our society and its direction for the future by placing value on human workers as the drivers of innovation and critical thinking. Industry 5.0 can redistribute access to knowledge coproduction from Big Data, democratizing it and creating further structure on the new concept of symmetrical innovation.

Thus, studies show that Industry 5.0 is poised to bring significant changes to the economy and society (Özdemir and Hekim, 2018; Xu *et al.*, 2021; Leng *et al.*, 2022). It can be stated with certainty that the world will be undergoing a major transformation, with innovation being its primary driving force.

## Women-Driven Innovation

By analyzing previous literature, it was discovered that innovation among women has been discussed through the lens of several terms such as women empowerment, women entrepreneurship, women-led growth, and successful women-run businesses. Thus, several studies that were considered in this research focusing on the responsible factors behind women-led innovation in the modern industry have also paid attention to the contributions by women in creating new entrepreneurship ventures, venture performance, business success, venture growth and venture survival (Tulus, 2009; Shane & Nicolaou, 2013; Gottschalk *et al.*, 2014). While innovation is crucial as it influences the success rate of women business owners, it is the quality of activities by entrepreneurs that are driven by innovation that creates value (Lai *et al.*, 2010; Ferraris *et al.*, 2018; Saiz-Alvarez & Martínez, 2019). The combination of entrepreneurship and innovation helps in developing the knowledge that can be used for cross-border entrepreneurship and co-creating value (Nair, 2016). Women are capable of bringing innovative ideas to the table through their differential perspectives toward society and community and well-honed managing skills that are advantageous to the economy in controlling unemployment and boosting economic growth (Kovid *et al.*, 2021; Kumari and Mor, 2021).

## Barriers to Women-Driven Innovation

Barriers to women-driven innovations, such as lower entrepreneurial ability, lack of funds, *etc.*, often inhibit women entrepreneurial innovations. While Nählinder *et al.* (2015) did not find much difference in innovativeness between men and women entrepreneurs, Neumeyer *et al.* (2019) reported differences in the ecosystem of entrepreneurship among male and female entrepreneurs.

### *Financial Barriers*

It is no surprise that women entrepreneurs have a severe lack of credit support and risk-covering possibilities at a financial level (Suseno and Abbott (2021); Kumari and Mor (2021)). In many developing and under developed countries, assets that yield financial capital, such as property or ancestral wealth, are only inherited. In these societies, the key inhibition to women's financial independence is the barrier to the claim to their rightful share of inherited property. This is due to the fact that there exists a widespread social practice that limits a woman's share of her money and dowry. Not only does it limit the amount of financial assets to the name of women, it also imposes the condition of marriage, often even kids, upon the woman. Such financial barriers restrict the woman's decision-making and independence. Women in many societies find it hard to own property, which could then create a barrier to collecting collateral to yield to banks and obtain loans. Other than inherited property, women are also not favored for gainful employment or capital lending in many economies. Several studies find that women are disproportionally rejected for loan applications. This is a major roadblock for first-time women business owners and especially so for women entrepreneurs in semi-urban and rural areas in developing economies.

### *Social and Institutional Barriers*

Fenwick and Huttons (2000) described that many women have narrated success with a subjective perspective, such as the freedom to choose their daily activity, the ability to balance between work and family, contribution to the social community around them, personal and family reputation, children and the overall quality of life that they establish. When the ability to work and innovate hampers this delicate work-life balance, women are de-incentivized to invest in discovering new avenues of growth and work. Additionally, the most common social barrier to women-led innovation is the lack of access to education and knowledge at early stages of life. Thus, it is no coincidence that areas with higher literacy rates also have more women entrepreneurs (Kelley *et al.*, 2016). Social constraints, such as preset expectations about the roles of female members of society, also hamper women from making visionary decisions. As per Bijedic *et al.* (2016), various institutional constraints contribute to women self-selecting into female-oriented professions. This becomes the major cause behind women being disinclined to lead new avenues of growth and discovery, which halts critical and innovative thinking. Even when they are self-motivated to lead new ideas forward, conventional organizational structures can discourage them from occupying lead positions and relegate them to middle-management or secretarial work positions (Nair, 2020; Henry *et al.*, 2016). Women are also in need of continuous incubatory support and training to overcome the lack of entrepreneurial and mindset training prevalent since decades of traditional role management in societies. Thus, where there is a lack of vocal and institutional support for facilitating women-driven ventures through government-aided schemes, the chances for women innovation are fairly slim (Badstue *et al.*, 2018; Al-Razgan *et al.*, 2021; Kumari and Mor, 2021). Based on this research, it can be said that social factors such as lack of education and training, absence of institutional support, and backward societal expectations can thus prohibit women from achieving their true potential and leading to innovative growth.

## Factors that Foster Innovation among Women Workers

The existing literature in the field of innovation among women workforce is spread across a wide array of fields, regions, and co-linked outcomes such as entrepreneurial success, women empowerment, overall economic growth, and sustainable social development. To understand the factors behind women-driven innovation in a modern context, it is important to take into context these related outcomes. Broadly, it was found that women-led growth happens due to a variety of factors that exist at a larger as well as individual scale (Suseno and Abbott, 2021; Kumari and Mor, 2021; Nair, 2020; Badstue *et al.*, 2018; Marvel *et al.*, 2015).

Individually, women-driven innovation can be linked to personal capacity factors that drive women leaders, whether they are a part of businesses or leading their own ventures as entrepreneurs. Innovativeness has been defined as a key trait and characteristic of entrepreneurs (Rauch & Freese, 2007; Rieger, 2012). A person with an innovative outlook refers to one who addresses problems, offers solutions, accepts responsibility and considers the outcomes (Rauch & Frese, 2007). According to Nurwahida (2007), an innovator's orientation toward taking chances in making an uncertain decision is considered to be risk-taking. In a widely cited study by Schumpeter (2013), entrepreneurs have been characterized as innovative as a result of their creativity and knowledge (Sledzik, 2013; LeBlanc, 2013). Innovation and creativity are two critical factors for the success of businesses that are run by female leaders (Lai *et al.*, 2010). As mentioned by Hassan *et al.* (2014), it is cited as the willingness of women to be involved in risky work. Peprah *et al.* (2022) further highlighted the importance of entrepreneurs who are creative and innovative because a lack of these characteristics might result in a low survival rate among women business owners. Hassan *et al.* (2014) interpreted that the creative and innovative abilities of entrepreneurs are crucial in introducing and bringing out new ideas for their businesses. However, as per Bakri and Mardziyah (2012), women leaders are usually more creative and adaptable when solving their problems for the growth of a business. According to Kumari and Mor (2021), gaining social currency and status for themselves and family is a core factor for women innovators to try new ventures. Researchers are of the reasoning that a motivating factor behind the success of teams is higher sensitivity to team members' personal ambitions and collective growth. This was determined as the abilities of team members to gauge and monitor the professional and personal needs of others to be able to respond proactively to those needs. Some studies also ascribe the superior ability of women to read complex emotions to lead their teams to a higher potential. Teams that constitute women are more likely to achieve a breakthrough because the diversity brings about greater creativity and fresh approaches to existing challenges (Hewlett *et al.*, 2013; Khursheed *et al.*, 2021; Friedman *et al.*, 2016; Kwakwa, 2015).

At a wider scale, there are several institutional factors that impact the trait of innovativeness among women workforce. Badstue *et al.* (2018) term these as social factors; these are factors that impact women's innovative capacity by virtue of existing as a woman under social constraints reflective of a particular community, time period, religion, or nationality. Previous studies show that one cannot ignore the role of social factors like education and access to knowledge for women in driving innovation in their work (Talukder, 2012; Kabasheva *et al.*, 2015; Kumari *et al.* (2021)). India ranks top in global rankings for having a considerable number of female graduates in the fields of science, technology, engineering and mathematics (STEM), with over one-third of women graduating from this field. Indian women are, thus, essentially the game changers in the fields of science and technology. Several studies in the literature relevant to this topic also refer to systemic or regulative factors. Researchers state that the creation of a new enterprise is a very complex process, inclusive of the actions, activities, mindset, thoughts, and processes (Lopez-Carlos and Mata, 2009). The literature also asserts that external factors are more dominant than internal ones in contributing to business success. To answer the question of how the barriers to women innovation can be addressed in the modern times, several solutions find common ground across multiple studies. For instance, Badstue *et al.* (2018) and Al-Razgan *et al.* (2021) indicate that the government should actively play a pivotal role toward skill training since most rural businesses are labor-intensive, which involve skills and creativity. It should also strive toward improving business competencies through more rigorous training. Thirdly, governments should invest in capital infrastructure and facilities for a conducive environment for local business.

Lastly, it should facilitate effective market support services in terms of product promotion, market accessibility and networking (Kabasheva *et al.*, 2015; Kariv, 2013; Badstue *et al.*, 2018; Al-Razgan *et al.*, 2021). Government policies that provide funding and resources for women-led startups and small businesses, as well as initiatives to increase the representation of women in leadership roles, can help create a working environment that is more motivating towards women's ideas and contributions. Similarly, social system policies, such as parental leave, flexible working arrangements, and unconscious bias training, can also help to reduce barriers and increase the participation of women in industry (Sarker and Palit, 2014). Organizational policies, such as diversity and inclusion initiatives, can help create a culture that values and supports the contributions of women in the workplace. All these policies combined can create an ecosystem that fosters and sustains innovation driven by women.

Table **1** provides a literature review summary of some active factors and sub-factors that impact women innovators in light of Industry 5.0 and sustainable women empowerment.

**Table 1. Critical factors behind women-led innovation.**

| Factors | Sub-factors | Citations |
|---|---|---|
| Regulatory Factors | Government policies | Nawaz (2009); Kelley *et al.* (2016); Al-Razgan *et al* (2021); Badstue *et al.* (2018) |
| | Organizational policies | Henry, Foss, & Ahl (2016); Bijedic *et al.* (2016); Friedman *et al.* (2016); Henry *et al.* (2016) |
| | Social system policies | Suseno and Abbott (2021); Bijedic *et al.* (2016) |
| Social factors | Availability of financial capital | Suseno and Abbott (2021); Kumari and Mor (2021) |
| | Education and access to information | Kelley *et al.* (2016); Kyaruzi and Hales (2009); Bijedic *et al.* (2016); Sarker and Palit (2014) |
| | Training for entrepreneurship | Nair (2020) ; Lai *et al.* (2010) ; Jovanovic and Lazic (2018); Sarker and Palit (2014) |

*(Table 1) cont.....*

| Factors | Sub-factors | Citations |
|---|---|---|
| Personal Factors | Risk-taking capacity | Marvel *et al.* (2015) ; Idris (2008); Hassan *et al.* (2014); Sarker and Palit (2014) |
| | Desire for achievement and recognition | Nair (2020), Hassan *et al.* (2014), Kumari and Mor (2021) |
| | Business acumen | Nair (2020), Neumeyer *et al.* (2018) |
| | Adaptability and higher EQ | Rani *et al.* (2018), Mendryk and Dylon (2014) ; Peprah *et al.* (2022) |
| | Market network | Henry, Foss, & Ahl (2016); Nair (2020); Badstue *et al.* (2018) |

## Critical Factors, Innovation and Sustained Growth

The review of literature in the current study clearly establishes that these critical factors play a significant role in fostering women-driven innovation in industry. The impact of these attributes that drive innovation in industry has been proven to be essential to the sustained success of not just the business but the society as a whole (Kumari and Mor, 2021). Limited resources, both in terms of financial capital and human capital, have been limiting the performance of women's innovative processes. It must be corrected in order to realize the full potential of half of our social workforce and achieve sustained growth and development. Women-led innovation in industry can lead to sustained women's development by creating opportunities for women to participate fully in the economy and society.

When women are given the opportunity to innovate and lead in industry, they are able to shape the direction of the industry, create new product lines and services, and drive economic growth. By encouraging women to start their own businesses, pursue careers in STEM fields, and take on leadership roles, women-led innovation can help to close the gender gap in the workforce and increase the representation of women in decision-making roles. This can, in turn, lead to better policies and programs that address the concerns of women and a more equitable distribution of resources and opportunities (Ingalagi *et al.*, 2021). Additionally, by highlighting the contributions of women in industry, women-led innovation can help to break down stereotypes and challenge traditional gender roles, ultimately leading to a more inclusive and equal society (Sarker and Palit, 2014).

Moreover, when women are empowered to innovate, they can bring new perspectives, ideas and solutions to the table. This is especially important in the context of Industry 5.0, which is characterized by rapid technological change and the need for new ideas and solutions to address complex challenges. Women-led innovation can also lead to more sustainable and responsible industry practices, as women tend to prioritize social and environmental concerns more than men. All of these factors, when combined, can contribute to a more equitable and sustainable future for all.

The 2030 Agenda also shows high expectations in how innovation by women and for women will play a central role in addressing SDGs. According to the agenda, the Sustainable Development Goals (SDGs), especially SDG 5 and 9, focus on catalyzing women's innovation-led entrepreneurship. Women's economic involvement leads to sustainable economic growth and aids in the development of nations.

**Strategies to Aid Policymakers**

- Establish mentorship and networking programs for women in industry, specifically in STEM fields. This will provide support and resources for women to develop their ideas and connect with other industry leaders.
- Establish a nationwide modified loan process that enhances transparency and simplicity. The demand of the time is for financial products that are women-friendly, including smaller and innovative collateral loans.
- Foster external growth opportunities for small business owners, enabling them to enhance their economic impact. These women entrepreneurs will significantly contribute to job creation and serve as inspiration for their female employees.
- Enhance the visibility of investors in women-led companies through mainstream and general media platforms, utilizing awards, publications, and media coverage. This approach aims to dismantle stereotypes and promote female role models. Investors and mentors of women entrepreneurs should form an ecosystem within the larger system to raise awareness effectively.
- Increase access to education and training opportunities for women in industry, particularly in STEM fields, to build a diverse and skilled workforce for Industry 5.0.
- Advocate for a reevaluation of corporate Human Resource norms to offer support and encouragement to women entrepreneurs in the corporate sector.
- Establish women-focused scaling accelerators and incubators with sponsorship from influential leaders.
- Promote and support collaboration and partnerships between industry, government, and academia to foster an environment of innovation and inclusion for women in industry.
- Establishing networks of successful male and female entrepreneurs to create a platform for exchanging ideas, information, capital, and mentorship.

In India, the government increased the budget for Women and Child Development by 14% in 2021. It set aside over Rs. 30,000 crores (US$ 3.97 billion) in FY 2021. Its key development schemes include business loan schemes such as Bhartiya

Mahila Bank Business Loan for offering collateral-free loans up to INR 1 crore, and sector-specific industrial loans under the Dena Shakti Scheme for offering loans at lower rates than the market. Additionally, organizations such as NITI Aayog promote women entrepreneurship by hosting workshops and educational events to motivate women and empower them to start their own ventures.

With the assurance of government support, law enforcement agencies, and institutional assistance, the number of women innovators is expected to increase in the future. Additionally, regulatory factors will positively influence the normative and cognitive aspects that affect women innovators. Therefore, it is crucial for the government and other institutions to take proactive measures to create a conducive business environment for women in the workforce. However, there is ample room for identifying additional factors by conducting further studies and considering a larger sample size in the future.

## FUTURE SCOPE

The study's findings aim to assist and guide practitioners seeking women-driven innovation to foster sustainable growth using this framework. Furthermore, this study expands our knowledge of women entrepreneurs. Just a decade ago, India was recognized as a country where owning a bank account was a significant accomplishment for its female population. This remarkable transformation highlights the potential of Indian women and their ability to lead the way through innovative solutions to contemporary challenges. The factors identified in this study as drivers of women-led innovation in the industry should be carefully examined and further researched to develop policies that facilitate progress in emerging sectors.

## CONCLUSION

The world is set to witness a major transformation thanks to women innovators in the industry with women domination. In Industry 5.0, women's roles will be crucial in the workplace. Industry 5.0 is built upon the recognition of human contribution to the success and encouragement of women leaders, which will lead to striking business development in the coming decade. The industry can multiply its growth manifold through the careful evaluation and development of social, regulatory, and personal factors behind women-led innovation. As a direct consequence of the same, the society as a whole will also witness sustained development and growth in the quality of life and output of its women, as targeted in the Sustainable Development Goals under the United Nations' Agenda 2030.

# BIBLIOGRAPHY

Abd Rani, S.H., Hashim, N., Abd Rani, S.H. (2019). The impact of networking among women entrepreneurial success. *Voice of Academia, 15*(3), 65-71.

Ahmad, N.H., Suseno, Y., Seet, P.S., Susomrith, P., Rashid, Z. (2018). Entrepreneurial competencies and firm performance in emerging economies: A study of women entrepreneurs in Malaysia. *Knowledge, learning and innovation.* (pp. 5-26). Cham: Springer.
[http://dx.doi.org/10.1007/978-3-319-59282-4_2]

Al-Razgan, M., Alrowily, A., Al-Matham, R.N., Alghamdi, K.M., Shaabi, M., Alssum, L. (2021). Using diffusion of innovation theory and sentiment analysis to analyze attitudes toward driving adoption by Saudi women. *Technol. Soc., 65*, 101558.
[http://dx.doi.org/10.1016/j.techsoc.2021.101558]

Badstue, L.B., Lopez, D.E., Umantseva, A., Williams, G., Elias, M., Farnworth, C.R. (2018). What drives capacity to innovate? Insights from women and men small-scale farmers in Africa, Asia, and Latin America. *J. Gender.Agric. Food Secur.*

Bakri, A.M.M., Mardziyah, A. (2012). *Developing sustainable growth model for women entrepreneur in Malaysia: case study in Johor Bahru.* (Doctoral dissertation, Universiti Teknologi Malaysia).

Balhara, S., Singh, A. (2015). Women entrepreneurship: A big motivation. *Business and economic research, 5*(2), 207-216.
[http://dx.doi.org/10.5296/ber.v5i2.8452]

Bijedić, T., Brink, S., Ettl, K., Kriwoluzky, S., Welter, F. (2016). Women's innovation in Germany–Empirical facts and conceptual explanations. *Research handbook on gender and innovation.* Edward Elgar Publishing.
[http://dx.doi.org/10.4337/9781783478132.00009]

Carayannis, E.G., Dezi, L., Gregori, G., Calo, E. (2022). Smart environments and techno-centric and human-centric innovations for Industry and Society 5.0: A quintuple helix innovation system view towards smart, sustainable, and inclusive solutions. *J. Knowl. Econ., 13*(2), 926-955.
[http://dx.doi.org/10.1007/s13132-021-00763-4]

Chatterjee, C., Ramu, S. (2018). Gender and its rising role in modern Indian innovation and entrepreneurship. *IIMB Manag. Rev., 30*(1), 62-72.
[http://dx.doi.org/10.1016/j.iimb.2017.11.006]

Fenwick, T., Hutton, S. (2000). Women crafting new work: The learning of women entrepreneurs. *Proceedings of 41st Annual Adult Education Research Conference,* Vancouver, Canada: University of British Columbia.127-132.

Ferraris, A., Santoro, G., Papa, A. (2018). The cities of the future: Hybrid alliances for open innovation projects. *Futures, 103*, 51-60.
[http://dx.doi.org/10.1016/j.futures.2018.03.012]

Friedman, H.H., Friedman, L.W., Leverton, C. (2016). Increase diversity to boost creativity and enhance problem solving. *Psychosociol. Issues Human Resour. Manag., 4*(2), 7.
[http://dx.doi.org/10.22381/PIHRM4220161]

Gottschalk, S., Greene, F.J., Höwer, D., Müller, B. (2014). If you don't succeed, should you try again? The role of entrepreneurial experience in venture survival. The Role of Entrepreneurial Experience in Venture Survival. ZEW-Centre for European Economic Research Discussion Paper, (14-009).
[http://dx.doi.org/10.2139/ssrn.2387508]

Hassan, F., Ramli, A., Mat Desa, N. (2014). Rural women entrepreneurs in Malaysia: what drives their success? *Int. J. Bus. Manag., 9*(4), 10.
[http://dx.doi.org/10.5539/ijbm.v9n4p10]

Hassan, S.H., Zeqiri, J., Ramadani, V., Zhen, T.S., Azman, N.H.N., Mahmud, I. (2020). Individual factors, facilitating conditions and career success: insights from Malaysian female entrepreneurs. *J. Enterp. Cult.,*

*28*(4), 375-400.
[http://dx.doi.org/10.1142/S0218495820500168]

Henry, C., Foss, L., Ahl, H. (2016). Gender and entrepreneurship research: A review of methodological approaches. *Int. Small Bus. J., 34*(3), 217-241.
[http://dx.doi.org/10.1177/0266242614549779]

Hewlett, S.A., Marshall, M., Sherbin, L. (2013). How diversity can drive innovation. *Harv. Bus. Rev., 91*(12), 30-30.

Hoe, C.H., Isa, F.M., Hin, C.W., Hashim, N., Yunus, J.M., Abdullah, H.H. (2012). Development of women entrepreneurs: The case of Malaysia. *WORLD, 2*(6), 124-145.

Huang, S., Wang, B., Li, X., Zheng, P., Mourtzis, D., Wang, L. (2022). Industry 5.0 and Society 5.0—Comparison, complementation and co-evolution. *J. Manuf. Syst., 64*, 424-428.
[http://dx.doi.org/10.1016/j.jmsy.2022.07.010]

Ingalagi, S.S., Nawaz, N., Rahiman, H.U., Hariharasudan, A., Hundekar, V. (2021). Unveiling the crucial factors of women entrepreneurship in the 21st century. *Soc. Sci., 10*(5), 153.
[http://dx.doi.org/10.3390/socsci10050153]

Jovanović, O., Lazić, M. Women entrepreneurship in Serbia: Potentials and constraints. *J. Women's Entreprene. Educ. twic. Year Scientific J.,* (3/4), 60-72.

Kabasheva, I. A., Rudaleva, I. A., Bulnina, I. S., Askhatova, L. I. (2015). Organizational factors affecting employee innovative behavior. *Mediterranean J. Soc. Sci., 6*(1 S3), 435.
[http://dx.doi.org/10.5901/mjss.2015.v6n1s3p435]

Kariv, D. (2013). *Female entrepreneurship and the new venture creation: An international overview..* Routledge.
[http://dx.doi.org/10.4324/9780203140987]

Kelley, D., Singer, S., Herrington, M. *Global entrepreneurship monitor.* Global Report,Global Entrepreneurship Research Association, London Business School, Regents Park.London NW1 4SA, UK:

Khursheed, A., Mustafa, F., Khan, A.A. (2021). Turning the COVID-19 crisis into entrepreneurial success: An exploratory study on women innovators of Pakistan. *Enterp. Dev. Microfinance., 32*(1), 57-67.
[http://dx.doi.org/10.3362/1755-1986.21-00009]

Kovid, R.K., Kumari, D., Pandey, S. (2021). Strategic response to the corona pandemic crisis: A case of Indian women entrepreneurs. *Stakeholder strategies for reducing the impact of global health crises.* IGI Global.
[http://dx.doi.org/10.4018/978-1-7998-7495-9.ch005]

Kumari, P., Mor, S. (2021). Entrepreneurship and source of finance: The case of Indian women microentrepreneurs. *Strateg. Change, 30*(4), 331-340.
[http://dx.doi.org/10.1002/jsc.2427]

Kyaruzi, I.S., Hales, C.A. (2009). Processes of incubating African female entrepreneurs: Some evidences from Senegal and Tanzania. *JWEE,* (3-4), 42-68.

Lai, K., Nathan, R., Tan, K., Chan, B. (2010). Effect of innovation to the success of female entrepreneurs. *J. Innov. Manag. Smal. Med. Enterpr., 2010*, 1-14.
[http://dx.doi.org/10.5171/2010.369877]

LeBlanc, A.A. (2013). *The effect of education and knowledge, experience, mentoring, and risk on the successful entrepreneur: A qualitative study.* (Doctoral dissertation, Capella University)..

Leng, J., Sha, W., Wang, B., Zheng, P., Zhuang, C., Liu, Q., Wuest, T., Mourtzis, D., Wang, L. (2022). Industry 5.0: Prospect and retrospect. *J. Manuf. Syst., 65*, 279-295.
[http://dx.doi.org/10.1016/j.jmsy.2022.09.017]

Lopez-Claros, A., Mata, Y.N. *The innovation capacity index: factors, policies, and institutions driving country innovation.* In the Innovation for Development Report 2009–2010 (pp. 3-65). Palgrave Macmillan,

London.
[http://dx.doi.org/10.1057/9780230285477_1]

Marvel, M.R., Lee, I.H., Wolfe, M.T. (2015). Entrepreneur gender and firm innovation activity: A multilevel perspective. *IEEE Trans. Eng. Manage., 62*(4), 558-567.
[http://dx.doi.org/10.1109/TEM.2015.2454993]

Mendryk, I., Dylon, D. Factors of professional success for self-employed women. Human Capital without Borders: Knowledge and Learning for Quality of Life, 933-938.

Nählinder, J., Tillmar, M., Wigren, C. (2015). Towards a gender-aware understanding of innovation: A three-dimensional route. *Int. J. Gend. Entrep., 7*(1), 66-86.
[http://dx.doi.org/10.1108/IJGE-09-2012-0051]

Nair, S.R. (2020). The link between women entrepreneurship, innovation and stakeholder engagement: A review. *J. Bus. Res., 119*, 283-290.
[http://dx.doi.org/10.1016/j.jbusres.2019.06.038]

Neumeyer, X., Santos, S.C., Caetano, A., Kalbfleisch, P. (2019). Entrepreneurship ecosystems and women entrepreneurs: A social capital and network approach. *Small Bus. Econ., 53*(2), 475-489.
[http://dx.doi.org/10.1007/s11187-018-9996-5]

Nurwahida, F. (2007). *Relationship between psychological characteristics and entrepreneurial success: A study of woman Entreprenuers in Malaysia.* Universiti Utara Malaysia.

Özdemir, V., Hekim, N. (2018). Birth of industry 5.0: Making sense of big data with artificial intelligence,"the internet of things" and next-generation technology policy. *OMICS, 22*(1), 65-76.
[http://dx.doi.org/10.1089/omi.2017.0194] [PMID: 29293405]

Peprah, A.A., Giachetti, C., Larsen, M.M., Rajwani, T.S. (2022). How business models evolve in weak institutional environments: The case of Jumia, the Amazon. com of Africa. *Organ. Sci., 33*(1), 431-463.
[http://dx.doi.org/10.1287/orsc.2021.1444]

Poutanen, S., Kovalainen, A. (2016). Innovating is not of the spirit world depicting a female inventor's unique path with materiality-friendly gender concepts. *Research Handbook on Gender and Innovation.* Cheltenham, UK: Edward Elgar Publishing.
[http://dx.doi.org/10.4337/9781783478132.00021]

Rauch, A., Frese, M. (2007). Let's put the person back into entrepreneurship research: A meta-analysis on the relationship between business owners' personality traits, business creation, and success. *Eur. J. Work Organ. Psychol., 16*(4), 353-385.
[http://dx.doi.org/10.1080/13594320701595438]

Rieger, K. (2012). *Phenomenological exploration of the characteristics of successful women entrepreneurs.* Northcentral University.

Saiz-Alvarez, J.M., Martínez, A.C. Entrepreneurial Quality and Economic Crisis in the Eurozone Countries Driven by Innovation. In Handbook of Research on Ethics, Entrepreneurship, and Governance in Higher Education (pp. 414-432). IGI Global.
[http://dx.doi.org/10.4018/978-1-5225-5837-8.ch019]

Sarker, S., Palit, M. (2014). Determinants of success factors of women entrepreneurs in Bangladesh : A study based on Khulna region. *Bus. Econ. Rev., 4*(2), 237.
[http://dx.doi.org/10.5296/ber.v4i2.6337]

Schumpeter, J.A. (2013). Economic theory and entrepreneurial history. *Explorations in enterprise.* Harvard University Press.

Shane, S., Nicolaou, N. (2013). The genetics of entrepreneurial performance. *Int. Small Bus. J., 31*(5), 473-495.
[http://dx.doi.org/10.1177/0266242613485767]

Śledzik, K. Schumpeter's view on innovation and entrepreneurship. Management Trends in Theory and

Practice,(ed.) Stefan Hittmar, Faculty of Management Science and Informatics, University of Zilina & Institute of Management by University of Zilina. [http://dx.doi.org/10.2139/ssrn.2257783]

Suseno, Y., Abbott, L. (2021). Women entrepreneurs' digital social innovation: Linking gender, entrepreneurship, social innovation and information systems. *Inf. Syst. J., 31*(5), 717-744. [http://dx.doi.org/10.1111/isj.12327]

Talukder, M. (2012). Factors affecting the adoption of technological innovation by individual employees: An Australian study. *Procedia Soc. Behav. Sci., 40*, 52-57. [http://dx.doi.org/10.1016/j.sbspro.2012.03.160]

Tulus, T. (2009). Women entrepreneurship in Asian developing countries: Their development and main constraints. *J. develop. Agricult. Econom., 1*(2), 027-040.

Ummah, S., Gunapalan, S. (2012). Factors influencing on entrepreneurial success: An empirical study on women headed families in Ampara and Batticaloa districts in Sri Lanka. *Int. J. Busin.Econom. Law, 1*(1), 141-148.

Xu, X., Lu, Y., Vogel-Heuser, B., Wang, L. (2021). Industry 4.0 and Industry 5.0—Inception, conception and perception. *J. Manuf. Syst., 61*, 530-535. [http://dx.doi.org/10.1016/j.jmsy.2021.10.006]

# CHAPTER 12

# Managing Knowledge Processes and Conceptual Review for Higher Education Institutions

**Neha Rastogi**[1,*], **Rajeev Ranjan**[2] and **Tilottama Singh**[3]

[1] *Doon Business School, India*

[2] *Uttaranchal University*

[3] *Uttaranchal Institute of Management, Uttaranchal University, Dehradun, India*

**Abstract:** Higher education is the backbone of any country, which decides where we stand and where we want to move ahead. The objective of higher education is to provide a platform for students to enhance their knowledge, skills and attitude in their chosen area of specialization. Each course has its objectives and learning outcomes, which are to be expected after completion of the particular course. Despite all efforts, there is a huge gap in terms of the right set of skills required to make a student employable. This is one of the bottlenecks in the entire system of the teaching-learning process. Do we just want to provide a degree that is a piece of paper, or do we want to create an ecosystem in which we want to produce the manpower that can create a difference after the completion of the chosen specialization? The dream of the middle class is to get their livelihood after completion of the course, but in the current scenario, it is very hard to get a job. Whatever the reasons are, we have to accept that we are not able to generate the right set of skills among the students pursuing higher education. The objective of education is not only to get a job but to increase overall learning and understanding of the overall human ecosystem. Creating an entrepreneurial ecosystem is another option, but it is very hard to arrange all the resources required to start an entrepreneurial setup. The author, through this research, wants to find out the gap in the system and will suggest a revised mechanism to achieve the objectives of higher education.

**Keywords:** Employability, Entrepreneurship, Higher education, Policy framework, Skill.

## INTRODUCTION

Students pursuing higher education have a dream that after completion of the chosen specialization, they will be able to get a job either in private or public service. 90% of middle-class students have a dream that after completion of their chosen specialization, they will get a job that will help them earn their livelihood.

[*] **Corresponding author Neha Rastogi:** Doon Business School, India; E-mail: acsneha89@gmail.com

**Sukanta Kumar Baral, Richa Goel, Tilottama Singh, Erdener Kaynak & Vishal Jain (Eds.)**

The students who have a family business have the option to either opt for a job or continue with their family business. Only a few of them think out of the box and dare to think of an entrepreneurial setup. The paper presents the picture of higher education with special reference to India. Earlier, pursuing higher education in a specified course was very tough because there was a limited number of institutions that provided higher education, and the students who were very bright would get admission to these selected institutions. Privatization has significantly shaped higher education. The main focus of private institutions is on admissions and creating infrastructure. Creating an infrastructure needs funds, and for generating funds, a source is very important. Admission of the students to these institutions is the only source of funds. This has led to the development of a new business model – the customer and service provider model (Commercial). The ancient Indians trusted in the proclamation "Thamasoma Jyotirgamaya"—light scatters dimness. The reality with regards to suggestions (Satyam), the decency innate in morals (Shivam) and the magnificence of involvement (Sundaram) are all light that drives us to that which perseveres. Since ages, the place from where one can get true education was called a University / Higher Educational Institutions. After this, we transferred our interest to finalize "What to teach and how to teach". Globalization has made us convert students with skills into marketable resources. By 2030, India will be among the countries with the most young population in the world. With almost 140 million individuals in the school-going age, one in every four alumni in the world will be a result of the Indian advanced education framework (Ernst and Young, 2013). Post-independence, on the basis of the belief that teaching and research would go ahead of grade specifications and lead to notable scholars who could bring revolution in the progress of the country, the foundation of the Centre of Excellency was laid down. In the current scenario, India's higher education system is the world's third largest in terms of scholars, next to China and the United States. India's 11% of youth is in higher education as compared to 20% in China. Even after having a substantial number of universities, none is among the top 150 Universities in the world (QS ranking 2020). Though IIT Mumbai, IIT Delhi (182) and IIS (184) rank 152, 182 and 184, respectively, according to the QS ranking 2020. The top-rated universities and institutes of India, like IITs, IIMs, Delhi University, Jawaharlal University *etc.*, require a student to be extra bright. What about other scholars? IITs, IIMs, and NITs have just 3% of the total students; the remaining 97% of students attend other higher educational institutes (central, state, deemed and private universities and affiliated colleges) in the country. As per the results of a survey across India, around 770 thousand undergraduate students were enrolled in private state universities in the academic year 2019. India is home to several private universities and institutes that were founded with the only objective of creating straightforward profit.

## REVIEW OF LITERATURE

Swati Sharma (2016), after reviewing literature, identified three key areas for future research. The first area of research is the link between education level and employment distribution. Second, there is a need to examine the differences among the various social groups in terms of the relationship between edifying level attainment and employment consequences. Third, additional research is required across various states to understand the relationship between education and employment outcomes. Thomas Asha E. and Bhasi. M (2018), in their findings, found that efforts need to focus on improving outcome-based learning. Instructional quality needs to be improved by providing better training and development to the teachers offering higher education. Low-skilled teachers need specific guidance to reach the acceptable level to teach the students. Coopers and Lybrand (1998) define the employability skills of the students in terms of four key skills: 1. Traditional intellectual skills. 2. Key skills in terms of communication. 3. Personal attributes like self-reliance and motivation. 4. Knowledge of organization about how they work. Dearing (1997) stated that students must be aware of their personal development well in advance before they apply for the job. The nature of the job and requirements should match the skill set before they apply for any job. Atkins (1999) stated that the criticism of the shortcomings of graduate recruits by the employer is not so much the result of the failure of the higher education curriculum, but it is a failure of the transfer process that matters a lot. Brennan *et al.* (1996), in a survey conducted on graduate students across Europe and the UK, found that teamwork, oral communication, skills for solving problems and working under pressure, are among the top 10 skills they viewed as important to make the students employable. Atlay and Harris (2000) commented that it is important to work on the culture and values in the institutions offering higher education. A nourished culture and values can help improve the learning environment for the benefit of the students and staff. Harpe *et al.* (2000) concluded in their findings that in academics, the concept of individualism exists and without the staff commitment, nothing can be achieved. Hussain (2005), in his study, stated that employment opportunities are less in higher education. Warrick, Daniels and Scott (2010) emphasized the collaborative relationship of the education system with employment. This will help in increasing employability among the students pursuing higher education. Tynjala, Valimaa and Sarja (2003) suggested the integration of education and working practices to enhance the productivity of a nation with practical knowledge. Sumanth S. Hiremath *et al.* (2016) concluded that the higher education system needs to be vibrant, competitive and meaningful. To cope with these changes, teachers are expected to excel in every sphere of higher education, which includes improved classroom teaching and live practical projects in practice with the regular classroom. The teacher has to perform the role of a counselor, administrator and policymaker to make the teaching-learning system effective in higher education. Vibhash Kumar (2013) suggested changing the teaching pedagogy to suit the requirements of the current environment so that students can relate to the changing environment. The curriculum should be based on the changing environment and as per current requirements, which need continuous monitoring and evaluation. The author also suggested creating industry-smart students to make them employable as per current market requirements. K. Manitombi Devi (2017) suggested that higher education institutions should ensure the availability of quality faculty and capacity building at all levels of employment. Annala, J., Lindén, J. and Mäkinen, M. (2016), in their research, found that the curriculum needs to be designed as per the changing dynamics of the environment. There should be a relationship between what is taught in the classroom in college/universities and the changing world and society as a whole. The authors also found that the concept of curriculum does not have a shared meaning in higher education. Devesh Nigam, M.P. Ganesh, and Suvashisa Rana (2020) emphasized a collaborative approach in the case of higher education, which includes collaboration at national and international levels on reforming the system of higher education such as quality assurance, credit recognition at the international level and designing a unified national qualification framework for higher education. Suresh. R, and B.C. Mylarappa (2012) suggested that to create a universal education system, India needs to enhance its priority for higher education. Nitesh Sanklecha (2017) addressed the following problems in higher education:

- Low enrolments of students in higher education.
- Unequal access to the students.
- Poor quality of higher education.
- Level of relevance in the higher education system in India.

The author also stated that research is an important area and its utility is also very important in teaching, but we should not forget that providing good knowledge is also equally important for the students in higher education. Singh, J. D (2016) concluded that higher education, as per current requirements, needs to be revised and updated in the policy framework. There is enough evidence from the existing literature that the existing system of higher education is inadequate and out of date. The author also suggested incorporating online classes and partnerships with foreign universities to improve the performance of higher education in India in the global market. Alam Zafrul (2018), in his research, concluded that the quality of higher education has a direct relationship with the admission criteria and curriculum content, which are dominant factors in improving the quality of higher education. Vnoučková L., Urbancová H. and Smolová H. (2017) found that five factors play a significant role in changing the perception of quality of higher education among students. These include Quality receptionists, Business oriented, Expert innovators, Distance learners and Arrangement oriented. Ching lian Mawi and Premlata Maisnam (2014) found that we need to develop a culture of high awareness, and in this, greater access on the part of parents, administrators and teachers is the key influencing factor for the success of higher education. E.N., Yildirim, E., Elvan, Ozturk, D. and Recepoglu, S. (2019) stated that the expectations and aspirations of the parents for their children are parallel to each other. The authors also found that there is limited literature available regarding the effect of parent expectations on the success of the students. Indu Bala and Franky Rani (2017) revealed that the perception of male and female candidates with regard to effective teaching in higher education is different. The female students are more sincere as compared to the male students. The authors also suggested that improvement is needed among the teachers in higher education, and they should be trained to improve their skills and knowledge as per the present working requirements. Pallavi Tomar Mishra, Abhishek Mishra, and Sudhinder Singh Chowhan (2019), in their research, concluded that in terms of employment generation, professional courses are contributing more as compared to traditional courses. The authors also suggested focusing on traditional degree courses to get more options for employment. Joseph Christian P. Oliquino (2019) suggested that in the 21$^{st}$ century, skill development will be the prime concern to make students employable. Mayuri J. Popat and Amit Ganatra (2017) revealed that companies have identified the gap between the academic outcomes and the expectations from the students. A strong relationship is needed to bridge the gap. Sodi Jasbir Kaur (2017) found that there is a gap between the industry and academic institutions. Kapil Prachi (2016) observed that companies have adopted new methods and strategies to acquire the best talent in their companies. They have their set skill parameter for selecting the employee in their company. Butt, B.Z. and Rehman, K. (2010) found that the largest factor influencing the satisfaction of the students pursuing higher education is the expertise of the teacher of a respective domain. Allam, Z. and Ahmad, S. (2013) found that the responses of stakeholders on the quality of higher education were different. The institutional factors and teaching-learning experience of the students are the most important factors contributing to maintaining the quality of higher education. Sulphey, M.M. and Allam, Z. (2017) mentioned that the mentoring model is one of the effective models that could contribute significantly to academic outcomes in higher education. Oldfield, B. M., and Baron, S. (2000) reported that the perception of quality is not permanent and could change over time with acceptable elements. Hill, F. M. (1995) discussed different methods for managing the quality of service in higher education and suggested that the service provider should meet the expectations of the students, who are the primary consumers, to improve the service quality of higher education. Athiyaman, A. (1997), in his research, built a link between perceived service quality and customer satisfaction based on the present scenario specific to higher education. Akareem, H. S. and Hossain, S. (2012), in their research, found that scholarship status, parentage, student age, where the student studied, and extracurricular activities, all play a significant role in influencing the quality of higher education. Fan, X. and Chen, M. (2001), in their research, found that parental expectations were the greatest impacting factor on the academic achievement of the students pursuing higher education. Carpenter, D. M. (2008) threw light on the future of the children as per their expectations, which were different from the parental aspirations. Rutchick *et al.*, 2009 found that high parental expectation positively influences children's motivation at the school level and continue at the societal level, which is carried forward at the college and university level. Pushkar (2013) identified that there is limited collaboration between industry and academia, due to which, higher education is facing a challenge in drafting a future-oriented course curriculum. Agarwal (2006) found that despite the stringent process of affiliation, the authorities are not able to control fake universities. The activities being carried out in institutions offering higher education are doubted and are not able to meet international standards. Motala (2000) concluded that education institutes should not only consider the aspect of quality as a concept but it should be incorporated into the institute's philosophy with commitment, along with the determination to put effort into the implementation of different aspects of the quality parameter in the education services like tangibility, attitude, competence, delivery, reliability, content, *etc.* Boaden and Dale (1992) observed that applying a quality feature is very difficult in higher education because it needs teamwork to achieve quality. Kirk, Lewis-Moss, Nilsen, and Colvin (2011) explained that the success of students in academics has a direct relationship with parental participation in education-oriented communication with the child. Rohde and Thompson (2007) found that the intrinsic motivation factor plays a very important role in the success of students. Walkey, McClure *et al.* (2013) suggested that factors like teachers, family and peers have an influence on the academic success of students. Jacobs & Harvey (2005) and Phillipson & Phillipson (2007) found that besides intelligence, the student's performance in the class is the key factor in the success of the students. Dandy & Nettelbeck (2002) and Davis-Kean (2005) found that parents' levels of education play a significant role in the student's success in academics. Almeida (2007), Tomé (2007), Berntson, Sverke, & Marklund (2008) Brown & Hesketh (2004) and Forrier & Sels (2003) found that desired skills and learning of the students pursuing higher education are the most important factors linked with employability among students pursuing higher education. Lambert *et al.* (2007), in their findings, suggested that in the context of entrepreneurialism as a curriculum, teaching and research should be the key parts of the scholarly enterprise. Fig. (**1**) depicts the learning goals through situational factors.

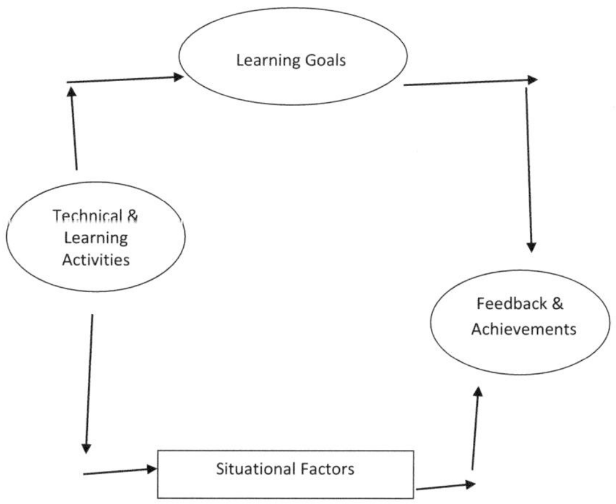


**Fig. (1).** Learning goals through situational factors.
Source: Developed by the Authors.

## RESULT AND DISCUSSION

Based on the review of the literature, we have come to know that there is enough evidence showing a clear gap between industry and academic institutions offering higher education. The skillset that the industry wants from students pursuing higher education does not match the expectations of the industry. The quality of the teachers imparting higher education needs to improve to meet the requirements of the current industry. None of the higher education institutions meet the expectations of the students pursuing higher education. The research indicates improvement in the teaching pedagogy and the teaching-learning ecosystem. There is a need to revise the policy framework for the institution offering higher education, which is supported by all the reviews discussed in the research. The professional courses, to some extent, are able to employ students, but not to the level that students expect after completion of the courses. There is a need to devise a new policy framework for the traditional courses according to the current market requirements, as they are outdated and not able to create the right set of skills. The need is to emphasize outcome-based learning not on paper but in real-time. A joint effort is required to improve the quality of higher education between industry and academia. A clear road map for employing completion of higher education is missing in the higher education ecosystem. The concept of entrepreneurship is only reflected in the policy draft, but in actual operation, its existence is missing. The rate of unemployment has increased in the recent past, but it has been found that there is an increase in the percentage of students who have completed their higher education. Enough evidence shows that the majority of the students who have completed their higher education are unable to find a suitable job. The evaluation system strictly needs to be designed if we want to improve the teaching-learning system for the institutions offering higher education. The syllabi of the subjects need intensive research, and the involvement of all the stakeholders is necessary to improve the quality of higher education. Interest-based teaching pedagogy can be introduced into the system, which must be linked with the industry requirement. The syllabi and subjects that are outdated and do not meet the current requirements should be eliminated. The courses that can generate employment should be emphasized to make the students employable. A uniform system of learning across the globe is required if we want to grow at a global level. A clear gap is observed in the research in this direction. The involvement of the parents is also necessary to guide the students in the right direction.

## BIBLIOGRAPHY

Abelha, M., Fernandes, S., Mesquita, D., Seabra, F., Ferreira-Oliveira, A.T. (2020). Graduate employability and competence development in higher education—A systematic literature review using PRISMA. *Sustainability (Basel), 12*(15), 5900.
[http://dx.doi.org/10.3390/su12155900]

Akareem, H.S., Hossain, S.S. (2016). Determinants of education quality: what makes students' perception different? *Open Review of Educational Research, 3*(1), 52-67.
[http://dx.doi.org/10.1080/23265507.2016.1155167]

Allam, Z., Ahmad, S. (2013). An empirical study of quality in higher education about stakeholders perspectives. *J. Am. Sci., 9*(12), 387-401.

Almeida, A.J. (2007). Employability, work contexts and the labour market in Portugal. *J. Educ. Sci., 2*, 51-58.

Allan, J., Clarke, K., Jopling, M. (2009). Effective Teaching in Higher Education: Perceptions of First-Year Undergraduate Students. *Int. J. Teach. Learn. High. Educ., 21*(3), 362-372.

Andrewson, J., Mitchell, H. (2006). *Employability for students: how to get the best from your education course, escalate: higher education academy.* Education Subject Centre.

Annala, J., Lindén, J., Mäkinen, M. (2015). Curriculum in higher education research. *In Researching higher education.*

Athiyaman, A. (1997). Linking student satisfaction and service quality perceptions: the case of university education. *Eur. J. Mark., 31*(7), 528-540.
[http://dx.doi.org/10.1108/03090569710176655]

Atlay, M., Harris, R. (2000). An institutional approach to developing students"transferable'skills. *Innov. Educ. Train. Int., 37*(1), 76-84.
[http://dx.doi.org/10.1080/135580000362115]

Atkins, M.J. (1999). Oven-ready and Self-basting: taking stock of employability skills. *Teach. High. Educ., 4*(2), 267-280.
[http://dx.doi.org/10.1080/1356251990040208]

Bala, I., Rani, F. (2017). *Perception of Students Towards Effective Teaching in Higher Education: A Mixed Analysis Approach.*
[http://dx.doi.org/10.21922/srjhsel.v4i23.9636]

Berntson, E., Sverke, M., Marklund, S. (2006). Predicting perceived employability: Human capital or labour

market opportunities? *Econ. Ind. Democracy, 27*(2), 223-244.
[http://dx.doi.org/10.1177/0143831X06063098]

Bhushan, S. (2009). *Restructuring Higher Education in India..* New Delhi: Rawat Publications.

Biggs, L.B., Moore, P.J. (1993). *the process of learning. Prentice-Hall, Sydney* .

Bowers-Brown, T., Harvey, L. (2004). Are there too many graduates in the UK? *Ind. High. Educ., 18*(4), 243-254.
[http://dx.doi.org/10.5367/0000000041667538]

Brennan, J., Koogan, M., Teichler, U. (1996). *Higher Education and work..* London: Jessica Kingsley.

Butt, B.Z., Rehman, K. (2010). A study examining the students satisfaction in higher education. *Procedia Soc. Behav. Sci., 2*(2), 5446-5450.
[http://dx.doi.org/10.1016/j.sbspro.2010.03.888]

Cappon, P. (2006). *CCL calls for clear, measurable goals in post-secondary education..* Canadian Council on Learning.

Carpenter, D.M., II (2008). Expectations, aspirations, and achievement among Latino students of immigrant families. *Marriage Fam. Rev., 43*(1-2), 164-185.
[http://dx.doi.org/10.1080/01494920802013078]

Cryer, P. (1997). How to get ahead with a PhD. *Times High. Educ. Suppl.*

Coffield, F. (1997). A tale of three little pigs: building the learning society with straw. In: Coffield, F., (Ed.), *A national strategy for Lifelong Learning.* Department of Education, University of Newcastle.

CVCP, D. (1998). Skills Development in Higher Education Short Report. *London: Committee of Vice-Chancellors and Principals.*

Dandy, J., Nettelbeck, T. (2002). A cross-cultural study of parents' academic standards and educational aspirations for their children. *Educ. Psychol., 22*(5), 621-627.
[http://dx.doi.org/10.1080/0144341022000023662]

Davis-Kean, P.E. (2005). The influence of parent education and family income on child achievement: the indirect role of parental expectations and the home environment. *J. Fam. Psychol., 19*(2), 294-304.
[http://dx.doi.org/10.1037/0893-3200.19.2.294] [PMID: 15982107]

Devi, K.M. (2017). India: Higher Education In Twenty-First Century Vision And Action. *Voice of Research, 5*(4), 19-21.

Dunne, E., Rawlins, M. (2000). Bridging the gap between industry and higher education: Training academics to promote student teamwork. *Innov. Educ. Train. Int., 37*(4), 361-371.
[http://dx.doi.org/10.1080/135580000750052973]

Tait, J., Knight, P. (1996). *The management of independent learning..* Psychology Press.

Fan, X., Chen, M. (2001). Parental involvement and students' academic achievement: *A meta-analysis. Educ. Psychol. Rev., 13*(1), 1-22.
[http://dx.doi.org/10.1023/A:1009048817385]

Forrier, A., Sels, L. (2003). The concept employability: a complex mosaic. *Int. J. Hum. Resour. Dev. Manage., 3*(2), 102-124.
[http://dx.doi.org/10.1504/IJHRDM.2003.002414]

Garraway, J. (2010). Knowledge boundaries and boundary-crossing in the design of work-responsive university curricula. *Teach. High. Educ., 15*(2), 211-222.
[http://dx.doi.org/10.1080/13562511003620035]

Gallagher, M., Ann, J. C. Kaufman Gender differences in mathematics: An integrative psychological approach, 246– 263..

Joseph Christian P. Oliquino (2019). 21st Century Skills of Students in a Technical Vocational Education and

Training Institution in the Philippines.. (2019). *Jurnal Pendidikan Progresif, 9*(2), 146-155.

Abelha, M., Fernandes, S., Mesquita, D., Seabra, F., Ferreira-Oliveira, A.T. (2020). Graduate employability and competence development in higher education—A systematic literature review using PRISMA. *Sustainability (Basel), 12*(15), 5900. [http://dx.doi.org/10.3390/su12155900]

De La Harpe, B., Radloff, A., Wyber, J. (2000). Quality and generic (professional) skills. *Qual. High. Educ., 6*(3), 231-243. [http://dx.doi.org/10.1080/13538320020005972]

Harvey, L., Bowers-Brown, T. (2003). The employability of graduates: cross-country comparisons.

Hao, L., Bonstead-Burns, M. (1995). Parent-child differences in educational expectations and the academic achievement of immigrant and native students. *Sociology of Education, 74*(3), 175-198.

Hill, F. M. (1995). Managing service quality in higher education: the role of the student as a primary consumer.. (1998). *Qual. Assur. Educ., 3*(3), 10-21.

Hasan, M., Parvez, J. (2017). Professional Development of 21st Century Teachers in Higher Education, Educational Quest. *An Int. IJEASS., 8*(1), 145-149.

Husain, I. (2005). Education, employment and economic development in Pakistan.

Jacobs, J.E., Davis-Kean, P., Bleeker, M., Eccles, J.S., Malanchuk, O. (2005). I can, but I don't want to. *The impact of parents, interests, and activities on gender differences in math.* In: Gallagher, A., Kaufman, J., (Eds.), *Gender difference in mathematics.*

Joseph Christian, P.O. (2019). 21st Century Skills of Students in a Technical Vocational Education and Training Institution in the Philippines. *JPP., 9*(2), 146-155.

Kamran, P.R. (2004). Qualitative Improvement in Teacher Education.

Prachi, Kapil (2016). Bridging the Industry-Academia skill gap A conceptual investigation with special emphasis on management education in India. *J. Bus. Manag., 16*(3), 8-13.

Kaur, S.J. (2017). Need for bridging the industry-academia gap. *IJERD., 5*(4), 1243-1255.

Kelly, A. V. (2009). *The curriculum: Theory and practice.*

Kirk, C.M., Lewis-Moss, R.K., Nilsen, C., Colvin, D.Q. (2011). The role of parent expectations on adolescent educational aspirations. *Educ. Stud., 37*(1), 89-99. [http://dx.doi.org/10.1080/03055691003728965]

Kumar, R. (2013). Quality improvement in Higher Education in India: A Review, International Journal of Educational Research and Reviews *1*(2), 44-46.

Kumar, V. (2013). Challenges and opportunities in higher education system in India. *Higher Education: Challenges and Opportunities in Higher Education System in India. Delhi Business Review, 14*(2), 29-42. [http://dx.doi.org/10.51768/dbr.v14i2.142201313]

Knight, P.T., Yorke, M. (2002). Employability through the curriculum. *Tert. Educ. Manag., 8*(4), 261-276. [http://dx.doi.org/10.1080/13583883.2002.9967084]

Kreber, C. (2002). Teaching excellence, teaching expertise and scholarship of teaching. *Innovative High. Educ., 27*(1), 5-23. [http://dx.doi.org/10.1023/A:1020464222360]

Lambert, C., Parker, A., Neary, M. (2007). Entrepreneurialism and critical pedagogy: reinventing the higher education curriculum. *Teach. High. Educ., 12*(4), 525-537. [http://dx.doi.org/10.1080/13562510701415672]

Leitch, S. (2006). *Prosperity for all in the global economy-world class skills.*. The Stationery Office.

Lettmayr, C.F. (2012). *From education to working life, the labour market outcomes of vocational education and training.*. Luxembourg: Publications Office of the European Union.

Little, B. (2001). Reading between the lines of graduate employment. *Qual. High. Educ., 7*(2), 121-129. [http://dx.doi.org/10.1080/13538320120060015]

Moon, J. (1999). *The role of reflection in learning and professional development.*. Oxon: Routledge Farmer.

Mohandass, S. (2017). Current Scenario of Higher Education in India: Reflections on Some Critical Issues. *SIJP., 4*(6), 86-92.

Tomar Mishra, P., Mishra, A., Singh Chowhan, S. (2019). Role of higher education in bridging the skill gap. *Univers. J. Manag., 7*(4), 134-139. [http://dx.doi.org/10.13189/ujm.2019.070402]

Nihal Lindberg, E. (2019). Parents' educational expectations: does it matter for academic success? *Int. J. Educ. Res.,, 6*(2), 150-160.

Nigam, D., Ganesh, M. P., Rana, S. (2020). Review of the expansion of higher education in India: Cardinal concerns in the traverse. *JCR., 7*(2), 97-102.

Nyamupangedengu, E. (2017). Investigating factors that impact the success of students in a Higher Education classroom: a case study. *J. Educ.,* (68), 113-130.

Oldfield, B.M., Baron, S. (2000). Student perceptions of service quality in a UK university business and management faculty. *Qual. Assur. Educ., 8*(2), 85-95. [http://dx.doi.org/10.1108/09684880010325600]

Impact of Current Higher Education System on Human Resource Development in the State of Uttarakhand. (2019). *PBRI., 12*(1), 116-122.

Phillipson, S., Phillipson, S.N. (2007). Academic expectations, a belief of ability, and involvement by parents as predictors of child achievement: *A cross-cultural comparison. Educ. Psychol., 27*(3), 329-348. [http://dx.doi.org/10.1080/01443410601104130]

Pinar, W.F. (2004). The Miseducation of the American Public in his What is Curriculum Theory? *Mahwah, NJ: Lawrence Erlbaum,* 15-34.

Pinar, W. F. (1995). *Understanding curriculum: An introduction to the study of historical and contemporary curriculum discourses .*

Robbins, L.R.B. (1963). *Higher Education: Report of the Committee appointed by the Prime Minister under the chairmanship of Lord Robbins, 1*(5), 1961-63.

Rohde, T.E., Thompson, L.A. (2007). Predicting academic achievement with cognitive ability. *Intelligence, 35*(1), 83-92. [http://dx.doi.org/10.1016/j.intell.2006.05.004]

Rutchick, A.M., Smyth, J.M., Lopoo, L.M., Dusek, J.B. (2009). Great expectations: The biasing effects of reported child behaviour problems on educational expectancies and subsequent academic achievement. *J. Soc. Clin. Psychol., 28*(3), 392-413. [http://dx.doi.org/10.1521/jscp.2009.28.3.392]

Ryan, T. (2011). Quality assurance in higher education: A review of literature. *High. Learn. Res. Commun., 5*(4). [http://dx.doi.org/10.18870/hlrc.v5i4.257]

Samarawickrema, G. (2009). The criteria of effective teaching in a changing higher education context. *High. Educ. Res. Dev., 29*(2), 111-124.

Sharma, S. (2016). Relation between education and employment outcomes in the Indian labor market: A critical review of the literature. *IJRESS., 6*(4), 43-55.

Steinmayr, R., Spinath, B. (2009). The importance of motivation as a predictor of school achievement. *Learn. Individ. Differ., 19*(1), 80-90. [http://dx.doi.org/10.1016/j.lindif.2008.05.004]

Sulphey, M.M., Allam, Z. (2017). Efficacy of mentoring in enhancing the academic outcome of business students in KSA. *Soc. Sci., 12*(8), 1384-1388.

Srimathi, H. (2019). Higher Education System In India: Challenges And Opportunities. *Int. J. Sci. Technol. Educ. Res., 8*(12), 2213-2215.

Suresh, R., Mylarappa, B.C. (2012). Development of Indian higher education in 21st century, International. *IJSSIR., 1*(10), 70-81.

Sanklecha, N. (2017). Current Scenario of Higher Education in India. *IJERST., 4*(8), 171-173.

Singh, J. (2016). Higher education in the 21st century: Issues and challenges. *Int. Educ. J., 2*(2), 33-41.

Nasir, Z.M., Nazli, H. (2000). *Education and earnings in Pakistan. https //ideas.repec.org/p/pid/wpaper/2000177.html.*

Stenhouse, L. (1975). *An introduction to curriculum research and development.*. London: Heinemann.

Thomas, A.E. (2017). Sustainable Education: Re-Visioning for Twenty-First Century. *Thomas Asha E. and M. Bhasi (2017). Sustainable Education: Re-Visioning for Twenty-First Century. Asian J. Res. Soc. Sci. Humanit., 7*(5), 47-62.

Tomé, E. (2007). Employability, skills and training in Portugal (1988-2000): evidence from official data. *J. Eur. Ind. Train., 31*(5), 336-357.
[http://dx.doi.org/10.1108/03090590710756792]

Vnoučková, L., Urbancová, H., Smolová, H. (2017). Factors Describing Students' Perception on Education Quality Standards. *ERIES., 10*(4), 109-115.
[http://dx.doi.org/10.7160/eriesj.2017.100403]

Walkey, F.H., McClure, J., Meyer, L.H., Weir, K.F. (2013). Low expectations equal no expectations: Aspirations, motivation, and achievement in secondary school. *Contemp. Educ. Psychol., 38*(4), 306-315.
[http://dx.doi.org/10.1016/j.cedpsych.2013.06.004]

Warrick, C.S., Daniels, B., Scott, C. (2010). Accounting students' perceptions on employment opportunities. *Res. High. Educ., 7*, 1.

Yabiku, S.T., Schlabach, S. (2009). Social change and the relationships between education and employment. *Popul. Res. Policy Rev., 28*(4), 533-549.
[http://dx.doi.org/10.1007/s11113-008-9117-2] [PMID: 21461188]

Yorke, M., Knight, P. (2003). *The undergraduate curriculum and employability.*. LTSN Generic Centre.

Zafrul, A. (2018). Students' perception of quality in higher education: An empirical investigation. *Management Science Letters, 8*, 437-444.

**CHAPTER 13**

# Implementation of Internet of Things (IoT) in Human Resource Management: An Overview

**Arpita Nayak**[1,*], **Ipseeta Satpathy**[1], **B.C.M. Patnaik**[1], **Sukanta Kumar Baral**[2] and **Flavio De Sao Pedro Filho**[3]

[1] *KIIT School of Management, KIIT University, Bhubaneswar, Odisha, India*

[2] *Department of Commerce, Indira Gandhi National Tribal University, Madhya Pradesh, India*

[3] *Department of Management and Economics, Federal University, Rondonia, Brazil*

**Abstract:** The Internet of Things (IoT) is one of the most significant technological advancements in recent years. Simply described, the Internet of Things is a mechanism in which all individuals, companies, and devices are linked to each other over a network segment to continually exchange data without the need for human participation, completely stirring up business. Because of these technologies, tracking efficiency has never been easier. Communication tools, wearable computing gadgets, trackers, and other technologies have had a greater impact on business and everyday life than ever before. In order to respond to technological advancements, executives are emphasizing the use of IoT, and human resource management is not exempted. HR managers utilize IoT to gather relevant information about some major components like future workers, as well as improve performance evaluation, recruitment, training and development, and employee engagement. This paper aims to give an overview of the implementation of IoT in HRM. From the evolution of a mobile job seeker to the incorporation of microchips to manage staff, the expanding nature of the Internet of Things (IoT) affects the way human resources function in companies as well as the way businesses operate.

**Keywords:** ATS, Actuators, Benefits of IoT, Compensation management, Employee engagement, Employee, Evolution, HRM, Human resource management, HR planning, Internet of Things (IoT), Job Performance, Performance evaluation, Recruitment, Sensors, Training and Development, Technology, Technological Innovation, Workplace.

* **Corresponding author Arpita Nayak:** KIIT School of Management, KIIT University, Bhubaneswar, Odisha, India; E-mail: 2181158@ksom.ac.in

**Sukanta Kumar Baral, Richa Goel, Tilottama Singh, Erdener Kaynak & Vishal Jain (Eds.)**

## INTRODUCTION

The phrase "Internet of Things" is 16 years old. However, the notion of connected devices has been around for a while—at least since the 1970s. At the time, the notion was known as "integrated internet" or "embedded devices". However, it was Procter & Gamble employee Kevin Ashton who invented the term "Internet of Things" in 1999. The business environment has evolved in light of the emergence of the information era and the increased rise of economic globalization. With 21.5 billion devices expected to be wired by 2025, IoT is currently present in every area and niche. It has indicated a paradigm change in the world of information technology. Millions of gadgets, ranging from high-end industrial equipment to children's toys, are now linked to the internet. Two main parts make up the Internet of Things. The first is a physical item or "thing" that you wish to link to make it intelligent. The connection, on the other hand, is handled by the embedded system. While the first half of this may seem simple, the second half involves a complicated procedure that could involve several sensors, actuators, interfaces, a data analysis layer, and other parts. Because of their interconnection, all of these things can be programmed, and communicated with one another and with people. Companies that do not consider training their personnel for the Internet of Things will fall behind. Indeed, according to a recent study published in CIO Magazine, 33% of firms would benefit from extra capabilities, while 47% of organizations lack IoT skills entirely. So, to stay ahead of the competition, create and train your personnel for the IoT age. IoT devices and structures enable enterprises to improve their safety ratings while also collecting vital data about their equipment, operations, clients, and much more. The Internet of Things ecosystem is made up of sensing and embedding components (sensors, actuators), communication (protocols, IoT gateways), IoT cloud, IoT analytics, data management, and end-user service interfaces. As a result, many businesses have begun to recognize the importance of maximizing the value of their human resources and using them as a source of advantage in competition. However, to accomplish this goal, we must not only develop sound HR planning but also use a variety of tools and techniques. Using IoT, all resources are connected to the internet and monitored remotely. IoT and personal safety include anything from surveillance systems (such as ADP, Ring, and Nest doorbells) to lights, cameras, and appliances that link to our phones, computers, or other devices *via* Wi-Fi Internet connections. The active gathering of data aims to give various workplace departments insights into existing or future concerns that may have a significant influence on the overall efficiency of their firm. This involves concerns such as employee mental health, occupational health, and the development of initiatives to provide employees with greater safety and security. IoT is changing how we live our lives, giving us a deeper understanding of how the world around us functions. Leaders in today's scenario look to have a good impact on the unification of management resources and thus lower management expenses by enhancing the design of HRM information technology . HRM informatization will greatly aid enterprise management, and they recommended that advanced management systems have features like "labor costing", "data report generation", "monitoring recruitment", "tracking compensation and benefits" and "automatic attendance" in addition to HR data management and payroll accounting. Organizations are already earning major benefits from IoT-based projects, according to a Harvard Business Review poll, with 58% reporting enhanced business cooperation. Video conferencing, which formerly required the use of fixed equipment, will soon be accessible from any area of a corporate base using a computer, laptop, iPad, or smartphone. HR management helps close the productivity gap between employees and the specific priorities of the organization. A strong HR management team leads the organization towards a better competitive environment. IoT in the workplace provides several interesting opportunities for the HR sector and employees to participate in novel ways and RE-CONSIDER their working environment. With just a few resources, it can be shown that the organization's development is appropriately maintained through the use of HRM procedures. High-performance information technology is used to sustain the evolution of human resource management. To sustain the change of HRM toward an attractive recruiting process, digital technologies are being leveraged more. This research seeks to provide an overview of IoT deployment in several key areas of human resource management, such as the recruitment process, training and development, compensation management, and performance management, and how it contributes to the efficient operation of the same. The IoT sector will see a $1 trillion and $3 trillion boom by 2025, according to forecasts, as a result of the transition from basic connections to IoT-powered apps, platforms, and services. IoT combines two essential components: a communication medium and connectivity with an increasing number of intelligent items. As connection increases the possibilities of the linked system and the connected devices, it contributes to the production of rich data whose analysis offers decision-makers incredibly important insights. Employees today arrive at work with smartphones or smart watches affixed to their wrists that provide high-speed Internet access, including the log-in and log-off time of their work time, along with other notifications, indicating a workforce embedded in and around IoT. The possible effects of these phenomena on HR practices, employees, and employers should be the focus of HR managers and employers. For example, IoT can assist a project planning tool in immediately communicating a company's employment needs to its hiring system or department. In organizations as a whole and HRM, in particular, IoTs are necessary to supervise efficiency, security, objectivity without bias, and straight forwardness. The direct connection between the use of data innovation, human resources and innovation assets enhances business performance. Recruitment, training and development, socialization, work plans, compensation management, assistance, career advancement, performance reviews, worker, and job security are the HRM focus areas. High-performance information technology is used to sustain the growth of human resource management. To sustain the change of HRM toward enticing recruiting processes, IoT in HRM solutions is being adopted more . Employee experience is enhanced through IoT with Internet-capable mobile devices, with employees, managers, and HR constantly connected. It would be beneficial for future generations to have flexible work environments. IoT would enable HR to create flexible offices with the ability to manage work using mobile and wearable technologies. To connect diverse gadgets and people, the IoT creates a worldwide digital nervous system with numerous devices and sensors. It affects human resource management because it takes in huge amounts of data from HRM. As a result, it provides HRM with the tactics they may employ to optimize agility, including the right to decide who makes up the workforce, combining the advanced key talents, such as teamwork, agility, organizational growth, cognitive flexibility, and even creativity, in the best possible way. To examine the efficacy of people's practices, procedures, and even initiatives, IoT can be employed in people analytics. It also aids in comprehending how information from social and data sciences may be used to make defensible and even impartial choices about individuals.

## Use of IoT in Recruitment

Lawrence Bossidy, the former CEO of Honey well, commented, "I am confident that nothing we do is more important than hiring and developing people." In the end, you bet on humans rather than techniques. The recruitment strategy is the most crucial component of the organization's human resources management system since it is critical to the organization's performance. An organization's hiring process is crucial since choosing the right applicant is essential to the development and growth of the company. Selecting the right candidates through the hiring process is a delicate procedure that presents several problems to the organization's HR administration. The traditional methods of recruiting have altered as a result of technological innovation. Many gadgets are now connected to the internet as computer and network connectivity technologies advance. The borders that separate the real world from the virtual world have become hazier since the introduction of IoT. Organizational HR managers utilize IoT to look up applicant information since it saves a variety of facts about things, people, and websites that are crucial for managing an organization's workforce and recruiting efforts generally. IoT can assist the project-planning tool in communicating a company's employment requirements straight to its recruitment system or department. Candidates' expertise and talents may be immediately matched to the specifications, and new hires can get the offer on their mobile devices. The usage of IoT enables the human resource manager to get hold of the candidate's information within a limited time, which helps in short listing the fittest individual for the position. The implementation of IoT has increased the recruitment of candidates by enabling the screening of applicants and the selection of the most qualified ones based on a large amount of information, leading to assistance in human resource management. One of the most obvious benefits of IoT is the availability of information and data *via* cloud backups. Recruiters and employment firms, for example, have massive databases that update candidate data regularly. The use of optimal cloud technologies can make managing this vast volume of data easier. The adaptation of a new way of recruitment as a cutting-edge business model has decreased hiring expenses as compared to conventional recruiting through magazines and newspapers and transformed conventional recruiting into a more effective "continuous mode".One of the most time-consuming activities for staffing companies is finding applicants. By utilizing IoT technology, you may go from shortlisting applicants to focusing on those who could be a good fit. IoT may assist in creating an intelligent workforce by employing an ATS (Applicant Tracking System) to reduce the number of candidates for each position rather than the tiresome and time-consuming procedure of going through mountains of resumes, thus reducing the workload for HR personnel. Another fantastic tool is Google Glass, a ground-breaking IoT application that businesses have adopted. Hiring firms have access to enormous databases of applicants, information about interviews, and candidate profiling, as well as the capability of recording interviews that can then be analyzed in the decision-making process. To back up their data in cloud computing infrastructure, hiring companies must employ cloud technology to its fullest potential. In this manner, there is no risk of disc failure or theft, and the data may be accessed from anywhere. HR management efficiency is demonstrated by how efficiently information is carried out; hence, IoT aids in the management of critical data. With the advent of IoT, various multi national companies have directed their focus on discovering the correct technologies to improve their recruiting and training procedures that deal with advanced management of human resources, corporate culture, employee commitment, and supervising employee performance *via* IoT. Human resource management (HRM) recruits employees through various channels with the use of IoT to find particular aptitudes of individuals regarding the company's policies, laws, and regulations. Virtual platforms also assist the HRM in recruiting and training. Posting a job opening, receiving candidates, tracking applicants, collaborating, interviewing prospects, and hiring are the key recruiting processes that are expedited by ATS, thus IoT helps managers build an intelligent workforce without the time-consuming and difficult process of sifting through piles of applications, but rather by using an ATS (Applicant Tracking System) to narrow down to a few candidates per opening. The internet is being utilized for more than simply online shopping and networking. Rather, it has infiltrated more basic human life processes, such as job-seeking behavior. As a result, IoT is a fantastic approach to replacing old hiring procedures with smart and more modern alternatives. IoT simplifies procedures such as making data more available, using digital recruitment, AI-driven recruitment, and automating recruitment operations. A study done by the Recruitment Process Outsourcing Association (RPOA) states that individuals are more tech-aware nowadays; everything is at the tip of one's finger; the internet is no longer used to merely communicate with pals on social media, engage in online games, or do Christmas shopping. It has infiltrated more essential processes in people's lives and in the workplace, including job-searching behavior. The Internet of Things emphasizes the importance of being extremely pro active on social media and inbound recruiting activities. Networking is the center of social networks, and your potential applicants virtually live there. With the connectivity of IoT, social media will play a key part in the recruiting process in the next years. Organizations can simply improve candidate evaluation by placing them in simulated circumstances using IoT technologies and HRMS integration. This will aid in testing the behavior of each applicant. India had the quickest rate of growth, accounting for 32% of all IoT job advertisements in the three months ending in May 2021 and 36.8% in the same period last year. The hiring process has been eased and accelerated by Internet technologies, resulting in smooth human resource management. In the past, an applicant had to wait for publications and offline job applications. You can now email a candidate and expect an immediate answer. The same holds for submitting a CV. It can now be posted online in minutes for worldwide viewing. Because of the internet, recruiters can now work on a much larger scale. As a result, if you are a recruit with Internet access, you may publish many job adverts for a variety of positions and handle those advertisements from a single location, such as your email, a particular website, or software. Every recruiter wants to be able to accomplish more work, hire more individuals, and advocate for more positions. Every human resource manager wants to properly manage the resource.

## The Application of IoT in Employee Engagement

Leaders and managers in organizations all over the world are concerned about employee engagement because it is understood to be a crucial factor in determining the level of organizational performance, creativity, and competitiveness and shows a sign of effective management of the human resource. Employee engagement, according to Gallup, is defined as workers' enthusiasm for their jobs and working environment. Employee engagement is an essential component of HR and larger organization as a whole. The usage of IoT in the workplace will brighten the future, especially in the fields of retention and engagement of employees. As the constraints on our time rise, participation in the work environment becomes increasingly important. Employers are always searching for methods to boost productivity, minimize employee attrition, save expenses, and manage employees. Technology can facilitate HR transformation and generate improved efficiency and effectiveness. The capacity to apply smart solutions to assess buildings, workplaces and people in areas such as intellect, convenience, occupation, fitness, light, sustenance, water, air, and sound is growing. It equips real estate and facilities managers with smart devices to inform, advise, and coach their personnel. Improving workspaces, employee engagement, and wellness necessitates the use of technology and metrics to offer information and feedback to maintenance personnel, real estate managers, and employees to fulfill workplace strategy objectives. Real estate and facilities managers will be required to deliver innovative workplace solutions that allow for increased flexibility and agility for both the organization and employees, as well as long-term rational action. Communication and employee engagement are critical for both the business and the employee, and doing so is a crucial foundation for the future of business. The business sector is frequently the subject of difficulties ranging from competitors to the rise of technology and information, economic issues and dynamic changes. Organizations must undertake adjustments in response to the problems. Price cuts, layoffs, and reorganizations are a few instances of organizational changes made in reaction to problems. However, businesses must acknowledge the need to restructure all of their divisions, from production management to human resources. Retaining people and increasing employee engagement will improve organizational performance and human resource management without the need for any radical adjustments. It has been discovered that workplace engagement enhances organizational performance. Employee engagement goes beyond the aspect of job satisfaction that has been extensively researched in recent years. Gall up assessments on the state of the American workplace reveal that 16% of the over 32 million employees are slackers, and as many as 51% of them are uninterested in their jobs . The internet is seen as an essential component of everyone's life. The internet allows people all over the world to communicate and exchange their thoughts, opinions, facts, and experiences. Improved employee interactions, employee growth, and the establishment of a better system for employee engagement are all made possible and empowered by the Internet of Things (IoT) . In today's world, technology is taking over all aspects of organizational tasks. Technology *via* one-to-one, immediate connection from anywhere, has a significant influence on generating a better experience in the shortest amount of time - all thanks to the help of our IoT gadgets. With the best human resource management, an IoT-enabled workplace may improve operational effectiveness, human-machine engagement, and productivity. The importance of engagement in the workplace grows as our time demands increase. Technology can facilitate HR transformation and generate improved efficiency and effectiveness. Remote-x encompasses remote employment, education, and telemedicine. We have all been influenced by a new manner of working style, which is working from home, due to the abrupt churn of time. Computer systems, mobiles, webcams, and mics are required for distant employees. IoT played a pivotal part in employee engagement *via* various platforms such as Zoom, WebEx, Microsoft Team Skype, and Google Meet. People adopted online platforms for personal usage due to the ease of use, availability of the internet, and breadth of applications. Human resource personnel feel at ease as they can manage and engage employees in the virtual platform. Employees want to accomplish more, but corporate technology expenditures typically focus solely on enhancing the productivity of employees. Connected devices may help workers at all levels execute their duties more efficiently, productively, and safely. Front-line employees are transitioning into information workers. That is the result of technology transforming individuals into amazing resources. Leading businesses have been able to leverage new technology that measures productivity, revenue, customer happiness, workflows, quality, and workplace interactions on a regular, if not real-time, basis. The Internet of Things and the creation of Smart and Learning Buildings can be an extremely good improvement that increases employee engagement. Measuring occupancy, air quality, acoustics, light, and even employee pleasure with smart technologies and sensors may help to optimize the workplace, employee engagement, management of employees, and organizational goals. 'Machine learning enables structures to learn and predict from gathered measurements and data, transforming them into 'Learning' structures' . Businesses should provide the optimal environment for information sharing to encourage employee involvement . Knowledge sharing (KS) has a large and favorable impact on employee engagement . Employee engagement and KS are influenced by organizational dedication, teamwork, and cohesion among co-workers. But, little is understood about what spurs workers to share information and how to encourage them to do so. Specifically, a few studies look at the extent to which the motivation to participate in the building of intellectual capital (IC) may inspire the objective of knowledge sharing . A study conducted by ITA Group states that the Internet of Things has distilled employee engagement into three important concepts: focus, feedback, and purpose. Data input and other manual chores will become obsolete as more devices are linked. People remain engaged when their actions are linked to their progress. A bigger goal can be found through its capacity to offer direction toward achievement. In the quickly evolving corporate environment, human resource management has experienced spectacular development and has become essential for the success of the corporation. The use of information technology in the corporate world has given workers numerous new opportunities. To guarantee that all users receive the required data in real time, businesses may connect and interact using smart devices thanks to the "Internet of Things". It offers new approaches to working, boosts output, improves the interactions people have with businesses, and smooths the flow of HRM. According to research, changes to an organization's operations can enhance each employee's engagement. IoT makes it possible for users to enjoy themselves more, which improves the workplace environment. IoT in the workforce is a potent invention that produces happier, more productive workers and a better working environment. We will be able to attract and retain our staff if we build and offer a great employee experience. IoT can design a personalized workspace for every kind of business. It can develop and provide tailored solutions to certain issues that arise at work. Remote employment, remote education, and healthcare are the three main subfields of Remote-x. Even before COVID-19, remote work was becoming popular, and this trend is expected to continue . IoT is the term used to describe the interconnection of offline equipment with the Internet to boost functionality using online tools. It substitutes office duties that are now performed at home offices for remote workers. The work calendar may alert employees regarding future activities and business responsibilities after being configured and connected to a web application like Alexa or Google Home, remarked Chris Muktar, the creator of the UK-based careers website WikiJob.co.uk. The HR officials were having difficulty engaging employees in work-from-home employment circumstances and were unsure how to tackle the issue because of the nature of IoT technology. Enterprises may now allow their employees to work from practically any location—flexibility that can provide considerable benefits to SMBs in particular. The Internet of Things revolution has expanded in small and medium-sized firms overhauling their business models, and hiring more comprehensive remote workers in "work from anywhere" roles is a favorable sign toward better human resource management.

## Effect of IoT on Training and Development

Training for employee development and progress is essential to be ahead in the game of businesses all over the world. In addition to giving employees the chance to grow their abilities, these programs also provide employers the chance to increase staff productivity, foster a positive workplace environment, and ensure enhanced HRM practices. According to the research by the 2020 Work Institute, they can also reduce employee attrition, which can have a big influence on a company's bottom line. According to the study, voluntary staff turnover costs US firms over $630 billion every year. Approaches for employee growth and organization productivity must include staff training and development. Research published in the Journal for Business and Management Research in 2019 found that 90% of workers agreed that activities for training and development improved their job performance. Employee T&D refers to an organization's continuing efforts to enhance the performance of its personnel. Employers train and grow their staff through several educational strategies and programs. In recent years, development and training have become increasingly significant components of the human resource strategic approach. More business owners now understand the importance of employee T&D as it not only keeps employees more engaged but also helps the company construct a highly skilled crew and a better way of managing human resources. The equipment used by apprentices in the future probably will be able to monitor their progress and provide real-time feedback. It is hoped that by receiving real-time feedback, seasoned workers with undesirable habits (such as a propensity to stroll in hazardous parts of a work site) may be able to unlearn risky behaviors while at work. This, in turn, can alter safety education, reduce fatalities and injuries in the workplace, and provide a better way of managing resources. IoT device adoption in the workplace gives manufacturers the chance to track and collect data and utilize that data to carefully manage a facility's operations and resources. Erika Melander, Manager of Travelers' manufacturing sector INDUSTRY *Edge*, has stated that with the use of new tools and machines, employees need to be made aware of the same. Manufacturers will want to guarantee that staff members are knowledgeable about how to operate and maintain sophisticated machinery as well as how to react to emerging technology. For instance, there are now wearables that allow immediate responses to risky behaviors or nearby threats. If the workers wearing them are trained in how to respond to alarms from their devices, just imagine how successful this IoT can be in minimizing fatalities. IoT network connections increased by 84% in the industrial sector in 2017. Manufacturers can improve productivity and safety by knowing how to handle IoT gear and equipment appropriately and safely. Additional training on IoT devices might be helpful for current workers who are learning new jobs or are unfamiliar with IoT-enabled machinery or equipment. Human resource workers can realize the need for training thanks to the Internet of Things' deep automation, analysis, and integration within many systems. They can monitor and maintain track of training data with their assistance. Manufacturers should include their IoT projects in their corporate safety culture to assist in dealing with change, from initial customization to staff onboarding, ongoing employee training and development, and post-incident reaction. One-third of the US employment and half of all workers in the form may work from home, as per the US Census Bureau. The number of individuals who work largely or entirely from home has been increasing for some years, but the COVID-19 pandemic has accelerated this trend. In recent years, the (IoT) has played an important role in linking businesses and workers. It has also become a significant part of the digital workspace in terms of employee training and performance tracking, as well as human resource management, and this is only feasible because of the quantity of data it can gather . With China's rapid growth in technology and science as well as industrial technologies, there has been a rise in the need for technical staff in recent years. The Internet of Things (IoT) is a relatively new field that concentrates on interdisciplinary principles and applications in fields such as communication, computing, network security, different sensors, and other data. A solution based on the IoT training practice system is offered to solve the issue of employment competence evaluation. The majority of this approach's content is based on research and analysis of an actual IoT training module. Based on the data features of IoT and the establishment of a realistic scenario, it has been determined that practical IoT building and development training systems are especially beneficial for assessing job capabilities and managing human resources. Allowing workers to review workplace training programs can improve continuing training and development by giving data on the programs' strengths and faults. Employers may be able to improve their programs as a result of this. Installing intelligent kiosks outside conference rooms, according to LinkedIn, allows employees to submit rapid feedback on the effectiveness of meetings and training courses. Employers may improve employee training by gamifying and rewarding employees with IoT-enabled technology such as machines and coffee makers. Employees can earn snacks and beverages by performing training-related activities satisfactorily or within a time restriction. The collection of data that is unique to each employee may allow this to be taken a step further through customized gamification that is targeted to individuals' specific aptitudes and skill sets. Previously, an engaging training session could only be obtained in person; IoT technologies now allow enterprises to give educational materials and skill sets training to remote workforces. Scan Creator, for example, is an IoT product that enables users to scan customizable text from books, papers, and other sources to access the information into a computer or tablet, where it can then be translated into 40 languages. Sweet Rush's solution, for instance, provides instructor-led training and incorporates aspects including competitive games and video and audio capabilities to increase engagement and retention. Sweet Rush created a virtual contact center setting financial institution that wants its call center staff to learn and practice skills without the need for in-person role play [30]. Making sure that the workplace is safe and there is proper management of human resources is the top responsibility of every business. The Internet of Things (IoT) and accident prevention software have raised the bar for workplace security. Whether it may be the time when employees undergo training or in the workplace, the deployment of IoT may act as a standard accident prevention program that is simple to incorporate into your company's safety system and helps to increase workplace safety. Every seven seconds, workplace incidents that cause employee injuries occur, as per the National Safety Council. The author explained the use of the Internet of Things as a tool for safety measures through an example, considering a warehouse management system powered by the Internet of Things that employs sensors to map not only the objects but also the machinery, robots, and humans present. The likelihood of accidents drops dramatically when everyone in the workforce has a more accurate understanding of the workplace. When one linked sensor activates, several possible threats may be quickly discovered and dealt with, which is where the usage of connected sensors comes in handy . The ability to provide employees with common educational and skill-based training resources has also been made possible by smart IoT technology. Even some of these training courses may be taken online. Regardless of what industry they work in, for both new and existing employees looking for training, connectivity is no longer an issue. Far-flung training facilities aid in the company's advancement rather than its stagnation, leading to a much more advanced way of HRM.

## Making Performance Evaluation Easier with the Help of the Internet of Things

Employee performance review is widely regarded to be a key managerial tool for every organization. Modern industrial and commercial organizations in the global economy must create effective ways of analyzing the performance of their human resources. One of the most important jobs of every firm is to thoroughly and methodically evaluate the performance of its employees. The data regarding the individuals are analyzed using various criteria based on the organization's aims. To produce a precise interpretation of knowledge, this information must be synthesized using certain criteria. It has been discovered that manual employee assessment methods may be effectively abolished by monitoring industrial personnel utilizing the omnipresent sensing capabilities of Internet of Things (IoT) devices. Manual employee assessment methods are especially sensitive to human biases since managers are given broad discretion in evaluating employee performance; a better HRM becomes the goal for organizations. Biases can occur due to human nature or when supervisors are not adequately trained to deliver impartial feedback. The evaluation of employee performance through the IoT tools would help in reducing the manual as well as any chance for biases in the evaluation process . The rapid growth of corporate organizations in their environments, whether public or private, has made us vulnerable. Given the high level of competitors in the economic sector, organizations tend to form alliances to maximize efficiency, increase the efficacy of their daily operations, and use various sorts of sophisticated technology to stand out in the market in contrast to other competitive firms. Because of the breadth of their offerings, the efficiency and usefulness of their HR Department, and the performance framework, an increasing number of businesses are drawn to automate the evaluation of workers' performance. A training program aids in speedier performance monitoring, resulting in a smooth flow of company activities and the completion of the HRM process . An effective performance evaluation approach for companies in today's changing climate is a complicated challenge given its financial scope. The performance evaluation system has become an integral part of the strategic policy of today's industries. Existing performance evaluation systems rely on manual estimates. Manual assessment approaches may demotivate employees since they are vulnerable to bias and opportunism. The author proposed a neuro-fuzzy-based paradigm to make this evaluation completely performance-driven. Sensors enabled by the IoT are used to detect and track employee actions, while an adaptive neuro-fuzzy inference system (ANFIS) is used for training and decision optimization. The suggested framework has an accuracy rate of 94.7%, and an estimated RMSE inconsistency value of 0.0717 was determined to be adaptable . The Internet of Things (IoT) has quickly made its way into daily goods, from vehicles to household appliances and wearables, transforming the way we live and work. In fact, according to IDC's Worldwide Semiannual Internet of Things Spending Guide, worldwide IoT spending is estimated to have reached about $1.4 trillion in 2021. According to MIT Technology Review's analysis, the top two advantages of application performance monitoring tools for IoT installations are enhanced performance and security. A key benefit of APM for IoT, according to 86 percent of study respondents, is the ability to swiftly identify performance concerns. A big advantage, according to 81%, is the ability to swiftly discover security vulnerabilities. This boosts dependability and retention, reduces total maintenance and assistance costs, and validates a smooth HRM process . Because of its great potential for innovation and meaningful advantages to the people, the Internet of Things (IoT) is a key pillar of the 4th Industrial Revolution. Companies' human resource management is increasingly focusing on handset communication and wearable computing devices. Because of the growing necessity for recording, assessing, and measuring employee performance, such adjustments are crucial. To establish a distributed network of devices, IoT devices combine sensors and computational power with strong interconnection. This ever-changing digital infrastructure may be used or upgraded to aid in workload monitoring. Wrist-worn gadgets, for example, may evaluate normal psycho physiological workload markers and are being utilized to improve worker safety in construction . Internet of Things (IoT) technology advancements have been efficiently used in several industrial sectors for surveillance, tracking, and remote decision-making. The capacity to obtain detailed information about everyday activities has created several prospects for applying this technology in sensitive fields such as national defense security. The author of this study has analyzed the performance and behavioral aspects of defense employees given their daily activities . One of the most important tasks of any Human Resources department is to provide frequent employee assessments and better management facilities to ensure that employees recognize their strengths and short comings, as well as how to grow and progress within a business. A graphical rating scale is a tried-and-true way of performance evaluation. It is a scale in which performance evaluation determines desired traits and behaviors for each role and then rates employees on a number scale on each of those. The characteristics might include timeliness, work quality, technical competency, teamwork, accountability, responsibility, and so on. This helps a corporation determine staff performance levels, increase efficiency and productivity, and make salary or promotion decisions. The HR personnel need a confidential and hassle-free method to do this process; when there is a desire for such, the Internet of Things comes into play because when the procedure is done virtually, it saves time and ensures secrecy, eliminating the possibility of prejudice . An employee performance tracker assesses an employee's performance. It uses measurements to assess how well an employee is performing. It typically examines performance every year and assists managers in determining staff competency levels. With the shift in working pattern, *i.e.*, working from home, keeping track of employee performance and evaluating methods were a struggle, but the Internet of Things has allowed devices to connect to the Internet, detect, gather, receive, and transmit data, and interact with one another and applications using IP technologies, frameworks, and networking solutions. Furthermore, according to Gartner, 81% of HR departments are upgrading their employee performance tracking measures for improved evaluation, resulting in increased efficiency and usability of user activity monitoring software . The use of video in HR technology is rapidly changing how executives do business throughout the world. Gayle Wiley, Chief People Officer at Lifesize, an Austin-based video, audio, and web-conferencing firm, puts her organization to test by employing video conferencing for recruitment purposes. “Externally, I utilize video-conferencing to interview applicants who are not in my immediate vicinity,” Wiley stated. “Internally, Skype is my primary communication platform for holding effective meetings with our whole global staff — for performance evaluations, town hall meetings, new employee onboarding, training and development, and more.” Face-to-face encounters with one click are critical in establishing human experience in today's increasingly fragmented workforce. Co-workers who could previously only communicate over the phone or *via* email may now see one another . Instead of wasting time on speculations, IoT-enabled HR software may deliver real-time data on performance evaluation. Employers will be able to determine if low employee performance is due to insufficient training or if it is influenced by environmental conditions such as humidity, brightness, temperature, or employees' physical health. This will provide insights into prospective areas of training and growth, in addition to helping HR to plan in a way that encourages improved efficiency and an easy way of evaluating performance . During this pandemic time, IoT has come in handy for various industries. Remote IoT apps make it possible for specialists to properly maintain functioning without equipment or the need for someone to be available at the site. IoT sensors coupled with cloud software packages may deliver actual information to the responsible party about machine status, use, and even temperature. Not only technicians but also HR personnel could track down the activities of the employees in case of attendance verification, productivity, or performance.

## IoT Integration in Global Corporations: A Global Perspective

In its "Worldwide Internet of Things Spending Guide", research company IDC forecasted a double growth rate in 2021, with an annual compound increase of 11.3% from 2020 to 2024. According to IDC, healthcare, insurance, and education are the industry leaders in IoT spending. Statista researchers forecast similar rapid development, estimating that the worldwide IoT market for end-user solutions will expand from $212 billion in 2019 to $1.6 trillion by 2025. IoT connections span the world and sectors, as well as penetrating individual homes, businesses, and automobiles. Traditional automobiles also have IoT connections, with manufacturers adding linked sensors to monitor efficiency and handle computerized systems. Municipal buses and business delivery vans are frequently outfitted with additional IoT technology, such as linked systems, to check for safety hazards. Personal automobiles and trucks may be outfitted with comparable equipment, which is usually provided by insurance companies to capture and send telemetry information to ensure safe driving practices . The Internet of Things is unquestionably seeing a global market boom. The current estimate for IoT-connected devices is 10 billion, with 1.5 trillion objects capable of connecting. Global enterprises have not missed the mark in terms of implementing IoT-enabled systems, with the widespread installation of connected smart devices and big data analytics; in fact, a report released notes that in Australia alone, 77 percent of corporate entities have already employed an IoT-focused strategy in some form or another. According to a Boston Consulting Group forecast, companies will spend €250 billion, or approximately US$285 billion, on IoT services and products, with manufacturing, transportation, and utility industries accounting for half of the total spend. The benefits of IoT from a global corporate perspective are desirable and wide, aimed at encourage perfect communication between devices at any location. In addition to increasing levels of citizen safety, the usage of Big Data analytics and broadband connections, for example, is fantastic news for worldwide employees. It will not only result in a considerable increase in situational awareness, but it will also result in a more effective decision-making process, all while increasing the force multiplier and lowering the total cost of corporate activities.

## CONCLUSION

Enterprises may now access the three essential components for functioning thanks to the Internet of Things (simplicity, scalability, and security). HRM has changed now, from the old method of working to the modern way of working. "A smart HR" has adjusted to the change in the workplace, and by applying the advanced way of working, the style of working has changed significantly. Whether it may be the case of recruitment, employee engagement, training, and development, or evaluation of employee performance, IoT has been a great help to Human Resource personnel. Today, it has become a reality that devices and household appliances may be linked to the web and invariably transmit and/or receive data from/to your smartphone, and this picture is only a prelude to an eternally linked world. However, it is a well-known truth that individuals spend the majority of their time at work, and as such, it is critical to grasp how the world of the Internet of Things (IoT) will affect the working environment in the future and how it is already changing the way businesses are conducted now. From the evolution of the mobile job seeker to the incorporation of microchips to manage personnel, the expanding nature of the IoT looks promising. The system combines, optimizes, collaborates, increases productivity, optimizes performance management, boosts employee motivation, improves real-time monitoring and control, offers strategic planning, reduces operational risks, increases entrepreneurship's ability to compete, and offers technical help for the enterprise's HRM strategy. Human resource management has benefited from the Internet of Things, and job searchers now turn to their smartphones rather than newspaper articles while looking for employment. Understanding how businesses and organizations are currently conducted can help you realize how IoT has positively affected HRM. Industry 4.0 is the digital evolution of industrial production and manufacturing, and it is associated with the value-creation process and industries. The IoT's participation in organizations, enterprises, and the organization-management process has positively altered how HR operates.

## BIBLIOGRAPHY


Abdussamad, Z., Tweneboah Agyei, I., Sipahi Döngül, E., Abdussamad, J., Raj, R., Effendy, F. (2022). Impact of internet of things (IOT) on human resource management: a review. *Mater. Today Proc., 56*, 3534-3543.
[http://dx.doi.org/10.1016/j.matpr.2021.11.247]

Ahn, C.R., Lee, S., Sun, C., Jebelli, H., Yang, K., Choi, B. (2019). Wearable sensing technology applications in construction safety and health. *J. Constr. Eng. Manag., 145*(11), 03119007.
[http://dx.doi.org/10.1061/(ASCE)CO.1943-7862.0001708]

Al-Jabri, I.M. (2020). Investigating the mediating role of knowledge sharing on employee engagement: evidence from a developing nation. *Int. J. Hum. Cap. Inf. Technol. Professionals, 11*(1), 47-63. [IJHCITP].
[http://dx.doi.org/10.4018/IJHCITP.2020010104]

Alti, A., Almuhirat, A. (2021). An Advanced IoT-Based Tool for Effective Employee Performance

Evaluation in the Banking Sector. *Ingénierie des systèmes d information,* *26*(1), 103-108. [http://dx.doi.org/10.18280/isi.260111]

Arokiasamy, L., Balaraman, R.A. (2019). The influence of the internet of things on employee engagement among generation Y at the workplace. *Glob. Bus. Manag. Res.,* *11*(1), 428-435.

Barata, J., Cunha, P.R.D. (2019). Safety is the new black: the increasing role of wearables in occupational health and safety in construction. *International Conference on Business Information Systems,* 526-537. [http://dx.doi.org/10.1007/978-3-030-20485-3_41]

Bhatia, M., Sood, S.K. (2018). Internet of Things based activity surveillance of defence personnel. *J. Ambient Intell. Humaniz. Comput.,* *9*(6), 2061-2076. [http://dx.doi.org/10.1007/s12652-017-0507-3]

Buchanan, G. (2019). *The importance of minimising and preventing the influence of unconscious bias in recruitment. The importance of minimising and preventing the influence of unconscious bias in recruitment | Cambridge Network. Retrieved from: https://www.cambridgenetwork.co.uk/news/importance-minimisin--and-preventing-influence-unconscious-bias-recruitment.*

Burnett, J.R., Lisk, T.C. (2019). The future of employee engagement: Real-time monitoring and digital tools for engaging a workforce. *Int. Stud. Manage. Organ.,* *49*(1), 108-119. [http://dx.doi.org/10.1080/00208825.2019.1565097]

Chintankar, J. (2022). *How IOT is enhancing the employee training experience: IOT now news and reports. IoT Now News - How to run an IoT enabled business. Retrieved from: https://www.iot-now.com/2022/05/05/121086-how-iot-is-enhancing-the-employee-training-experience/.*

Devanesan, J. (2020). *Has 2020 ushered in a new era of 'intelligent education' ICT? Tech Wire Asia. Retrieved from: https://techwireasia.com/2020/09/has-2020-ushered-in-a-new-era-of-intelligent-education/.*

Dhir, K., Chhabra, A. (2019). Automated employee evaluation using fuzzy and neural network synergism through IoT assistance. *Pers. Ubiquitous Comput.,* *23*(1), 43-52. [http://dx.doi.org/10.1007/s00779-018-1186-6]

Fait, M., Cillo, V., Papa, A., Meissner, D., Scorrano, P. (2023). The roots of "volunteer" employees' engagement: The silent role of intellectual capital in knowledge-sharing intentions. *J. Intellect. Cap.,* *24*(2), 399-429. [http://dx.doi.org/10.1108/JIC-04-2020-0133]

Franklin, E. (2022). *Enabling and streamlining the recruitment process with IOT.*https://www.iotforall.com/enabling-and-streamlining-the-recruitment-process-with-iot.

Gasparovich, E.O., Uskova, E.V., Dongauzer, E.V. (2020). The impact of digitalization on employee engagement. *An International Online Forum named after A. Ya. Kibanov Innovative Personnel Management,* 143-150.

Gravina, N., Nastasi, J., Austin, J. (2021). Assessment of employee performance. *J. Organ. Behav. Manag.,* *41*(2), 124-149. [http://dx.doi.org/10.1080/01608061.2020.1869136]

Gronau, N., Ullrich, A., Teichmann, M. (2017). Development of the industrial IoT competencies in the areas of the organization, process, and interaction based on the learning factory concept. *Procedia Manuf.,* *9*, 254-261. [http://dx.doi.org/10.1016/j.promfg.2017.04.029]

Gao, H., Xiao, Y., Yan, H., Tian, Y., Wang, D., Wang, W. (2020). A Learning-Based Credible Participant Recruitment Strategy for Mobile Crowd Sensing. *IEEE Internet Things J.,* *7*(6), 5302-5314. [http://dx.doi.org/10.1109/JIOT.2020.2976778]

*How IOT can help in the recruitment process? Things of IOT. Retrieved from : https://www.thingsofiot.com/blog/how-iot-can-help-in-the-recruitment-process.*

Hristova, P., Rusev, R., Ivanova, B. (2021). Training of administrative staff for providing information

security in a remote work environment. *INTED Proc.,* 9899-9905.
[http://dx.doi.org/10.21125/inted.2021.2060]

Huhman, H.R. (2017). *4 ways technology improves the Human Resources (and human) experience. Entrepreneur. Retrieved from https://www.entrepreneur.com/science-technology/4-ways-technol-gy-improves-the-human-resources-and-human/29670.*

Ilieva, G., Yankova, T. (2020). IoT in distance learning during the COVID-19 pandemic. *TEM Journal, 9*(4), 1669-1674.
[http://dx.doi.org/10.18421/TEM94-45]

Isaac, O., Abdullah, Z., Ramayah, T., Mutahar, A.M. (2017). Internet usage, user satisfaction, task-technology fit, and performance impact among public sector employees in Yemen. *IJILT., 34*(3), 210-241.
[http://dx.doi.org/10.1108/IJILT-11-2016-0051]

Jha, S., Khanna, P. (2020). Study of enhancing employee engagement at workplace by adopting internet of things. *IJBSR., 14*(3), 341-361.
[http://dx.doi.org/10.1504/IJBSR.2020.108282]

Jindal, A. (2018). *Unlock the value of IOT with performance monitoring: Blog. AppDynamics. Retrieved from: https://www.appdynamics.com/blog/product/unlock-the-value-of-iot-with-performance-monitoring/.*

Jindal, A. (2019). *Unlock the value of IOT with performance monitoring: Blog. AppDynamics. Retrieved from: https://www.appdynamics.com/blog/product/unlock-the-value-of-iot-with-performance-monitoring/.*

Juan, S. H., Ting, I. W. K., Kweh, Q. L., Yao, L. (2018). How does knowledge sharing affect employee engagement? *Institutions and Economies, 10*(4).

Kamran, P.R. (2004). Qualitative Improvement in Teacher Education. *In SOUVENIR, State Level Seminar cum Workshop on Quality Improvement in Teacher Education. Ferozepur: Dev Samaj College of Education for Women, 5*, 54-67.

Kaur, N., Sood, S.K. (2017). A game theoretic approach for an IoT-based automated employee performance evaluation. *IEEE Syst. J., 11*(3), 1385-1394.
[http://dx.doi.org/10.1109/JSYST.2015.2469102]

Khan, Y. (2020). *5 Components of an IoT Ecosystem. Learn Hub. Retrieved from: https://learn.g2.com/iot-ecosystem.*

Kumar, R. (2018). *How IOT improves employee engagement and retention. SightsIn Plus. Retrieved from: https://sightsinplus.com/hrtech/artificial/how-iot-improves-employee-engagement-and-retention/.*

Lee, I. (2017). An exploratory study of the impact of the internet of things (IoT) on business model innovation: Building smart enterprises at fortune 500 companies. *The Internet of Things.* Breakthroughs in Research and Practice.
[http://dx.doi.org/10.4018/978-1-5225-1832-7.ch020]

Lloret, J., Garcia, M., Catala, A., Rodrigues, J.J.P.C. (2016). A group-based wireless body sensors network using energy harvesting for soccer team monitoring. *IJSNet., 21*(4), 208-225.
[http://dx.doi.org/10.1504/IJSNET.2016.079172]

Macey, W.H., Schneider, B., Barbera, K.M., Young, S.A. (2011). *Employee engagement: Tools for analysis, practice, and competitive advantage.* John Wiley & Sons.

Mary, A., Fulzele, S., Rokade, V., Nomani, M.Z.M., Jaiswal, S., Salahuddin, G. (2023). The Integrated Framework of Environmental Internet of Things Based Recruitment Process and the Impact Created by IoT in Inventory Management. *Proceedings of Second International Conference in Mechanical and Energy Technology,* 199-206.
[http://dx.doi.org/10.1007/978-981-19-0108-9_21]

Moyeenudin, H.M., Anandan, R. (2021). IoT Implementation at Global Enterprises for Progressive Human Resource Practices. *Proceedings of First International Conference on Mathematical Modeling and Computational Science,* 109-117.

[http://dx.doi.org/10.1007/978-981-33-4389-4_12]

Nižetić, S., Šolić, P., López-de-Ipiña González-de-Artaza, D., Patrono, L. (2020). Internet of Things (IoT): Opportunities, issues and challenges towards a smart and sustainable future. *J. Clean. Prod., 274*, 122877-122877.
[http://dx.doi.org/10.1016/j.jclepro.2020.122877] [PMID: 32834567]

Nor, N.I.M., Arokiasamy, L., Balaraman, R.A. (2018). The influence of the Internet of Things on employee engagement among generation Y at the workplace. *In SHS Web of Conferences, 56.*

Özçelik, G. (2015). Engagement and retention of the millennial generation in the workplace through internal branding. *Int. J. Bus. Manage., 10*(3), 99.
[http://dx.doi.org/10.5539/ijbm.v10n3p99]

Parra, D.T., Guerrero, C.D. (2020). Decision-making IoT adoption in SMEs from a technological perspective.
[http://dx.doi.org/10.23919/CISTI49556.2020.9141045]

Pratt, M.K. (2022). *Top 8 IOT applications and examples in business. IoT Agenda. Retrieved March 30, 2022, from https://www.techtarget.com/iotagenda/tip/Top-8-IoT-applications-and-examples-in-business.*

Pont, S. (2013). *Digital state: How the Internet is changing everything..* Kogan Page Publishers.

Pütz, S., Rick, V., Mertens, A., Nitsch, V. (2022). Using IoT devices for sensor-based monitoring of employees' mental workload: Investigating managers' expectations and concerns. *Appl. Ergon., 102*, 103739.
[http://dx.doi.org/10.1016/j.apergo.2022.103739] [PMID: 35279467]

Rahmani, A.M., Bayramov, S., Kiani Kalejahi, B. (2022). Internet of things applications: opportunities and threats. *Wirel. Pers. Commun., 122*(1), 451-476.
[http://dx.doi.org/10.1007/s11277-021-08907-0] [PMID: 34426718]

Rahmani, A.M., Ehsani, A., Mohammadi, M., Mohammed, A.H., Karim, S.H.T., Hosseinzadeh, M. (2022). A new model for analyzing the role of new ICT-based technologies on the success of employees' learning programs. *Kybernetes, 51*(6), 2156-2171.
[http://dx.doi.org/10.1108/K-02-2021-0164]

Sceulovs, D., Shatrevich, V., Gaile-Sarkane, E. (2017). Evaluation of E-recruitment as a Business Model through Internet of Things Approach. *J. Bus. Econ. Res., 2*(1) [JBER].

*State of the American Workplace,,* 1-214.

Sergi, B.S., Popkova, E.G., Bogoviz, A.V., Litvinova, T.N. (2019). *Understanding industry 4.0: AI, the internet of things, and the future of work..* Emerald Group Publishing.

Sharples, S., Megaw, T. (2015). The definition and measurement of human workload. *Evaluation of human work,* 516-544.

Soltani, S. (2022). B2B engagement within an internet of things ecosystem. *J. Bus. Ind. Mark., 37*(1), 146-159.
[http://dx.doi.org/10.1108/JBIM-05-2020-0224]

Thomas, M. (2022). *Internet-of-Things (IoT) Companies You Should Know. Built-In. Retrieved from: https://builtin.com/internet-things/iot-internet-of-things-companies.*

Truong, N.B., Lee, G.M., Um, T.W., Mackay, M. (2019). Trust evaluation mechanism for user recruitment in mobile crowd-sensing in the Internet of Things. *IEEE Trans. Inf. Forensics Security, 14*(10), 2705-2719.
[http://dx.doi.org/10.1109/TIFS.2019.2903659]

Vidros, S., Kolias, C., Kambourakis, G. (2016). Online recruitment services: another playground for fraudsters. *Comput. Fraud Secur., 2016*(3), 8-13.
[http://dx.doi.org/10.1016/S1361-3723(16)30025-2]

Vijayalakshmi, N. S., Lourens, M. E. (2022). The role of the Internet of Things (IoT) is to improve the overall recruitment and manpower management system of an organization. *International Journal of*

*Mechanical Engineering,* *7*(1).

Vivekananth, P. (2016). The impact of Internet of Things (IoT) in human resource management. *IPASJ International Journal of Management (IIJM),* *4*(9).

Wu, F., Wu, T., Yuce, M. (2018). An internet-of-things (IoT) network system for connected safety and health monitoring applications. *Sensors (Basel),* *19*(1), 21. [http://dx.doi.org/10.3390/s19010021] [PMID: 30577646]

Yang, Y., Yu, D. (2022). Research and Exploration on the Training of New Engineering Personnel from the Perspective of Artificial Intelligence. *In 2022 2nd Asia Conference on Information Engineering (ACIE),,* 102-106.

Zhang, X. (2022). Development and Construction of Internet of Things Training Practice Platform for Employment Skills Assessment. *J. Sens.,* *2022*, 1-7. [http://dx.doi.org/10.1155/2022/3014565]

# CHAPTER 14

# Artificial Intelligence (AI): A Metamorphic Transformation in Healthcare Services

**B.C.M. Patnaik**[1], **Ipseeta Satpathy**[1,*] and **S. K. Baral**[2]

[1] *KIIT School of Management, KIIT University, Bhubaneswar, Odisha, India*

[2] *Department of Commerce, Indira Gandhi National Tribal University, Madhya Pradesh, India*

**Abstract:** Artificial intelligence plays a key role in all aspects of human existence, and technology is meant to improve human well-being. In this aspect, healthcare is a major field, and artificial intelligence is us hering in rapid progress. Artificial intelligence has provided several solutions that were previously un attainable, such as diagnosis, treatment, prevention, and therapy. Medical experts have traditionally been responsible for prediction, forecasting, as well as identification or decision-making, which are the main objectives of Artificial Intelligence (AI). AI is capable of providing a better healthcare service in the form of smart devices. By integrating artificial intelligence with the Internet of Things (IoT), compact and mobile devices are now making human life more comfortable. Aside from diagnosing diseases such as Alzheimer's, these devices are also used to provide appropriate treatment for various brain disorders. Considering the relevance of the same, the study is undertaken to understand the patient's and healthcare provider's (doctors and nursing staff) perception of AI. The scope of the study includes super specialty private hospitals in the capital region of Odisha and Vizag of Andhra Pradesh. Around 387 samples were collected for analyzing the data, which included 142 patients, 153 nursing staff, and the rest were doctors. The period of the study was six months, from December 2021 to May 2022. The entire analysis was done under nine parameters: Robot-assisted surgery, virtual nursing assistants, administrative workflow assistants, fraud detection, prescription error recognition, automated image diagnosis, cyber security, connected medical devices, and identification of clinical trial participants with 33 attributes.

**Keywords:** Artificial intelligence, Clinical error, Health care, Patient data, Patient safety, Report analysis.

* **Corresponding author Ipseeta Satpathy:** KIIT School of Management, KIIT University, Bhubaneswar, Odisha, India;
E-mail: ipseeta@ksom.ac.in

**Sukanta Kumar Baral, Richa Goel, Tilottama Singh, Erdener Kaynak & Vishal Jain (Eds.)**

## BACKGROUND OF THE STUDY

AI offers significant opportunities for progress and innovation since it solves cognitive problems that would normally require human intelligence. Voice recognition, recommendation systems, and self-driving cars are all examples of the practical successes of AI in various domains. Future developments in AI are likely to become even more significant. Spending on artificial intelligence is predicted to increase to 97.9 billion by 2023, according to the International Data Corporation. AI has a lot of potential to improve people's health and well-being since electronic health records (EHRs) and other patient-related data are becoming increasingly available, *e.g.*, by augmenting clinicians' diagnostic work, signaling prevention opportunities, and offering personalized treatment recommendations, among other things. Even though some simple assistive tools have been deployed in the field.

AI research, development, and deployment is growing in the health sector as well. This is due to the potential of AI to promote healthy lifestyles, detect infectious diseases and environmental hazards early and treat them, and prevent diseases from occurring. For example, the World Health Organization (WHO) has set a target called "triple billion" that aims to improve the health and well-being of 1 billion people by providing universal health coverage, reducing the risk of health emergencies, and enhancing the protection against health emergencies. AI is expected to help it achieve these goals.

A new potential is emerging for improving patient safety outcomes and the quality of care with the integration of artificial intelligence (AI) into the healthcare system. AI can be broadly defined as a computer program that is capable of making intelligent decisions. Artificial intelligence is defined in this review as the ability to analyze healthcare data, identify risks, and reveal hidden knowledge. Several healthcare-related areas have been improved with artificial intelligence, including diagnosis, drug development, and personalized medicine. Clinicians may be able to make better diagnoses with the help of artificial intelligence. As a means of identifying, assessing, and mitigating threats to patient safety, artificial intelligence (AI) has also been embedded in electronic health record (EHR) systems. Clinical efficiency is not necessarily a function of AI accuracy. Artificial intelligence can be used in both clinical as well as diagnostic settings in the healthcare industry. The application of artificial intelligence to healthcare presents a powerful tool for revealing subtle patterns in data, which are then interpreted by clinicians for identifying new medical and health-related problems. Research on AI in diagnosis, such as the identification of diseases, has focused mainly on recent studies and reviews.

AI is gradually changing medical practice. Several AI applications in medicine can be used in a variety of medical fields, such as clinical, diagnostic, rehabilitative, surgical, and predictive practices. Other critical areas of medicine where AI is making an impact are clinical decision-making and disease diagnosis. AI technologies can ingest, analyze, and report large volumes of data across different modalities to detect disease and guide clinical decisions.

Health services management and patient care can also benefit from these technologies. Clinical creativity and critical thinking will be emphasized by using technology to reduce care costs and repetitive operations. Fig. (**1**) depicts the four dominant variables for AI healthcare, and Fig. (**2**) explains Artificial Intelligence (AI) route to patient safety *via* "Clinical" and "Diagnostic" level interventions DSS: decision support.

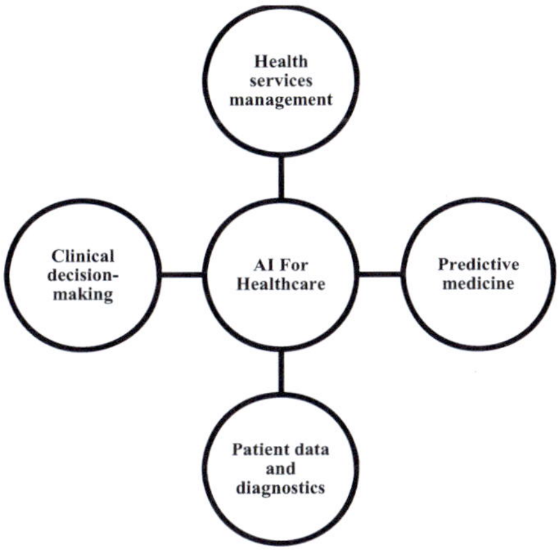


**Fig. (1).** Four dominant variables for AI healthcare: health services management, clinical decision-making, predictive medicine, and patient data and diagnosis.
Source – Author's Elaboration.

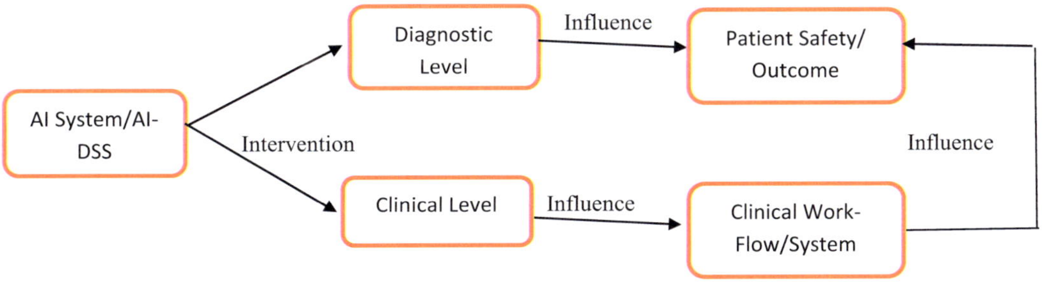


**Fig. (2).** Artificial Intelligence (AI) route to patient safety via "Clinical" and "Diagnostic" level interventions DSS: decision support.
Source – Author's Framework.

## Objectives of the Study

- To understand the patient's and health care provider's (doctors and nursing staff) perception of artificial intelligence.
- To contribute to the existing literature.

## Scope of the Study

The scope of the study includes super specialty private hospitals in the capital region of Odisha, including KIMS Hospital, Sum Ultimate Medicare, Apollo Hospital, Kalinga Hospital, Utkal Hospital, Care Hospital, Sparsh Hospital, and AIIMS Hospital. In Vizag (AP), the hospitals include Apollo Health City Hospital, Omni RK Super Specialty Hospital, Seven Hills Hospital, Mycure Hospital, and Kala Hospital.

## Research Design

Both primary and secondary data were used in this study. Patient, nursing staff, and doctor data were collected as primary data. The total period was spread over six months. The variables were mostly derived from core group discussions, and some were from the review of literature. In this regard, eight core group discussions were made consisting of patients, doctors, and nursing staff of various super specialty hospitals in Odisha and Andhra Pradesh. Initially, more than 38 attributes were identified; however, after continuous deliberations with various groups, the attributes were finally restricted to 33 under nine different parameters.

## Sample Size Determination for Unknown Populations

$N= Z^2 (P) (1-P)/ C^2 = (1.96)^2(0.5) (1-0.5)/ (0.05)^2 = 384$

Where Z= Standard normal deviation set at 95% confidence level, which is 1.96, P= Percentage picking choice or response, which is 0.5, and C=Confidence interval, which is 0.05

For the collection of data cluster and random sampling method used, 783 people were approached for the data; however, only 387 respondents responded in proper form. All the responses were included for a better representation.

## Tools Applied

A simple weighted perception score method was used for the various sub-variables considered for the study. A 5-point Rensis Likert scale was used to measure each attribute. Weights of 5 were assigned to completely agreeing responses, weights of 4 were assigned to agreeing responses, weights of 3 were assigned to neutral stands, weights of 2 were assigned to disagreeing responses, and weights of 1 were assigned to completely disagreeing responses, as mentioned in the Table **1**, **2**, and **3**.

**Table 1. Sampling frame.**

| Place | Name of the Hospital | Questionnaire Distributed | Collected | Rate of Response (%) |
|---|---|---|---|---|
| **Bhubaneswar – Odisha** | | | | |
| | KIMS Hospital | 50 | 31 | 62 |
| | Sum Ultimate Medicare | 50 | 29 | 58 |
| | Apollo Hospital | 50 | 28 | 56 |
| | Kalinga Hospital | 50 | 28 | 56 |
| | Utkal Hospital | 50 | 32 | 64 |
| | Care Hospital, | 50 | 31 | 62 |
| | Sparsh Hospital | 50 | 29 | 58 |
| | AIIMS Hospital | 50 | 26 | 52 |
| Total | | 400 | 234 | 58.66 |
| **Vizag- Andhra Pradesh** | | | | |
| | Apollo Health City | 60 | 32 | 53 |
| | Omni RK Super Specialty Hospital | 60 | 29 | 48 |
| | Seven Hills Hospital | 60 | 33 | 55 |
| | My Cure Hospital | 60 | 28 | 47 |
| | Kala Hospital | 60 | 31 | 52 |
| Total | | 300 | 153 | 51 |

**Table 2. Break up of sampling frame.**

| **Bhubaneswar- Odisha – 234** | | | **Vizag- Andhra Pradesh -153** | | |
|---|---|---|---|---|---|
| Patients | Nurses | Doctors | Patients | Nurses | Doctors |
| 84 | 97 | 53 | 58 | 56 | 39 |

**Table 3. Data analysis.**

| Variables | Patients @BBSR | Nurses @BBSR | Doctors @ BBSR | Patients @Vizag | Nurses @ Vizag | Doctors @ Vizag |
|---|---|---|---|---|---|---|
| **Robot-assisted Surgery** | | | | | | |
| Lower risk of infections | 364 | 409 | 236 | 243 | 246 | 163 |
| Less pain, scarring, and blood loss | 343 | 425 | 243 | 247 | 245 | 168 |
| Shorter hospitalization and faster recovery | 363 | 426 | 225 | 233 | 239 | 166 |
| Quicker return to daily routines | 344 | 426 | 243 | 246 | 226 | 165 |
| **Total score** | 1414 | 1686 | 947 | 969 | 956 | 662 |
| **Maximum Possible Score** | 1680 | 1940 | 1060 | 1160 | 1120 | 780 |
| **Least Possible Score** | 336 | 388 | 212 | 232 | 224 | 156 |
| **% of the total score to the maximum possible score** | 84.17 | 86.90 | 89.34 | 83.53 | 85.36 | 84.87 |
| **Average Score** | 85.70 | | | | | |
| **Virtual nursing assistants** | | | | | | |
| 24/7 access to medical support | 356 | 444 | 248 | 249 | 247 | 175 |
| Round-the-clock patient condition monitoring | 370 | 444 | 243 | 251 | 236 | 162 |
| A quick response to medication and illness questions. | 349 | 434 | 240 | 240 | 242 | 163 |
| **Total score** | 1075 | 1322 | 731 | 740 | 725 | 500 |
| **Maximum Possible Score** | 1260 | 1455 | 795 | 870 | 840 | 585 |
| **Least Possible Score** | 252 | 291 | 265 | 174 | 168 | 117 |
| **% of the total score to the maximum possible score** | 85.32 | 90.86 | 91.95 | 85.06 | 86.31 | 85.47 |
| **Average score** | 87.50 | | | | | |
| **Administrative workflow assistants** | | | | | | |
| Decisions about operational tasks are made faster and more accurately by healthcare professionals | 360 | 436 | 239 | 231 | 256 | 173 |
| By focusing solely on patients, doctors can deliver better-quality care | 373 | 439 | 243 | 249 | 248 | 174 |
| Prioritizing requests and automating patient discharges ensure that patients with critical conditions receive timely care | 357 | 442 | 243 | 242 | 259 | 176 |
| The cost of running a practice is lower because fewer people are needed to maintain it. | 376 | 494 | 242 | 238 | 254 | 171 |

*(Table 3) cont.....*

| Variables | Patients @BBSR | Nurses @BBSR | Doctors @ BBSR | Patients @Vizag | Nurses @ Vizag | Doctors @ Vizag |
|---|---|---|---|---|---|---|
| **Robot-assisted Surgery** | | | | | | |
| **Total score** | 1466 | 1811 | 967 | 960 | 1017 | 694 |
| **Maximum Possible Score** | 1680 | 1940 | 1060 | 1160 | 1120 | 780 |
| **Least Possible Score** | 336 | 388 | 212 | 232 | 224 | 156 |
| **% of the total score to the maximum possible score** | 87.26 | 93.35 | 91.23 | 82.76 | 90.80 | 88.97 |
| **Average score** | 89.06 | | | | | |
| **Fraud detection** | | | | | | |
| Faster insurance processing and patient dispatch | 359 | 433 | 243 | 247 | 254 | 176 |
| A reduction in the cost of care and patient premiums | 356 | 434 | 240 | 254 | 240 | 173 |
| Higher personal healthcare data security | 366 | 419 | 224 | 260 | 235 | 170 |
| Higher patient satisfaction rates | 374 | 419 | 245 | 254 | 252 | 164 |
| **Total score** | 1455 | 1705 | 952 | 1015 | 981 | 683 |
| **Maximum Possible Score** | 1680 | 1940 | 1060 | 1160 | 1120 | 780 |
| **Least Possible Score** | 336 | 388 | 212 | 232 | 224 | 156 |
| **% of the total score to the maximum possible score** | 86.61 | 87.89 | 89.81 | 87.5 | 87.59 | 87.56 |
| **Average score** | 87.83 | | | | | |
| **Prescription error recognition** | | | | | | |
| Prevent overdosing and health risks by improving the quality of care. | 316 | 451 | 234 | 245 | 244 | 166 |
| Clinical documentation for drugs requiring approval can be submitted, authorized, and reviewed electronically | 355 | 439 | 232 | 242 | 246 | 178 |
| Monitor patients' medication adherence | 343 | 439 | 220 | 238 | 246 | 182 |
| **Total score** | 1014 | 1329 | 686 | 725 | 736 | 526 |
| **Maximum Possible Score** | 1260 | 1455 | 795 | 870 | 840 | 585 |
| **Least Possible Score** | 252 | 291 | 265 | 174 | 168 | 117 |
| **% of the total score to the maximum possible score** | 80.48 | 91.34 | 86.29 | 83.33 | 87.62 | 89.91 |
| **Average score** | 86.50 | | | | | |
| **Automated image diagnosis** | | | | | | |
| The reduction of human error and the improvement of diagnostic accuracy. | 357 | 463 | 246 | 239 | 237 | 172 |

*(Table 3) cont.....*

| Variables | Patients @BBSR | Nurses @BBSR | Doctors @ BBSR | Patients @Vizag | Nurses @ Vizag | Doctors @ Vizag |
|---|---|---|---|---|---|---|
| **Robot-assisted Surgery** | | | | | | |
| Well-recorded and reliable monitoring of a patient's progress. | 364 | 440 | 243 | 236 | 250 | 167 |
| More transparency in diagnosis | 349 | 433 | 226 | 241 | 253 | 157 |
| Automatic diagnosis report generation | 351 | 432 | 236 | 257 | 247 | 165 |
| **Total score** | 1421 | 1768 | 951 | 973 | 987 | 661 |
| **Maximum Possible Score** | 1680 | 1940 | 1060 | 1160 | 1120 | 780 |
| **Least Possible Score** | 336 | 388 | 212 | 232 | 224 | 156 |
| **% of the total score to the maximum possible score** | 84.58 | 91.13 | 89.72 | 83.88 | 88.13 | 84.74 |
| **Average score** | 87.03 | | | | | |
| **Cyber security** | | | | | | |
| Eliminating threats to patients' safety | 364 | 449 | 229 | 241 | 255 | 177 |
| Achieving reputation protection and preventing lawsuits for hospitals | 360 | 436 | 235 | 236 | 245 | 178 |
| Reducing costs associated with breach recovery | 360 | 433 | 241 | 242 | 245 | 182 |
| **Total score** | 1084 | 1318 | 705 | 719 | 745 | 537 |
| **Maximum Possible Score** | 1260 | 1455 | 795 | 870 | 840 | 585 |
| **Least Possible Score** | 252 | 291 | 265 | 174 | 168 | 117 |
| **% of the total score to the maximum possible score** | 86.03 | 90.58 | 88.68 | 82.64 | 88.69 | 91.79 |
| **Average score** | 88.07 | | | | | |
| **Connected medical devices** | | | | | | |
| Care tailored to the activity and physiological needs of the patient | 378 | 434 | 236 | 229 | 255 | 180 |
| Insights gathered from diverse data sources lead to better clinical results | 376 | 432 | 225 | 254 | 252 | 172 |
| Monitoring and alerting patients in real time to prevent life-threatening crises | 368 | 433 | 212 | 253 | 258 | 177 |
| Optimized hospital workflows based on care prioritization | 364 | 438 | 238 | 246 | 253 | 184 |
| **Total score** | 1486 | 1737 | 911 | 982 | 1018 | 713 |
| **Maximum Possible Score** | 1680 | 1940 | 1060 | 1160 | 1120 | 780 |
| **Least Possible Score** | 336 | 388 | 212 | 232 | 224 | 156 |

*(Table 3) cont.....*

| Variables | Patients @BBSR | Nurses @BBSR | Doctors @ BBSR | Patients @Vizag | Nurses @ Vizag | Doctors @ Vizag |
|---|---|---|---|---|---|---|
| **Robot-assisted Surgery** | | | | | | |
| **% of the total score to the maximum possible score** | 88.45 | 89.54 | 85.94 | 84.66 | 90.89 | 91.40 |
| **Average score** | 88.48 | | | | | |
| **Identification of clinical trial participants** | | | | | | |
| Ease the strain on resources | 359 | 435 | 236 | 237 | 245 | 186 |
| Free up time for doctor-patient interaction | 353 | 445 | 218 | 239 | 247 | 198 |
| Diagnose diseases faster with the accuracy of top medical experts | 363 | 429 | 240 | 244 | 251 | 180 |
| Develop tailored, precise treatment strategies | 351 | 416 | 242 | 249 | 241 | 176 |
| **Total score** | 1320 | 1725 | 936 | 969 | 984 | 740 |
| **Maximum Possible Score** | 1680 | 1940 | 1060 | 1160 | 1120 | 780 |
| **Least Possible Score** | 336 | 388 | 212 | 232 | 224 | 156 |
| **% of the total score to the maximum possible score** | 78.57 | 88.92 | 88.30 | 83.53 | 87.86 | 94.87 |
| **Average score** | 87 | | | | | |

**Source:** Annexure A, B, C, D, E and F
Maximum possible score= responses X Variables X maximum score
Least possible score = responses X variables X least score

## RESULTS AND DISCUSSIONS

Responding to the questions related to the benefits of robot-assisted surgery, the perception score against the maximum possible score for the patients, nursing staff, and doctors of Bhubaneswar was 84.17%, 86.90%, and 89.34%, respectively, and for the same category of respondents of Vizag, it was 85.53%, 85.36 and 84.87%, respectively. It indicates that the various sub–variables considered for the study under this category have a very significant impact on changing healthcare scenarios. In the case of virtual nursing, the actual percentage of score against the maximum possible score for the patients, nursing staff, and doctors in the case of Vizag was 85.06%, 86.31%, and 85.47%, respectively, and in the case of Bhubaneswar respondents, it was 85.32%, 90.86%, and 91.95%, respectively. The majority of the respondents felt that nursing assistance services had made a lot of improvements due to AI revolutions.

Answering the questions related to the AI benefits for administrative workflow support, the percentage of opinions of doctors, nurses, and patients in the case of Bhubaneswar was 91.23%, 93.35%, and 87.26%, respectively, and the same for the Vizag respondents was 88.97%, 90.80%, and 82.76%, respectively. This shows that AI has simplified the administrative support service in recent times in the case of healthcare providers. Participating in the questions related to the role of AI in fraud detection, the percentage of opinions of patients, nursing staff, and doctors in Bhubaneswar were 86.61%, 87.89%, and 89.81%, respectively. However, in the case of Vizag responses, they were 87.5%, 87.59%, and 87.56%, respectively.

Regarding the benefits of prescription error recognition, the percentage of actual score to maximum possible score for the patients, nurses, and doctors in the case of Vizag was 83.33%, 87.62%, and 89.91%, respectively, and the same for the Bhubaneswar respondents was 80.48%, 91.34%, and 86.29%, respectively. This shows that AI has reduced prescription errors. Responding to the benefits of automated image diagnosis due to AI, the perception score to the maximum possible score for the patients, nurses, and doctors in the case of Bhubaneswar was 84.58%, 91.13%, 89.72%, respectively, and the percentage of opinions of the Vizag respondents for the same was 83.88%, 88.13%, and 84.74%, respectively.

In the case of AI benefits related to cyber security, the actual perception score percentage to the maximum possible score for the doctors, nurses, and patients of Bhubaneswar was 88.68%, 90.58%, and 86.03%, respectively, and the same for the respondents of Vizag was 91.79%, 88.69%, and 82.64%, respectively. It concludes that AI has contributed a lot in this direction. Answering the AIs benefits related to connected medical devices, the percentage of responses of the patients, nursing staff, and doctors of Bhubaneswar was 88.45%, 89.54%, and 85.94%, respectively, and the same for the Vizag respondents was 84.66%, 90.89%, and 91.40%, respectively. It shows that AI facilitates connecting medical devices to deliver better healthcare facilities.

Similarly, in the case of questions related to the benefits of identification of clinical trial, the percentage of actual score to the maximum possible score in the case of patients, nursing staff, and doctors of Vizag was 83.53%, 87.86%, and 94.87%, respectively and same for the participants of Bhubaneswar was 78.57%, 88.92%, and 88.30%, respectively. Fig. (**3**) depicts the average score for the AI benefits by the respondents.

## Data Inclusion and Exclusion Criteria

The respondents were only those patients, nursing staff, and doctors who volunteered during the study and agreed to participate in the collection of data. It was a very challenging job to classify the exclusion and inclusion criteria; however, the researchers managed to collect the desired sample size.

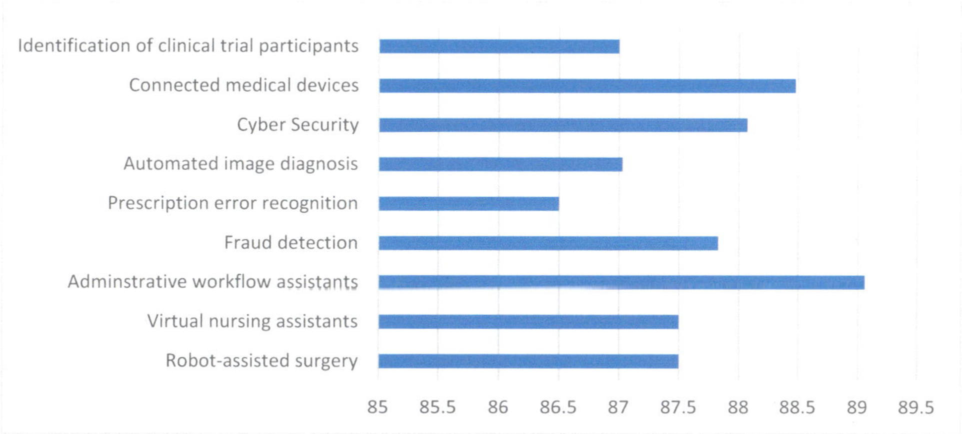


**Fig. (3).** Average Score for the AI benefits by the respondents.

# CONCLUSION

The innovation of science, technology and AI has redefined healthcare services. It is a blessing for mankind. Traditional healthcare services are still present in most parts of the country, but those super specialty hospitals that adopted technology-based healthcare services for their patients have made tremendous changes in the healthcare services. With the adoption of artificial intelligence, the various benefits of healthcare services have increased a lot. In the study, it was found that it contributed to a lower risk of infection, less pain, shorter hospitalization, faster recovery, 24/7 access to medical support, timely care, reduction in operational cost, faster processing of insurance settlements, higher personal healthcare security and transparency in diagnosis in addition to other benefits. So, it is in the interest of the hospitals to survive in the new environment and adopt modern technology for better service to mankind.

# BIBLIOGRAPHY

Banerjee, I., Li, K., Seneviratne, M., Ferrari, M., Seto, T., Brooks, J.D., Rubin, D.L., Hernandez-Boussard, T. (2019). Weakly supervised natural language processing for assessing patient-centered outcome following prostate cancer treatment. *JAMIA Open, 2*(1), 150-159.
[http://dx.doi.org/10.1093/jamiaopen/ooy057] [PMID: 31032481]

Bahl, M., Barzilay, R., Yedidia, A.B., Locascio, N.J., Yu, L., Lehman, C.D. (2018). High-risk breast lesions: a machine learning model to predict pathologic upgrade and reduce unnecessary surgical excision. *Radiology, 286*(3), 810-818.
[http://dx.doi.org/10.1148/radiol.2017170549] [PMID: 29039725]

Bhardwaj, R., Nambiar, A.R., Dutta, D. (2017). A study of machine learning in healthcare.
[http://dx.doi.org/10.1109/COMPSAC.2017.164]

Bhagyashree, S.I.R., Nagaraj, K., Prince, M., Fall, C.H.D., Krishna, M. (2018). Diagnosis of Dementia by Machine learning methods in Epidemiological studies: a pilot exploratory study from south India. *Soc. Psychiatry Psychiatr. Epidemiol., 53*(1), 77-86.

[http://dx.doi.org/10.1007/s00127-017-1410-0] [PMID: 28698926]

Burton, R.J., Albur, M., Eberl, M., Cuff, S.M. (2019). Using artificial intelligence to reduce diagnostic workload without compromising detection of urinary tract infections. *BMC Med. Inform. Decis. Mak., 19*(1), 171.
[http://dx.doi.org/10.1186/s12911-019-0878-9] [PMID: 31443706]

Cho, B.J., Choi, Y.J., Lee, M.J., Kim, J.H., Son, G.H., Park, S.H., Kim, H.B., Joo, Y.J., Cho, H.Y., Kyung, M.S., Park, Y.H., Kang, B.S., Hur, S.Y., Lee, S., Park, S.T. (2020). Classification of cervical neoplasms on colposcopic photography using deep learning. *Sci. Rep., 10*(1), 13652.
[http://dx.doi.org/10.1038/s41598-020-70490-4] [PMID: 32788635]

Chen, H., Engkvist, O., Wang, Y., Olivecrona, M., Blaschke, T. (2018). The rise of deep learning in drug discovery. *Drug Discov. Today, 23*(6), 1241-1250.
[http://dx.doi.org/10.1016/j.drudis.2018.01.039] [PMID: 29366762]

Ciervo, J., Shen, S.C., Stallcup, K., Thomas, A., Farnum, M.A., Lobanov, V.S., Agrafiotis, D.K. (2019). A new risk and issue management system to improve productivity, quality, and compliance in clinical trials. *JAMIA Open, 2*(2), 216-221.
[http://dx.doi.org/10.1093/jamiaopen/ooz006] [PMID: 31984356]

Ciervo, J., Shen, S.C., Stallcup, K., Thomas, A., Farnum, M.A., Lobanov, V.S., Agrafiotis, D.K. (2019). A new risk and issue management system to improve productivity, quality, and compliance in clinical trials. *JAMIA Open, 2*(2), 216-221.
[http://dx.doi.org/10.1093/jamiaopen/ooz006] [PMID: 31984356]

Dalal, A.K., Fuller, T., Garabedian, P., Ergai, A., Balint, C., Bates, D.W., Benneyan, J. (2019). Systems engineering and human factors support of a system of novel EHR-integrated tools to prevent harm in the hospital. *J. Am. Med. Inform. Assoc., 26*(6), 553-560.
[http://dx.doi.org/10.1093/jamia/ocz002] [PMID: 30903660]

*European Commission, High level expert group on artificial intelligence. Ethics guidelines for trustworthy AI. Published in Brussels:(2019). Retrived from: pa.eu/newsroom/dae/document.cfm?doc_id.*

Ekins, S., Puhl, A.C., Zorn, K.M., Lane, T.R., Russo, D.P., Klein, J.J., Hickey, A.J., Clark, A.M. (2019). Exploiting machine learning for end-to-end drug discovery and development. *Nat. Mater., 18*(5), 435-441.
[http://dx.doi.org/10.1038/s41563-019-0338-z] [PMID: 31000803]

Eloff, J., Bihina Bella, M., Eloff, J., Bella, M. B. (2018). *Software failures: An overview. Software Failure Investigation: A Near-Miss Analysis Approach,* 7-24.

Guan, M., Cho, S., Petro, R., Zhang, W., Pasche, B., Topaloglu, U. (2019). Natural language processing and recurrent network models for identifying genomic mutation-associated cancer treatment change from patient progress notes. *JAMIA Open, 2*(1), 139-149.
[http://dx.doi.org/10.1093/jamiaopen/ooy061] [PMID: 30944913]

Grossman, L.V., Choi, S.W., Collins, S., Dykes, P.C., O'Leary, K.J., Rizer, M., Strong, P., Yen, P.Y., Vawdrey, D.K. (2018). Implementation of acute care patient portals: recommendations on utility and use from six early adopters. *J. Am. Med. Inform. Assoc., 25*(4), 370-379.
[http://dx.doi.org/10.1093/jamia/ocx074] [PMID: 29040634]

Ghebreyesus, T. (2018). *Artificial intelligence for good global summit (2018). World Health Organization. Retrived from: http://www.who.int/dg/speeches/2018/artificial.*

Hashimoto, D.A., Rosman, G., Rus, D., Meireles, O.R. (2018). Artificial intelligence in surgery: promises and perils. *Ann. Surg., 268*(1), 70-76.
[http://dx.doi.org/10.1097/SLA.0000000000002693] [PMID: 29389679]

He, J., Baxter, S.L., Xu, J., Xu, J., Zhou, X., Zhang, K. (2019). The practical implementation of artificial intelligence technologies in medicine. *Nat. Med., 25*(1), 30-36.
[http://dx.doi.org/10.1038/s41591-018-0307-0] [PMID: 30617336]

*International Data Corporation (2019). worldwide spending on artificial intelligence systems will be nearly*

*$98 billion in 2023, according to new IDC spending guide, 2019. Retrived from: https://www.idc.com/getdoc.jsp?containerId.*

Jiang, F., Jiang, Y., Zhi, H., Dong, Y., Li, H., Ma, S., Wang, Y., Dong, Q., Shen, H., Wang, Y. (2017). Artificial intelligence in healthcare: past, present and future. *Stroke Vasc. Neurol., 2*(4), 230-243. [http://dx.doi.org/10.1136/svn-2017-000101] [PMID: 29507784]

Kong, H.J. (2019). Managing unstructured big data in healthcare system. *Healthc. Inform. Res., 25*(1), 1-2. [http://dx.doi.org/10.4258/hir.2019.25.1.1] [PMID: 30788175]

Keane, P.A., Topol, E.J. (2018). With an eye to AI and autonomous diagnosis. *NPJ Digit. Med., 1*(1), 40. [http://dx.doi.org/10.1038/s41746-018-0048-y] [PMID: 31304321]

Lee, R.F., Lober, W.B., Sibley, J., Kross, E.K., Engelberg, R.A., Curtis, J.R. (2019). Identifying goals-of-care conversations in the electronic health record using machine learning and natural language processing. *A22.* Facilitating palliative and end-of-life care. [http://dx.doi.org/10.1164/ajrccm-conference.2019.199.1_MeetingAbstracts.A1089]

Li, Q., Zhao, K., Bustamante, C.D., Ma, X., Wong, W.H. (2019). Xrare: a machine learning method jointly modeling phenotypes and genetic evidence for rare disease diagnosis. *Genet. Med., 21*(9), 2126-2134. [http://dx.doi.org/10.1038/s41436-019-0439-8] [PMID: 30675030]

Meskó, B., Drobni, Z., Bényei, É., Gergely, B., Győrffy, Z. (2017). Digital health is a cultural transformation of traditional healthcare. *mHealth, 3*, 38. [http://dx.doi.org/10.21037/mhealth.2017.08.07] [PMID: 29184890]

Ronquillo, J.G., Erik Winterholler, J., Cwikla, K., Szymanski, R., Levy, C. (2018). Health IT, hacking, and cybersecurity: national trends in data breaches of protected health information. *JAMIA Open, 1*(1), 15-19. [http://dx.doi.org/10.1093/jamiaopen/ooy019] [PMID: 31984315]

Rajkomar, A., Oren, E., Chen, K., Dai, A.M., Hajaj, N., Hardt, M., Liu, P.J., Liu, X., Marcus, J., Sun, M., Sundberg, P., Yee, H., Zhang, K., Zhang, Y., Flores, G., Duggan, G.E., Irvine, J., Le, Q., Litsch, K., Mossin, A., Tansuwan, J., Wang, D., Wexler, J., Wilson, J., Ludwig, D., Volchenboum, S.L., Chou, K., Pearson, M., Madabushi, S., Shah, N.H., Butte, A.J., Howell, M.D., Cui, C., Corrado, G.S., Dean, J. (2018). Scalable and accurate deep learning with electronic health records. *NPJ Digit. Med., 1*(1), 18. [http://dx.doi.org/10.1038/s41746-018-0029-1] [PMID: 31304302]

Sahli Costabal, F., Matsuno, K., Yao, J., Perdikaris, P., Kuhl, E. (2019). Machine learning in drug development: Characterizing the effect of 30 drugs on the QT interval using Gaussian process regression, sensitivity analysis, and uncertainty quantification. *Comput. Methods Appl. Mech. Eng., 348*, 313-333. [http://dx.doi.org/10.1016/j.cma.2019.01.033] [PMID: 32863454]

Salahuddin, L., Ismail, Z., Hashim, U.R., Ismail, N.H., Raja Ikram, R.R., Abdul Rahim, F., Hassan, N.H. (2020). Healthcare practitioner behaviours that influence unsafe use of hospital information systems. *Health Informatics J., 26*(1), 420-434. [http://dx.doi.org/10.1177/1460458219833090] [PMID: 30843460]

Tonekaboni, S., Joshi, S., McCradden, M.D., Goldenberg, A. (2019). What clinicians want: contextualizing explainable machine learning for clinical end use. *In Machine learning for healthcare conference*

Topol, E.J. (2019). High-performance medicine: the convergence of human and artificial intelligence. *Nat. Med., 25*(1), 44-56. [http://dx.doi.org/10.1038/s41591-018-0300-7] [PMID: 30617339]

Zhou, L., Blackley, S.V., Kowalski, L., Doan, R., Acker, W.W., Landman, A.B., Kontrient, E., Mack, D., Meteer, M., Bates, D.W., Goss, F.R. (2018). Analysis of errors in dictated clinical documents assisted by speech recognition software and professional transcriptionists. *JAMA Netw. Open, 1*(3), e180530. [http://dx.doi.org/10.1001/jamanetworkopen.2018.0530] [PMID: 30370424]

Zhang, Y., Padman, R., Levin, J.E. (2014). Paving the COWpath: data-driven design of pediatric order sets. *J. Am. Med. Inform. Assoc., 21*(e2), e304-e311. [http://dx.doi.org/10.1136/amiajnl-2013-002316] [PMID: 24674844]

Zhang, X., Pérez-Stable, E.J., Bourne, P.E., Peprah, E., Duru, O.K., Breen, N., Berrigan, D., Wood, F., Jackson, J.S., Wong, D.W.S., Denny, J. (2017). Big data science: opportunities and challenges to address minority health and health disparities in the 21st century. *Ethn. Dis., 27*(2), 95-106. [http://dx.doi.org/10.18865/ed.27.2.95] [PMID: 28439179]

# SUBJECT INDEX



**Sukanta Kumar Baral, Richa Goel, Tilottama Singh, Erdener Kaynak & Vishal Jain (Eds.)**

**D**



**E**



**F**

## L



## M



## N



## O



## P



## R



## S

## T



## V

## W

Made in United States
Cleveland, OH
04 November 2026

47649313R00167